Amy Sugeno

A Sourcebook for Helping People with Spiritual Problems

by
Emma Bragdon, Ph.D.

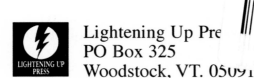

Lightening Up Pre
PO Box 325
Woodstock, VT. 05091

D1157972

Praise for the Sourcebook:

"This Sourcebook is a valuable resource for anyone interested in spiritual experiences and their relationship to psychological health and pathology. It is a clear, concise statement about the nature of spiritual emergencies and appropriate treatment modalities. It deserves careful reading by mental health professionals as well as laypeople who are exploring their own spiritual growth. It provides a well balanced perspective and a wealth of useful information." **- Frances Vaughan, Ph.D., past president of the Association for Transpersonal Psychology and author of** *Beyond Ego* **and** *Paths Beyond Ego.*

"It fulfills a real need among people who might otherwise be labeled mentally ill..." **- John Mack, M.D., professor of psychiatry at Harvard Medical School and founding director of the Center for Psychology and Social Change.**

"Bragdon's books are not only scholarly but communicate a clear message...they are really exceptional." **- Winafred Lucas, Ph.D., author of** *Regression Therapy: A Handbook for Professionals,* **diplomate of the American Board of Professional Psychology.**

"Once the concept of Spiritual Emergence is understood, psychotherapy will have broken the sound barrier. I trust that this book will make an important contribution to this hoped for breakthrough." **- Brother David Steindl-Rast, author & leader in interfaith dialogue.**

Lightening Up Press • P.O. Box 325 • Woodstock, VT 05091• USA

Email: pr@emmabragdon.com
Website: http://www.emmabragdon.com/
Library of Congress Cataloging-in-Publication Data
Bragdon, Emma
ASourcebook for Helping People
with Spiritual Problems

Includes References, Index, Glossary
Tables, Referrals, and Six Articles of Interest

1. Psychology 2. Religion 3. Consciousness 4. Spirituality

I. Title

LC# 93-091814
Second Edition

(Formerly A Sourcebook for Helping People in Spiritual Emergency)

References updated in January 2006

This book is formatted as an ebook and is available
for sale in softcover and as an ebook on
http:// www.emmabragdon.com/

Printed in the United States of America
ISBN 0-9620960-1-6

® SOFTCOVER IS PRINTED ON RECYCLED PAPER

Dedication

This new edition of the Sourcebook is dedicated to Mother Meera, Sogyal Rinpoche, Lama Zopa Rinpoche and His Holiness the Dalai Lama XIV – human beings who bring the wisdom of the East to the West with true inspiration and openness.

Acknowledgments

Christina and Stanislav Grof, M.D., coined the term "spiritual emergency" and published the seminal work differentiating mental disorder and spiritual emergence phenomena. Christina Grof identified the need for people in spiritual emergence to have special support and initiated the Spiritual Emergency Network in 1980. David Lukoff, Ph.D., also stands out as a pioneer during the initiation of this new arena of psychology. Without the pioneering work of these people this Sourcebook would never have taken form in its first or second editions.

I also acknowledge the many other voices from the East and West who have strained to find a common language to speak about the phenomena of spiritual emergence. The individual voices from religion, psychology, philosophy, anthropology and metaphysics are too many to list, but their energy, insight and brilliance contributed to the synthesis of ideas presented here.

I am indebted to the fortitude, skill and good humor of Keith S. Gordon who assisted me in the graphic design of this edition. Carolyn Hengst, MSW-ACP, and Francis Lu, MD., generously contributed their professional knowledge and editing skills for which I am very grateful. Ron Jue, PhD., made suggestions regarding films which illustrate spiritual emergence phenomena. Innumerable friends offered suggestions and encouragement. Thank you all for your love and attention.

J ust as the ink is drying from the newly issued fourth edition of the *Diagnostic and Statistical Manual (DSM-IV)*, which for the first time contains the category of spiritual problems, here appears the first-ever book devoted exclusively to the diagnosis and treatment of spiri¬tual problems. Religious problems, which make up the other half of the official DSM-IV diagnostic category, "Religious or Spiritual Problem," have received much more attention in the clinical and research literature. There's a handbook (Wicks, Parsons, and Capps, 1985) and four journals devoted to pastoral counseling, several more to "Christian psychiatry," as well as professional organizations and conferences that address religious problems. Unfortunately, there is nothing comparable for spiritual problems. *The Journal of Transpersonal Psychology* has published several articles on spiritual problems (Lukoff, 1985; Ossoff, 1993; Waldman, 1992), but there is no journal devoted to this topic. This is surprising since surveys have shown that mental health professionals routinely see clients with spiritual problems. In one survey, psychologists reported that 4.5% of their clients brought a mystical experience into therapy within the past year (Allman et al., 1992). Thus mental health professionals often work with spiritual problems, but many do not have appropriate training. Scott Peck, a psychiatrist who has written several books on the spiritual dimensions of life, including the best selling *The Road Less Traveled,* gave an invited address which drew a standing-room only crowd at the 1992 Annual Meeting of the American Psychiatric Association. He pronounced that psychiatrists are "ill-equipped" to deal with either religious /spiritual pathology or health. Continuing to neglect religious/spiritual issues, he claimed, would perpetuate the predicaments that are related to psychiatry's traditional neglect of these issues: "occasional, devastating misdiagnosis; not infrequent mistreatment; an increasingly poor reputation; inadequate research and theory; and a limitation of psychiatrists' own personal development" (Peck, 1993, p. 243).

Fortunately, in addition to the incorporation of spiritual problems as a diagnostic category in the *DSM-IV,* progress is occurring on other fronts. Francis Lu, M.D., has been working with the American Psychiatry Association and the Residency Review Committee to develop new guidelines for the Essentials for Psychiatry Residency Training, which sets forth the criteria used in the accreditation of all residency programs in the U.S.. These proposed criteria would be used to assess whether psychiatry residency programs are providing training in current American cultures and subcultures, especially related to gender, ethnicity, sexual orientation, and religious/spiritual beliefs. The adoption of these criteria would mandate that training programs for psychiatrists explicitly address religious and spiritual problems. In psychology, others such as Vaughan (1991), Krippner and Welch (1992) and Shafranske and Maloney (1990) have been bringing spiritual issues to the attention of clinical psychologists. Reviews of the research on psychoreligious and psychospiritual dimensions of healing (Lukoff, Turner, & Lu, 1992; 1993) indicate that recognition of these factors has been increasing in all of the allied mental health professions including rehabilitation, addiction counseling, nursing, and social work.

Like Dr. Bragdon, I also underwent the type of spiritual problem known as a spiritual emergency which temporarily impaired my ability to function in consensual reality and everyday social life. Also, like Dr. Bragdon, I was able see the experience through to a positive resolution with the support of my friends and family, obviating the need for traditional psychiatric intervention that might have resulted in hospitalization or medication. Since becoming a licensed psychologist and working at Camarillo State Hospital, the UCLA Clinical Research Center for Schizophrenia and its associated clinic, and currently at the San Francisco VA Day treatment Center, I have often found myself face-to-face with individuals in the same state of consciousness that I had been in: convinced that they were reincarnations of Buddha and Christ (or similar great spiritual figures), reporting communication with many spiritual and religious figures, believing they had a messianic mission to save the world, and preparing a "Holy Book" that would form the basis for a new religion. Since writing about this experience in Shaman's Drum (Lukoff, 1991), and giving workshops on "Psychosis; Mysticism, Shamanism or Pathology?" at the Ojai Foundation with Joan Halifax, I have been contacted by many other mental health professionals and ones in training who have told me about their similar experi¬ences. As in my own case, these spiritual emergencies served as "callings" into their vocations as psychologists, social workers, etc. Dick Price, co-founder of Esalen, who seeded the development of the Spiritual Emergency Network by providing staff support and office space for its founding at Esalen, also had such experiences. However, he was not as lucky as Dr. Bragdon and I were, and twice landed in a psychiatric hospital. The harsh treatment he received at these facilities led to his support for creating SEN. Similarly, Christina Grof, who founded SEN, underwent a spiritual emergency.

However, most spiritual problems are related to spiritual emergence rather than emergency. Many spiritual practices have been observed to induce some distress as part of the process, (e.g. kundalini as part of yogic practices; anxiety, derealization and depersonalization during meditation practice. In these instances, individuals might choose to consult a spiritual teacher about these problems rather than a mental health professional. It should also be mentioned that spiritual experiences are not spiritual problems per se. Most spiritual experiences do not require diagnosis or intervention by mental health professionals. Some people who have mystical experiences or intense opening experiences during meditation, for example, do not experience distress. They may be able to immediately integrate these spiritual experiences into their lives. However, research on near-death experience (NDE), which is the most well-researched spiritual problem, shows that most individuals experience anger, depression, and interpersonal difficulties after the NDE, and therefore could benefit from therapy with a sensitive and knowledgeable clinician.

Many of the founders of psychology and psychiatry have been "wounded healers" whose "creative illness" involved intense spiritual problems that ultimately were transformative (Goldwert, 1992). The sensitive treatments for spiritual problems, as outlined in Dr. Bragdon's book, can be administered in any setting, whether a therapist's office, a 24-hour residential facility, family home or ashram. This book will enable readers and those they are helping to survive the perils of the spiritual path and reap the benefits of a consciously lived spiritual life.

Table of Contents

Table of Contents

Note that in all case examples, names and other identifiable details
have been altered to protect confidentiality.

Preface

This sourcebook was written for professionals and para-professionals in the field of human services as a guide for helping someone with spiritual problems. Spiritual Problems is a new diagnostic category in the Diagnostic and Statistical Manual (DSM-IV) arising out of the profound disorientation and instability that sometimes accompany spiritual experience. In its most intense manifestation, lasting between minutes and weeks, spiritual problems can create a crisis. In this case, spiritual emergency, it appears similar to an acute psychotic episode excepting that the episode eventually has a positive transformative outcome (Dabrowski, 1964; Grof, 1985; Lukoff, 1986). People with spiritual problems or in spiritual emergency have needs for care usually unavailable from therapists, doctors, or in hospitals dealing with more well-known mental disorders.

Although this sourcebook is written for medical practitioners, healers, professional therapists, pastoral counselors, paraprofessional people working in crisis situations, and students in training for these positions, it will also be useful to leaders and teachers in spiritual and religious communities who are faced with the care of people with spiritual problems catalyzed, in part, by their spiritual practice. The sourcebook is written from a "transpersonal" orientation — it assumes that beyond our normal ego functioning there are dimensions of superior perception and function. [See Appendix E for a glossary of terms]. When we enter the transpersonal domain we can access intuitive wisdom, creativity, brilliance, compassion as well as extraordinary energy, peace of mind and healing abilities. People have generally labeled these as "expanded states of consciousness" or "altered states of consciousness."

Since the publication of the first edition of this book in 1988 there has been an upsurge of interest in spiritual emergency. Where the term, "spiritual emergency," was hardly recognized 5 years ago, it is now more commonly heard. This is due, in part, to the publication of several books and lead articles on the topic, as well as new programs designed specifically to attend those in spiritual emergency [See Appendix D for referrals and references].

In mid-1993, the editors of the *Diagnostic and Statistical Manual,* (DSM), decided to include a diagnostic category for "spiritual and religious problems" in the up-coming edition of the DSM-IV due to be circulated in 1994. Since the *DSM* is used by physicians, psychiatrists, psychologists, clinicians, hospital administrators and insurance agencies to categorize and communicate about mental disorders, inclusion of a category regarding spiritual problems is formal recognition that spiritual experiences interact in a meaningful way with emotional well-being and may initiate periods of emotional distress. Prior to the designation of this new category in the *DSM,* health care providers relying on the *DSM* and conventional education were led to assume that phenomena associated with spiritual experiences were symptomatic of deep pathology because the phenomena could so easily be confused with indicators of psychosis, mania, depres¬sion, schizophrenia or borderline personality disorder. The new diagnostic label, spiritual problem, gives health providers a way to speak about spiritual experiences, including mystical states of unity, without having to regard the symptoms automatically as pathological.

This new edition of the *Sourcebook for Helping People with Spiritual Problems* can be used as a study guide and reference manual to learn about the phenomena of spiri¬tual problems, how these problems can be differentiated from mental disorders, and appropriate care for those in spiritual emergency. This sourcebook includes updated references to books, articles, audio-tapes and movies which illustrate the dynamics of spiritual development and spiritual emergency. Readers will come to recognize how widespread these phenomena are. It also includes information regarding new treatment modalities which are appropriate for people wanting to accelerate *spiritual emergence,* growth into transpersonal realms or treat spiritual emergency. Resources for 24-hour care have also been updated. These include a range of licensed psychiatric units, residential treatment centers and spiritual retreat centers. Information about institutes which train people to work with spiritual emergency is also updated.

In this current edition I have attempted to simplify the definition of the spiritual emergence process so it can readily be identified as a natural part of human development. I have also significantly added to the definition of spiritual emergency by including more information on mystical states, possession, and UFO abduction (Chapter One). Chapter Five, "Ongoing Support" now includes a more thorough discussion of treatment modalities. I have not substantially changed the chapters which define when spiritual experiences happen (Chapter Two), Diagnosis (Chapter Three), Initial Interaction: Client and Helper (Chapter Four), the Role of the Helper (Chapter Six), or Case Study (Chapter Seven). Table Two, "Psychiatrists and Psychologists who Recognize Spiritual Emergency," in Chapter Three has been expanded. I have made some additions to "Global Trends Catalyzing Spiritual Emergence" (Chapter 8). I have dropped the chapter on suggestions for the future of the Spiritual Emergence Network as this organization is currently in the process of manifesting many of the ideas which were formulated in the 1980's. Appendices A and B still include "Identifying Community Resources," "Evaluating Your Knowledge of Spiritual Emergency/ Emergence" in order to help you or your group identify your particular skills and the resources of your community in attending someone in spiritual emergency. Appendix C,

"Articles of Interest," now includes "Toward a More Culturally Sensitive *DSM-IV:* Psychoreligious and Psychospiritual Problems" by David Lukoff, Ph.D., Francis Lu, MD and Robert Turner, MD., published first in the November, 1992, issue of the *Journal of Nervous and Mental Disease* proposing the new diagnostic category to be included in the DSM-IV. I hope this inclusion will stimulate more discussion about training programs for psychiatrists, psychologists, and counselors.

Again, I have attempted to write this book in a language which is accessible to laypeople as well as professionals. In the past 6 years I have received many letters from laypeople in the USA and in Europe who have said that the Sourcebook helped save their lives. I want to continue to reach out to help those people who are looking for a conceptual framework to understand their spiritual crisis and a path to appropriate help, as well as address the health care providers who are trying to work effectively with this realm of human experience. There is still a scarcity of written material on the subject and I recognize that this book attends to the needs of a wide audience.

However, this manual is not a substitute for professional help and I advise anyone in crisis to seek appropriate counsel. If you need a referral in your area, a supportive friend who has had a spiritual emergency and/or a professional who can give you guidance, please call the Center for Psychological and Spiritual Health, (415) 575-6299. This international referral service can give you names and telephone numbers of people who may be able to address your needs relating to spiritual emergence phenomena. This network has several satellite offices throughout the world that offer support services as well as referrals. You can search the WWW for "SEN", and find independent offices in many areas.

Finally, it is my pleasure and honor to transmit the following information to those interested in spiritual emergence and spiritual emergency. I applaud the leaders in the field of Spiritual Emergency who attended the SEN conferences in 1985 (listed in Appendix D). Their pioneering contributions formed the initial seed of this sourcebook. I also applaud the people who have taken professional and personal risks to explore and become skillful in helping others in spiritual emergency when this field is only beginning to have credibility in conventional psychology. I am personally grateful for the opportunity to contribute to the expansion of knowledge about facilitating spiritual growth and providing safety and guidance for those in the process of personal transformation. The people who are called to integrate the brilliance which is our human potential are those who can lead us to a brilliant future. My writing and teaching is my contribution to personal, interpersonal and world peace. May it serve as a stepping stone to help all beings realize the wisdom and compassion which unites us all so we can live cooperatively in harmony. It is time.

Emma Bragdon, Ph.D.
Winter, 1993

Chapter One _____

Spiritual Experience, Spiritual Problems and Spiritual Emergency

How many people have had spiritual experiences? Do spiritual experiences ever create a problem with psychological well-being? Are spiritual experiences related to psychological disturbance? What is the difference between a spiritual problem and a religious problem? What is spiritual emergence and what happens to people who experience it? How does it differ from spiritual emergency? How has spiritual emergency been confused with psychopathology?

This chapter addresses these questions and gives a theoretical foundation that will be the basis for later chapters on giving care to individuals with problems related to spiritual emergence.

Spiritual Experiences and Psychological Well-Being

Gallup polls and numerous studies in the last 20 years conclude that 30 to 40% of the population have had "mystical experiences." This spiritual experience is a transient, extraordinary episode marked by feelings of unity, harmonious relationship to the divine and everything in existence, as well as euphoric feelings, noesis, loss of ego functioning, alterations in time and space perception, and the sense of lacking control over the event (Lukoff, Lu and Turner, 1992). Many of these mystical experiences are the result of a Near Death Experience (NDE), when a person approaches clinical death for a short period of time and then comes back to life. As someone revives from this experience, he or she reports statements like,

> *"I came out of my body and felt like I was floating on the ceiling, looking down at the people who were operating on me."*

> *"As I lifted out of my body I was greeted by an exquisitely beautiful, kind being who made me feel very safe and loved. I have never felt so peaceful and comfortable."*

> *"I now know that the spiritual dimension exists. I have no doubts."*

"I am no longer afraid of death. I know it is a joyful transition."

"I feel moved to do more work in service to my fellow man. Material goals are just not very important."

According to a Gallup survey in 1982, people who have had near-death experiences number at least 8 million in North America. How does this kind of spiritual experience affect psychological well-being? Clearly, those who choose to accept their inner experience as valid find a renewed appreciation for life as they have realized new dimensions and new resources of love and peace; this, together with the loss of fear of death and the conviction that there is life after death brings great comfort. Those who feel threatened by their experience or are told to believe that their experience is delusional, a hallucination, unreal, etc., gain no psychological benefit. Those who find their religious convictions challenged by their spiritual experience may likewise be uncomfortable until they resolve their questions. (Pastoral counseling or psychological counseling may be called upon to help a person resolve their questions in these instances.)

The people who have experienced a greater reality through spiritual experience and integrated it into their lives are likely to be better educated, more economically successful, less racist, and substantially higher on scores of psychological well-being (Allison, 1967; Greeley, 1975; Hood, 1974, Thomas and Cooper, 1977, Vaughan and Walsh, 1980). "An appreciation of the holistic, unitive, integrated nature of the universe and one's unity with it" (Vaughan and Walsh, 1980) is further evidence of the positive changes which can come from integrating spiritual experience. Thus, it appears to be a contribution to individuals to help them integrate mystical experiences.

As our resuscitation technology improves increasingly more people will have these experiences when they are revived from near-death. Similarly, people anesthetized with ketamine and a variety of other anesthetics, will find themselves having NDE-like experiences (Rogo, 1984). Psychotropic drugs such as LSD and MDMA (Ecstasy), street drugs which are readily available, although illegal, also may facilitate the phenomena of spiritual experience.

A recent study (Allman et al., 1992) indicates that 4.5% of clients seeing full-time psychologists wanted to talk about their mystical experiences. Obviously, people who unexpectedly drop their fear of death or waylay doubts that the spiritual dimensions exist, or feel complete love and peace for the first time are having experiences which will have a profound impact on psychological health. These changes often include radical changes in values, radical changes in relationship to family and work, and new behaviors. Religious conversion may or may not be central to this transformation as people often move away from established religion and prefer a more spontaneous spiritual expression in alignment with a sense of the underlying unity of all religions.

Other spiritual experiences include the awakening of expanded perceptual abilities that are not related to paranoid ideation and have a positive, transformative impact. These abilities might include:

precognition: the ability to see into the future through awake vision or dream. This might include extraordinary inspiration such as Mozart hearing a whole symphony or Einstein seeing a new theorem through tapping resources that transcend logical processing.

clairvoyance: the ability to perceive constellations of energy through inner sight which are imperceptible to ordinary vision. Clairvoyant perceiving might include "seeing" roots of problems manifesting as physical disease, mental disturbance, or relationship difficulties. Clairvoyant "seers" can be used for health diagnostics and psychological counsel and are extraordinary resources for knowledge that transcend the limitations of time, space and technology.

clairsentience: the ability to feel energies in one's own body which duplicate the emotions, physical wellness, or thoughts of another being. Similar to clairvoyance, clairsentience can be useful in human health services as well as having applications in personal problem solving. When people feel their unity with the earth itself, it can be a source of great comfort and inspiration.

clairaudience: the ability to hear messages from a source of intelligence which goes beyond the rational information of the present life.

Examples include speaking with nonphysical spiritual guides or angels who give uplifting, positive direction and open the person to increased resources of compassion for all beings.

healing: the ability to manifest health-giving changes in the physiology or psychology of oneself or another being through laying on of hands, prayer, or psychic transmission.

psychokinesis: the ability to move material objects through psychic transmission.

Both the influences of medical and pharmaceutical experiences in our lives and psycho-social factors discussed in Chapters 2 and 8 contribute to this being a time in history when many people are able to have spiritual experiences, acquire some of the abilities mentioned above, and make the passageway to the increased well-being that spiritual experiences can promote. The following table published by A. Greeley in *American Health* in January, 1987, illustrates polls which indicate that spiritual experiences in the USA are on the rise. This is further evidence that the spiritual aspect of life increasingly plays a major role in the psychological lives of the majority of the population.

TABLE 1:

Increases in paranormal experiences in 1973 (in parentheses) and 1986.

Americans Who:	1973	1986
Had contact with the dead (adult pop.)	(27%)	42%
Had contact with the dead (widows)	(51%)	67%
Had visions	(8%)	29%
Experienced ESP	(58%)	67%
Experienced deja vu	(59%)	67%
Experienced clairvoyance	(24%)	31%
Believe in life after death	(*)	73%
Believe the afterlife is Paradise	(*)	68%
Believe that after death they'll be reunited with dead loved ones	(*)	74%

(*) No figures available

National surveys by the Gallup Organization bolster Greeley's polls showing paranormal experiences in the United States are on the rise:

Had an unusual spiritual experience	43%	('85)
Had a near-death experience	15%	('81)
Believe in life on other planets	46%	('81)
Believe in life after death	71%	('81)
Believe in reincarnation	23%	('81)
Believe in God or a Universal Spirit	95%	('81)
Believe Jesus is God	70%	('83)
Believe in angels	67% of teenagers	('86)
Believe in heaven**	71%	('80)
Believe in hell	53%	('80)
Expect the afterlife to be boring	5%	('81)

**Of those who believe, 20% think their chances of going to heaven are excellent.

Spiritual Experiences and Psychological Disturbance

Can the above-mentioned spiritual experiences cause psychological disturbance or be symptomatic of pre-existing pathology? The advent of these spiritual experiences often do stimulate a process of re-evaluation of values and convictions. New perceptual abilities and a greater sense of relatedness to spiritual forces may be disorienting at first. But, the spiritual experiences themselves, if they stimulate increased compassion, deeper relatedness and peace of mind, are not indicators of psychological disturbance. On the contrary, they are openings to higher states of well-being and more effective functioning in the world.

People who are becoming increasingly fearful, more isolated, less trusting, less energetic, and less interested in life, without remission, are psychologically disturbed. Some of these people may report hearing voices which tell them what to do or think, or feeling things in their body which do not belong to them, or seeing visions which impel them to destructive thinking or destructive behavior. An inner experience which robs a person of his or her free will, peace of mind or positive relatedness to others is indicative of psychological disturbance. People with these experiences should have a thorough physical examination checking for physical disease that can cause psychological imbalance as well as be attended to by someone skilled in psychiatric differential diagnosis. Mental health professionals need to recognize the varieties of spiritual experiences and learn to differentiate them from paranoid ideation, delusions, and hallucinations. People absorbed in integrating spiritual experiences are breaking through to higher levels of functioning. People absorbed in inner experiences which leave them chronically drained, fearful and isolated are breaking down and need skilled psychological intervention. The subtleties of differential diagnosis come to play when a person seems to be having both spiritual experiences and symptoms of mental disturbance. These issues are discussed in Chapter 3, Diagnosis.

Unfortunately, neither psychiatrists nor mental health professionals are given adequate training to prepare them to deal with issues arising in the realm of spiritual experiences or the subtleties of differentiating spiritual experiences from the symptoms of mental disturbance (Peck, 1993). Excerpts from the article in Appendix C by Drs. Lukoff, Lu and Turner (1992), relate: "Few psychiatrists are trained to understand religion, much less treat it sympathetically. Similarly, in a survey of members of the American Psychological Association, 83% reported that discussions of religion in training occurred rarely or never (Shafranske and Malony, 1990.) A study of training directors of the Association of Psychology Internship Centers found that 100% indicated they had received no education or training in religious or spiritual issues during their formal internship. Yet 72% reported that they had addressed those issues, at least occasionally, in clinical practice."

The people having spiritual experiences and needing counseling may well find themselves with clinicians who are not adequately trained to work effectively with this aspect of human experience. The conventional psychologist or psychiatrist is typically trained to interpret any experience of communication with invisible beings, perceptual distortions of time and space, and/or a sense of unity with larger forces as indicative of a radical debilitating psychological disturbance, a psychosis or mania. The aforementioned phenomena are perceived as indicators that the patient is "out of touch with reality." The administration of psychiatric drugs is the most often used therapeutic intervention for those perceived as manic or psychotic. This medical treatment may be the most compassionate intervention for someone who is psychologically disturbed, but may be debilitating for someone in the process of integrating spiritual experiences (Breggin, 1991).

The new diagnostic category in the DSM-1V for "spiritual or religious problem" is an important step in bringing the arena of spiritual experiences out of the shadows where it has been summarily confused with mental disease. Placed in the category of "other conditions that may be a focus of clinical attention," these problems can now be viewed as natural changes that may demand psychological and social adjustments but are not in themselves necessarily indicative of illness. Health professionals will now have a codified alternative to assuming that all spiritual experiences are indicative of pathology.

The Difference Between Spiritual and Religious Problems

Is there a difference between spiritual and religious problems? Perhaps not, if we believe that all problems that emerge in relation to one's religious life are essentially spiritual in nature. However, there are specific problems which arise which have to do with one's relationship to the beliefs and practices of an organized religious institution, or conversion to a particular faith. For the purposes of this book, I will call these specific problems "religious." Problems relating to spiritual experience and the transcultural experience of relationship with higher forces will be "spiritual" in nature. These problems include: shifting values, changes in relationship to one's self-concept when there are surges in physical energy, emotional reactions to spiritual experiences, as well as resistance to further spiritual experiences.

Spiritual Emergence

Spiritual emergence is the process of creating a meaningful context to integrate spiritual experiences as one matures. This process involves re-evaluating conceptual frameworks for what is real and what is meaningful in life. As such, it is an intellectual process regarding values. But, it also involves the emotions and the body as it calls us to a deeper experience of relatedness with ourselves and others. The spiritual emergence most often includes expanded perceptual abilities, increased energy, creative expression and the strong desire to take action in being of service in the world. Brother David Steindl-Rast, a Benedictine monk, describes the process in the following way:

> *Spiritual emergence is a kind of birth pang in which you yourself go through to a fuller life, a deeper life, in which some areas in your life that were not yet encompassed by this full-ness of life are now integrated or called to be integrated or challenged to be integrated... Breakthroughs are often very painful, often acute and dramatic breakthroughs (happen) on all levels: what we call material, spiritual, bodily—all levels.*
>
> *(Steindl-Rast, 1985)*

From this description, spiritual emergence is a kind of awakening to a more expanded way of being. It vitalizes a profound step in personal evolution.

In order to perceive phenomena of spiritual emergence as distinct from the dark realms of pathology it can be useful to see it as having a place in our natural unfolding. The map of the development of consciousness by Ken Wilber, Ph.D., (1980) gives a manageable linear illustration of spiritual emergence.

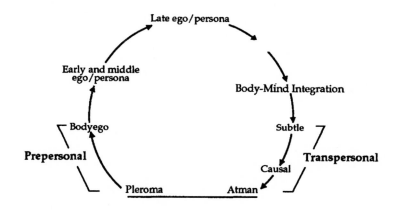

The Complete Life Cycle

According to this diagram, an individual begins life arising out of unity with infinite consciousness and proceeds through his or her unique life drawn toward mystical transpersonal experience. Biological development demands that one first identifies as an organ of the mother, then at birth begins a journey of disidentification with the mother and identification with the more independent self as a body first, then an independent mind and independent emotional and spiritual being. Adulthood is marked by the recognition that an individual is a separate being who is responsible in fulfilling his or her own needs.

At the top of the circle, the late ego, you can picture the adult who has a job, a satisfying intimate relationship, a satisfying connection to a wider community, adequate material wealth in order to be safe and fed, and the self -

discipline to continue maintaining this life. Further development takes a person into questions about the meaning of life and the impulse for self-actualization. People who identify with this later stage of life may start a spiritual practice, intensify their involvement in religion, attend workshops to stimulate personal growth and/or dedicate themselves to helping others.

The last stage in Wilber's diagram marks the final state of ultimate unity, or Atman. It is difficult to describe in words because it transcends all of our conceptual frameworks. Wilber writes, "Consciousness henceforth operates, not on the world, but only as the entire world process, integrating and interpenetrating all levels, realms and planes, high or low, sacred or profane." This is a multi-dimensional awareness that is not limited to time and space. It belongs to a particular person, but is not limited by any of the identifications of that person. This is a rare state of consciousness. No one, as yet, has devised a way to measure how many people have achieved it. Yet, however extraordinary it is, it has been described in the literature of ancient world religions as well as in modern anthologies. We can call it the state of enlightenment, or God, which has drawn people to experience awe and ecstasy throughout the ages.

In keeping with Wilber's spectrum, it is important to note that we never totally leave behind any stage of identification; we are not like a caterpillar metamorphosing into a butterfly that can no longer go back to being a caterpillar. Instead, we take the experiences of one identification with us as we continue through the cycle, a bit like nesting dolls where the next-larger doll holds the previous dolls, fully intact, within it. So our identification rests with the larger doll, the most expanded sense of self, even though we hold the smaller dolls, with their limited sense of self, within and can choose to identify with one of them as well.

In the personal realms on the left side of Wilber's spectrum of consciousness identifications may sound like: I am a child, I am a good girl, I am a student, I am rich, I am poor, I am black, I am white, I am an adult, I am a psychologist, I am a wife. When a person has identified with the more advanced realms of consciousness, he will describe himself as: I am a soul; I am a spirit; I am here to learn certain lessons before proceeding on to another dimension; I have many personal identifications within me, but I am more than those social roles and beliefs about myself.

As a person has more and more spiritual experiences, his or her sense of identity may include: I am one with the earth, I am one with God, I feel close to my spiritual guidance, I feel at one with nature, I feel the sensations of universal energy moving through me. In the final stage, there is no sense of an "I" which is separate from anything. In that consciousness the mind does not conceptualize "I" nor speak about "I," but still has the power to identify with a more limited identity in order to function in the world. This advanced consciousness holds all others within itself.

There are increasingly more autobiographies available which recount spiritual experiences individuals have had which have expanded their sense of identity to these advanced levels of consciousness. (Appendix D lists a number of these books.) Gopi Krishna (1971), an East Indian man, tells about one of his most dramatic experiences, a result of his meditation practice:

> *Suddenly, with a roar like that of a waterfall, I felt a stream of liquid light entering my brain through the spinal cord... The illumination grew brighter and brighter, the roaring louder. I experienced a rocking sensation and then felt myself slipping out of my body, entirely enveloped in a halo of light. It is impossible to describe the experience accurately. I felt the point of consciousness that was myself growing wider, surrounded by waves of light. It grew wider and wider, spreading outward while the body, normally the immediate object of its perception, appeared to have receded into the distance until I became entirely unconscious of it. I was now all consciousness, without any outline, without any idea of a corporeal appendage, without any feeling or sensation coming from the senses, immersed in a sea of light simultaneously conscious and aware of every point, spread out, as it were, in all directions without any barrier or material obstruction. I was no longer myself, or to be more accurate, no longer as I knew myself to be, a small point of awareness confined in a body, but instead was a vast circle of consciousness in which the body was but a point, bathed in light and in a state of exaltation and happiness impossible to describe.*

After having these kind of experiences Gopi Krishna developed an Institute for the Study of Kundalini, the universal energy in humans that contains the potential for extraordinary mental acuity, brilliant creativity, and love which usually lies dormant until awakened by spiritual practice. Gopi Krishna's life exemplified how life is transformed after these potent experiences. After his kundalini awakening he was able to learn a foreign language in a matter of days and needed very little sleep, only 1-2 hours a day. He wrote several books, while simultaneously maintaining a research institute and a school for boys, as well as traveling and teaching.

Yogananda, another East Indian in the 20th century, had similar experiences :

> *Soul and mind instantly lost their physical bondage... In my intense awareness I knew that never before had I been fully alive. My sense of identity was no longer narrowly confined to a body....People on distant streets seemed to be moving gently over my own remote periphery.... An oceanic joy broke upon the endless calm shores of my soul.*
>
> *(Yogananda, 1946)*

Yogananda was also inspired to be very active in the world as a result of his spiritual transformation. He founded the Self-Realization Fellowship, an international organization that melds the Christian and Hindu paths in order to facilitate spiritual emergence. This fellowship is still in existence, having close to a million members throughout the world. In addition to having extraordinary amounts of energy, less need for sleep, and a profound dedication to helping vast numbers of people, Yogananda was able to die consciously, at peace.

The powers that become accessible through identification with spiritual realms of consciousness go beyond many of our ideas of what is considered normal human limitation. The most advanced Tibetan spiritual adepts have been known to die and then to dissolve their physical body leaving only hair and fingernails behind (Sogyal, 1992). These feats demonstrate the enormous power contained in the spiritual dimensions within us. However, the magical demonstration of extraordinary power is not the issue here. The value that comes from realizing these dimensions is not in the extraordinary feats but the capacity to help others to a better life.

People who have integrated experiences of the highest spiritual realms often become spiritual teachers. In their presence one feels the deep wisdom they have attained and the loving compassion which they freely give to all. Rama et al., (1976) described it:

> *There is no more of the alternation of pain and pleasure, only a constant and pervasive joy...(He/ She) reflects an inner discipline and an inner peace—through a relaxed body and harmonious coordination, and through patience, confidence, clear thinking, and an unselfish attention to the needs of others.*

People in the news who best exemplify these characteristics are H.H. the Dalai Lama XIV of Tibet, winner of the Nobel Peace Prize in 1988, and Mother Theresa. There are many others who are less well known because they are not in the public eye.

Spiritual Emergency

When spiritual emergence catapults an individual into experiences at the high end of the spectrum of consciousness before that person has completed the stages of developing a mature ego, spiritual problems may result. At its most intense crisis point these problems may create a spiritual emergency. In this case, the immature ego, the "I," is disoriented and needs to withdraw from ordinary life for a time in order to find a context to integrate the spiritual experience(s). If given the appropriate support, this time out can be a time of accelerated learning and personal growth after which the individual is either ready to assume a more expanded sense of self, or prepared to do the necessary "self" work in preparation for that step. Without the appropriate support, an individual may become fixated on the spiritual experience, so the bodymind is energetically bound up in the experience without being able to use it as a stepping stone to higher functioning. In the latter case the bodymind deals with it as a trauma that has threatened the "I." Poor memory, fatigue, depression, anxiety, sleep disturbance and loneliness are indicators of spiritual experiences that have not been integrated.

The individual needs a conceptual framework to understand the experience as well as deal with emotional and physical reactions to the experience. Appropriate books and stories, especially personal interaction with people who have integrated spiritual experiences, are very reassuring to anyone in spiritual emergency. Bodywork, including psychophysical exercises like Yoga, T'ai Chi, and Chi Kung, help prepare the bodymind to adjust to the expanded energy levels which come with spiritual emergence. Psychotherapy and/or service work are useful guides for an individual to make the emotional steps needed to stabilize the ego so the "I" can accommodate the expanded energy levels.

If we consider that it is the work of this lifetime to expand spiritually, then there is a natural impulse in all of us to reach for the most expanded levels of consciousness. The conflict which arises when the moral code or conventional thinking of our family and friends does not accept this impulse for growth can inhibit spiritual emergence. If the growth wants to happen and is denied, the scene is set for a crisis to occur. A. Mindell (1988) suggests that it is our wrestling with convention which is responsible for spiritual emergency; J. W. Perry (1986) concurs:

> *(spirit)...is constantly striving for release from its entrapment in routine or conventional mental structures...if this work of releasing spirit becomes imperative but is not undertaken voluntarily with knowledge of the goal and with considerable effort, then the psyche is apt to take over and overwhelm the conscious personality with its own powerful processes.*
>
> *(J.Perry, 1986)*

When individuals have access to appropriate support for spiritual emergency, the intensely disturbing aspects of the crisis may be minimized. When individuals do not have appropriate support, the disturbing aspects may well become magnified. A lifetime punctuated by isolation, emotional turmoil and psychosomatic illness is not an unusual outcome for those who have not had the benefit of appropriate support during spiritual emergency.

The capacity to integrate spiritual experiences into one's self-concept and functioning in the world is the key determinant in the outcome of intense spiritual experiences. A natural spiritual emergence process is more likely to turn into a spiritual emergency when:

1. Someone has no conceptual framework to support the experience, or to understand and accept the phenomenon with equanimity.

2. Someone has neither the physical nor emotional flexibility to integrate the experiences into life.

3. The family, friends, and/or helping professionals of a person having the experience see the phenomenon in terms of psychopathological symptoms which have no possibility of being positive.

The pressure placed on persons to perceive themselves as crazy in the midst of an intense spiritual experience is often one of the most influential elements turning an emergence process into an emergency. Conversely, the willingness of a helper to accept the phenomena of spiritual experience and to have faith in a positive outcome is one of the most powerful elements in changing a spiritual emergency to a process of spiritual growth.

Examples of Spiritual Emergency

A good example of spiritual emergency is the case of Everest (Lukoff & Everest, 1985). When he was a young man in his early twenties, Everest brought himself into a transcendent state of consciousness through study and concentration. Because his psychological development was too immature to manage his state, he had to act out many of the themes of his inner process at inappropriate times, much to the bewilderment of his family and friends. He told them, in the midst of his intense experience:

> *"I have been through the bowels of Hell, climbed up and out, and wandered full circles in the wilderness. I have ascended through the Portals of Heaven where I established my rebirth in the earth itself, and now have taken my rightful place in the Kingdom of Heaven. ...I hoped my friends would make a similar connection and enter into an odyssey themselves. I urged them to create their own mythic vehicles and use them as guides into an odyssey as I had done."*
>
> *(Everest and Lukoff, 1985)*

His father, a general practitioner, committed Everest to a psychiatric ward soon after Everest entered his altered state of consciousness and began to talk and behave differently. This state continued for two months in the hospital, during which time he had very little interaction with the staff. He was given Thorazine, an antipsychotic medication, to inhibit the psychotic-type symptoms. Even without personal support from the hospital staff, family or friends, Everest never questioned the positive value of the experience his son was having. Everest was also able to cultivate his transpersonal experiences through his study of symbols and rituals.

At the end of two months, when Everest left the hospital, he was totally exhausted physically, emotionally, and mentally; however, he was capable of maintaining a part-time job that afforded him time to rest. Part of his exhaustion may have been a side effect of taking thorazine in the hospital. He discontinued all medication on his release.

In 1985, Everest wrote about his early experience:

> "*I have gained much from this experience. I am sorry for the worry and hurt that it may have caused my family and friends. These wounds have been slow to heal. I am deeply grateful for the great victory of my odyssey. With the dawning of a new vision of life has come a new sense of purpose. From a state of existential nausea, my soul now knows itself as part of the cosmos. Each year brings an ever increasing sense of contentment.*"
>
> *(ibid.)*

He has never been rehospitalized, has led a stable work life, and has joined a church group. He is involved with community work and maintains close relationships with his family and friends. His integration of his experience is still deepening.

Everest's story illustrates a spiritual emergency in which

psychological immaturity did not allow full integration of the spiritual experience at the time it was happening. His family, friends, and doctors considered Everest's experience as mental pathology, and did not support his entering it more deeply. His own understanding of his "odyssey," however enabled him to enter it fully and reap its transformational benefits.

Another example of spiritual emergency is taken from Chamberlin (1986) who worked with a group of 15-yearold boys in a psychiatric ward at the Menninger Foundation.

> *(He) taught (them) a variety of ways of altering their consciousness as a way of exposing them to alternatives to drug use. One of these methods involved biofeedback training with the eventual focus being on theta-wave training. During the time that the focus was on the theta-wave training and immediately following it, some of the teenagers developed some out-of-the-ordinary abilities. One of them began to have precognitive experiences that he perceived as strong intuitions and he needed to discuss these, particularly to validate them. Another person's reaction was more disruptive as he began to develop healing abilities. He was initially frightened by this ability. Later, he also began to notice that his electronic equipment was malfunctioning and that people in areas in which he would go would also report malfunctioning of electronic equipment. He was given some helpful suggestions about focusing his energy, at which point the electrical disruptions*

stopped. It appeared that this person was devel-oping some shamanistic abilities, which in other cultures would have been given a lot of support. He was given articles to read about shamanism, and this reading resulted in a con-ceptual framework that was a great deal of comfort to him. However, he felt these abilities were something he did not have the time to work with and so he moved away from them. By not using them they appeared to stop.

(Chamberlin, 1986)

Conceptual Frameworks and Supportive Contexts

The reactions of Chamberlin's adolescents illustrates the importance of an appropriate conceptual framework and supportive social context for persons in spiritual emergence.

Persons in spiritual emergency are deeply influenced by their community of friends, family and health care work-ers. The mini-culture in Chamberlin's ward supported spir-itual emergence in contrast to Everest's social community. Unlike most Western cultures, some cultures, like that in Tibet, hold a view of the world that allows spiritual expe-rience to be integrated into normal life.

(The Tibetan culture is built on the knowing that). . .all dharmas are dreamlike, all phenom-ena are dreamlike. It's seen from the very beginning from that perspective...Since it's seen from that point of view, when the world actually begins to fall apart in one's

31

experience, it doesn't become that much of a clash, of a contradiction...I think what has been happening in the West is the concretization of the world as really something solid, a permanent thing. This has been something that has been built on since the development of sciences and Cartesianism, so that the (dream-like quality of existence) has been "kind of kept under control so to speak." Sometimes people have these kind of (spiritual emergencies) because the real nature of existence has been so repressed, and then suddenly these energies themselves spontaneously become a little bit overwhelming.

(Sogyal, 1985)

There is no comparable perspective in Europe or North America that supports spiritual awakening as part of natural human development. Thus, most of us Westerners are afraid of spiritual phenomena. They are strange to us. We need some conceptual context to help us make sense of these phenomena so that we can be more at peace with our own and more supportive of others' spiritual awakening.

Patterns of Spiritual Experiencing

All spiritual experiences, as mentioned previously, are indicators of the spiritual emergence process. Sometimes an episode of various intense spiritual experiences will happen in a meaningful pattern. If one intense spiritual experience is a shocking opening for an individual, a pattern of several intense spiritual experiences are even more apt to catalyze a spiritual emergency.

For the sake of creating some order we can take the liberty on paper to differentiate eight different patterns of spiritual emergency. It is important to bear in mind, however, that these patterns in actuality usually overlap and often occur simultaneously. Imagine trying to understand human physiology at birth from the perspective of just understanding the changes in the digestive system. You have to take into consideration all the various systems in the body — breathing, perceiving, absorbing, circulating, and eliminating — in order to understand the full impact of change occurring in the newborn. Likewise, if you try to understand the evolutionary crisis of spiritual emergency from the point of view of only one pattern of spiritual emergency, you will miss the full dimensions of the transformation in progress. Thus, although the patterns of spiritual experiencing do not function like interdependent systems (as in the body), they are usually profoundly interwoven.

Christina Grof and her husband, Dr. Stanislav Grof, have made many contributions to creating a transcultural conceptual framework for understanding the patterns of spiritual emergence. They draw from the work of many spiritual teachers, shamans, anthropologists, psychologists and psychiatrists. Each pattern has certain characteristic features, or elements. A familiarity with these elements is essential for anyone working with people with spiritual problems.

The following eight patterns were first named by the Grofs (1985). The definitions I use supplement the definitions referred to by the Grofs.

1. Awakening of the Serpent Power (Kundalini)
- A radical transformation in the individual's relationship to his or her bio-energy and openness to transpersonal levels of experience. This awakening is usually accompanied by powerful sensations of heat and energy streaming up the spine, tremors, violent shaking, unusual auditory sounds, and the impulse to perform complex movements similar to yogic postures. These phenomena are associated with a letting go of chronic muscular tensions connected to past trauma and/or patterns of holding the body associated with particular beliefs, i.e., a person afraid of the world will hold his body in one way, a bully will hold his body in another, etc. Physical indicators may run the spectrum from debilitating illness to extraordinary perceptions of light that bring on ecstatic feelings of bliss. Although the opening of the energetic system occurs in all spiritual emergence, not all people experience intense episodes of muscular spasm or unusual sounds and the impulse to move in strange ways.

2. Shamanic Journey
- In this pattern the individual is often focused on elements of nature like animal guides, earth spirits, plant spirits, energies of the directions of north, south, east, west. On an inner level the individual is dealing with physical suffering and a personal encounter with death followed by rebirth. Descent to the underworld or ascent to the upperworlds are familiar aspects of the shamanic journey. Visions and premonitions of the future are often perceived in the intensity of this pattern. In shamanic cultures, these visions are seen as evidence of an individual's being a person able to heal others through access to

extraordinary dimensions. In ancient cultures Shamanic Journey was often created through fasting and isolation in the wilderness because it was clearly a powerful opening to the inner resources of wisdom and compassion.

3. Psychological Renewal through Activation of the Central Archetype - This pattern is marked by an inner experience of perceiving oneself as being in the center of all things and dealing directly with the dramatic universal experiences of life like the tension between good and evil, male and female, dark and light, life and death. Ordinary happenings take on mythic symbolic proportion. There is an emphasis on themes of death, afterlife and the return to the beginnings of creation. If this period of absorption in symbols and archetypal themes is validated as positive and respectable, the outcome can be a profound psychological renewal. If this episode is perceived as pathological and the individual is medicated, phenomena of spiritual emergence are pushed into the subconscious and become unavailable as powerful catalysts for psychological renewal.

The next three patterns demand a thorough evaluation of reincarnation and the law of karma. Karma, a concept from Far Eastern religious philosophies, refers to the law of cause and effect in personal life, e.g., if one is a victimizer at one time, one draws to oneself the effect of being victimized at another time. In the West we have an axiom which parallels the law of karma: "one reaps what one sows." The law of karma goes further by suggesting that when we have learned the lessons offered in duality we are no longer completely dominated by this duality. Eastern spiritual practices are devoted to mastering this transcendent stage of consciousness to benefit all of life.

4. Psychic Opening - This pattern is marked by a striking accumulation of instances of extrasensory perception - clairvoyance, clairsentience and clairaudience -or psychokinesis. It may include out of body experiences (OOBE). It may be stimulated by stress, spiritual focusing exercises, a powerful dream, an interaction with an extraterrestrial or a non-physical entity.

5. Emergence of a Karmic Pattern - If the psychic opening happens with a sense of sudden vivid recollection of a life or lifetimes before this life, it triggers a focus on karmic patterns. Frequently these openings deliver profound insight on current interpersonal problems. Perceiving karmic patterns gives an individual the opportunity to resolve dynamic inner conflicts and essential life lessons (Weiss, B. ,1988 & 1992).

6. Possession States - This pattern involves a person recognizing that either a disembodied soul that used to inhabit a body or a diabolical entity is having a manipulative or parasitic relationship with his or her vital energy and free will. This possessing entity may be a fragment of the self, a part of the shadow that has been rejected, a negative habit that has been passed down through the lineage of the family, or a victimizing outside force. Whether it is indigenous or foreign to the person, possession states make a demand that an individual review his or her ideas regarding the identity of the soul, free will, the power of the shadow and what happens to the soul after death. Some literature (Crabtree, 1985) suggests that Multiple Personality Disorder and addictive behavior (Lucas, 1993; Weiss, 1988) may be the result of possessing entities. Resolving issues of possession require someone skilled in exorcising these unusual phenomena. In addition to various paraprofessionals and shamans skilled in depossession there are some clinical psychologists who practice "spirit releasement" in the context of ongoing therapy. Apparently they can differentiate personal shadow material from entity possession and the exorcisms they initiate have been highly effective in stopping unwanted behavior, obsessions and fears. See References in Appendix D.

7. Encounters with Extra-terrestrials (ET's) - After conducting a thorough screening of hundreds who claim to have had an encounter with ET's, John Mack, MD, psychiatrist and professor at Harvard Medical School, believes that some people literally seem to have truly encountered extra-terrestrials. He believes their UFO abductions cannot be described by any of the psychiatric literature which means they are not an hallucination, a delusion or a projection (Harvard Magazine, March-April, 1992). These people are challenged to find a new conceptual framework to relieve the profound shock of their unexpected experiences. Often people feel they have been initiated into transpersonal states of consciousness through their abduction because the ET's seem to live at higher stages of consciousness than our own. Other dimensions and other space-time continua become real to abductees. The telepathic communication with ET's opened up channels within them that had been closed before. People who have an encounter with ET's in a vivid dream or spontaneous waking vision may also feel psychically opened by the experience and be compelled to re-examine their beliefs about extra-terrestrials and the other dimensions of reality these beings represent.

8. The Inter-life and other Mystical Experiences:
As mentioned above, the mystical experience is defined by a state of complete peace and at-one-ness with all that is. Individuals reach this state through a variety of ways. It may happen by being in communion with nature, through a Near Death Experience, through a powerful experience of love, direct neurological stimulation, or as a result of spiritual practice. The profound peace it brings has a healing effect since it allows one to feel whole within oneself as well as connected in a meaningful way to the world around. This mystical state can be stimulated through regression therapies which gently take people into the state of "being in the light" between lives, the Inter-life *(Lucas, 1993)*.

The phenomena associated with these forms of spiritual emergency can be bizarre and terrifying for someone who experiences them without understanding. In one case, a woman in childbirth was seized by a spontaneous kundalini experience that created strong, uncontrollable vibrations throughout her body. She was frightened for her and her child's life. Her nurses and doctors offered no explanation and only attempted to do what they could to make the vibrations stop through medication. No one had the knowledge to suggest that she may have been blessed with an experience of the Divine or had attained a level of self-realization which was not only valid, but which gave her extraordinary resources as a human and as a mother. For 10 years after the experience she was afraid to talk or think about the experience until finally she read about kundalini and understood she had had a spiritual awakening during childbirth.

Sympathetic and knowledgeable support at the birth could have helped her enjoy the extraordinary joy that comes with the rise of kundalini.

Confusion with Pathology
Some of the phenomena of spiritual emergence have been misconstrued as indicators of pathology. For instance, some criteria for the diagnosis of psychosis (DSM-III, 1980) are observable in spiritual emergency:

1. A disorientation which makes a person less interested in work, in social contacts and in self-care.

2. A difficulty in communicating about one's experience to others (in spiritual emergency this is the result of the noetic quality of the experience, not symptomatic of confused thinking).

3. Dissociation (in spiritual emergency this dissociation is a transitory part of the process of integrating one's experience.)

These phenomena subside after a spiritual emergency whereas in a chronic psychosis they do not.

The DSM-1V (1994) categorizes possession states as an example of "Dissociative Disorders Not Otherwise Specified." Examples include "Dissociative trance disorder: single or episodic alterations in the state of consciousness that are indigenous to particular locations and cultures. Dissociative trance involves narrowing of awareness of immediate surroundings or stereotyped behaviors or movements that are experienced as being beyond one's control. Possession trance involves replacement of the customary sense of personal identity by a new identity, attributed to the influence of a spirit, power, deity, or other person, and associated with stereotyped "involuntary" movements or amnesia" (American Psychiatric Association, 1993).

This clearly raises a question about differentiating between Dissociative Disorders which are mental disorder and possession states which are indicative of spiritual problems. Perhaps the longevity of the dissociative state will determine if mental disorder is the appropriate diagnosis? Or, perhaps it is not the symptom itself which determines the diagnosis but the individual's attachment to the mechanism of dissociating. Refer to Chapter 3, Diagnosis, for a more complete discussion on determining whether a person is in spiritual emergency or is sufferring from a mental disorder.

Many types of experiences involving a spiritual awakening have resulted in a person being humiliated and invalidated rather than celebrated. Hundreds of stories from people who have had spiritual emergencies, and have been misdiagnosed as having mental disease were collected by Ring (1984) and the Grofs (1989, 1990). Because our Western culture generally has not accepted spiritual emergence phenomena as the product of a sane mind, most of the people who have had Near Death Experiences (NDE) are inhibited from talking about their experiences from fear of being considered, and treated, as crazy.

According to Ring, people who have NDE are usually counseled by their doctors, nurses, and clergymen to forget the memories of the experience...as if it was only a hallucination or a bad dream attributable to stress. Many NDEr's who have not had people to validate their experience wonder if they were crazy. Some, however, spend their lives affirming the truth of their experience in spite of their community's lack of support.

Ring (1984) wrote about one woman who met a divine being during a NDE. Later, during the birth of her child she experienced a "surge of great joy" when she realized that her child would be able to go with the divine being she met when she was in her NDE. After her baby died a few days after birth, she did not experience the grief her doctor and minister expected her to go through. She wrote:

> *Well, I soon realized that my acceptance back into this world depended upon 'pretending' to forget, and 'pretending' to grieve the loss of my baby. So, I did this for everybody else's sake - except my husband, who believed me, and gained some comfort from it, second-hand. It was a dropped 'subject,' but never forgotten.*

Clearly a change in the attitudes of the public in general and health-care professionals in particular toward the validity of NDE phenomena might produce dramatic benefits. We might not fear death, might believe in the existence of divine beings, and might feel we could talk about the transpersonal phenomena that have a profound impact on our lives.

Summary

Spiritual emergence is a personal realization of a reality beyond ego reality, and, ultimately, one's unity with all things. The outcome of a spiritual experience may be gradual spiritual emergence or problems related to spiritual emergency. When the individual with spiritual problems is given an appropriate conceptual framework and community support, spiritual emergence is made more likely.

When a person with spiritual problems is perceived as out of touch with reality, he or she may be subjected to an inappropriate diagnosis and course of treatment which intensifies the problems. The new DSM-IV (1994) category allows us to differentiate spiritual experiences as a "condition that may be a focus of clinical attention" but is not neccarily indicative of mental disorder. Thus, spiritual experiences are not neccessarily symptomatic of mental disorder. However, there is still a considerable lack of clarity about distinguishing "spiritual problems" from Dissociative Disorder Not Otherwise Specified. Possession states, out -of- body experiences and other spiritual experiences could be diagnosed as indicators of spiritual problems or a dissociative disorder. Further study is needed to clarify these distinctions.

Chapter Two _____

When Do Spiritual Experiences Occur?

Spiritual experiences are more likely to happen at specific times and under particular circumstances. These circumstances may be personal (as discussed in this chapter) or be more involved with issues involving change on community, national or international levels (discussed in Chapter 8). At the personal level, there are spiritual practices and psychopharmaceutical interventions that can serve as catalysts for spiritual experience and spiritual problems. In addition, times of physical or emotional distress can provide the conditions for a spiritual experience to occur.

This chapter includes discussion of the following personal circumstances that are often associated with spiritual experience:

I. Openness to Change vs. Rigidity

II. Time of Life:
    1. Dark Night
    2. Destiny Calls

III. Spiritual Practice:
    1. Intensive Practice

IV. Physical Distress:
    1. Athletes and Yogis
    2. Near-Death Experience
    3. Surgery
    4. Pregnancy and Childbirth
    5. Natural Disaster

V. Emotional Distress:
    1. Emotional Intensity
    2. Fragmentation
    3. Emotional Deprivation

VI. Intense Sexual Experience

VII. Substance Use / Abuse
    1. Depressants
    2. Stimulants
    3. Barbiturates
    4. Opiates
    5. Marijuana
    6. Empathogens
    7. Psychedelics

Openness to Change vs. Rigidity

The factor which most contributes to spiritual experiences becoming problems is lack of personal flexibility and openness to change regarding cognitive values as well as emotional and physical patterns of behavior. Spiritual problems are less likely to occur when a person can weather a life-changing situation gracefully, by both letting go of what has been lost and opening with a positive, trusting attitude toward the future. Spiritual problems are more likely to occur when a person rigidly holds on to a belief about how life should be and resists change. People who are completely identified with narrow beliefs about the expression of spiritual life will tend to have more trouble with spiritual problems than people who are welcoming about spiritual life manifesting in a myriad of ways.

When a person is open to change, inner experiences are interesting, even welcome or exciting. When a person is not open to change, inner experiences may be threatening and evoke mental confusion as well as physical stress responses. A person who feels threatened may be ashamed to reach out for guidance and help. They may relegate their spiritual experiences into their shadow through a variety of defense mechanisms or deny the experience altogether. If such a person has a kundalini awakening sending streams of energy through the body, he or she is apt to feel overwhelmed, as if the very structure of life has been shaken and might try to resist the sensations by contracting muscles and breathing shallowly. A person who feels overwhelmed is not likely to redirect his or her attention away from the trauma. A more flexible person may experience bliss and openness during a kundalini awakening as he or she can trust in the process and easily surrender control. Such a person is more likely to be able to shift easily from personal experiences to interpersonal experiences that demand more objective attention. This person can go through a period of personal transformation and still maintain a household, an active role in the family, and a productive role in society.

As this chapter discusses the personal circumstances that are often associated with spiritual experience, bear in mind that it is not the circumstance, per se, which determines the possibility of spiritual problems but the mental, physical and emotional attitude toward the circumstance. Another determinant will be the element of surprise. Has the person had any foreknowledge of the experience or are the changes abruptly demanding a shift into a completely new way of perceiving the self and the world?

Time of Life

Spiritual experiences can happen at anytime and in any-place. Extra-sensory perception can, and usually does occur quite unexpectedly. Very common is 'deja-vu,' a sense of having been somewhere or known someone before—without any reference point from this lifetime. Also common is the knowing who is calling on the phone before the phone rings. People often experience a sense of total rightness in the world that sometimes comes as if by 'grace.' These spiritual experiences are windows into the extraordinary. Psychokinesis, psi phenomena, occult knowledge, or mystical experience are within this same category of experience. They happen to infants, young children, adolescents, and adults of all ages without regard to time, place, or circumstance.

The Dark Night

Although spiritual experience can happen at all ages, mid-life is a time that often precipitates spiritual awakenings, particularly among individuals who have achieved some real level of stability, even prosperity, in the world.

They've got it, to put it in the vernacular, they've got the two kids, they've got the two cars in the garage, they've got a house in the suburbs, or whatever the New Age equivalents of those things are. They've come to some level of personal ego (development). There's a self-sense, a definition of self that's relatively well-established. Then it still doesn't work. Life still doesn't work. These very subtle, elusive feelings of emptiness begin to emerge, feelings of, "So what? What have I done this for?" As one of my clients put it so eloquently, using the Lennon and McCartney song, "Nowhere Man, ... I have become a real 'Nowhere Man." There is a yearning for something more, but not knowing exactly what it is. It's certainly not something more tangible. It's certainly not something more material. It's something more enigmatic, something that's immaterial. It's my belief that what's happening in this kind of a crisis is that the Soul/Spirit is asking, demanding to be

> *recognized on some very deep level. That may not
> be what the client presents. In fact, most of the time
> it's not, but my experience is that as we unwind and
> go further into the material that the client presents,
> it's very often a yearning for the Spirit, for a greater
> sense of wholeness that includes an abiding, eternal
> principle.*
>
> *(Wittine, 1985)*

This experience is a modern aspect of the Dark Night of
the Soul, that is, the existential encounter with mean-
inglessness which meets any man or woman who has
reached material goals and has still not found inner satisfaction. This is the Dark Night of the Ego in which it is no
longer satisfying to just pursue ego gratification (Vaughan,
1985). Gopi Krishna pointed out that such an experience
may also occur to an adolescent, not only the more typical
mid-lifer.

> *...at a certain critical state in the development of
> the human mind the unanswered "Riddle of Life"
> attains an urgency which no treasure of the earth
> can counteract. This is the state of mind of millions
> of disillusioned young people of the world today
> ...when thwarted in its mission, the impulse can
> lead to social and political unrest...craving for
> drugs, promiscuity or other social evils and even to
> violence.*
>
> *(Gopi Krishna, 1975)*

The longing for something more may precipitate a search
for or spontaneous experience of transpersonal level
phenomena. If this longing is not met satisfactorily, the

effects may be disastrous for the individual and have a negative impact on society. The following passage illustrates this:

> *...about 30 Americans under 21 years of age commit suicide every day, indicating a three fold increase in the rate of suicide among American youth over the past decade. Also more than half the admitted to mental hospitals in the United States are young people...the main cause of the increase in the number of suicides and mental disorders among the youth is the increasing hollowness and senselessness of life of the society and the younger generation's distaste for profit.*
>
> *(Treffert, personal quote to Gopi Krishna, 1975)*

Destiny Calls

People who do not experience the Dark Night may instead be 'grabbed by the eternal' (Kennett Roshi, 1982) through a dramatic dream, a chance meeting with an inspiring person, a drug experience, or a spontaneous awakening. These experiences impel people to advance their developmental process into transpersonal levels. This is particularly true with adolescents and young adults who are looking for a meaning to their life.

Anne Armstrong's story illustrates the autonomous quality of spiritual experience when it almost forces itself on one, regardless of one's openness to it. Anne was a young wife and mother, a Girl Scout leader, living an ordinary life in a very normal suburb. She was not the least bit interested in psychic phenomena, yet, she spontaneously began to experience psi phenomenon that would not cease. By meditating and undergoing hypnotherapy, she cultivated her relationship to these spontaneous psychic happenings. Whenever she would stop these practices, she was saddled with migraine headaches. From her perspective, the transpersonal realm forced itself on Anne, as if it was her destiny to develop and become a psychic counselor (Armstrong, 1986).

Spiritual Practice

It is commonly believed that most people have entered transpersonal levels of consciousness by means of an intent to grow spiritually coupled with an intense dedication to spiritual discipline. Religious traditions of the Far East and ancient cultures have significantly influenced how people learn to reach transpersonal levels of consciousness. Lesser known esoteric Christian texts offer this same knowledge. However, Hindu and Buddhist literature, among others, offers a language for transpersonal states of consciousness that is far more detailed than anything we have in the English language.

Practitioners of both Eastern and Western religious disciplines are capable of reaching transpersonal levels and equally face the difficulty arising coming from intense spiritual practice.

Intensive Practice
Intensive practice of prayer, meditation or devotional work in both Eastern and Western religious practice can

catalyze spiritual emergency. Following is Baraz's description of the types of difficulty arising from intensive meditation, and the corresponding psychological stress that can catalyze spiritual emergency processes.

> *One meditation teacher calls practice "one insult after another." You see all the stuff that's in there. So it takes a lot of kindness and compassion with what you see and patience with the process. You see what's there and perhaps you have an image of what you'd like to be like. You know, a spiritual person who's loving and kind; and you see rage and fear and whatever, sadness, and that discrepancy can be very discouraging. That's where patience and compassion and kindness are essential. That's where it's very helpful to have someone around to check in with when you start getting lost in your despair. So that's the first level of difficulty that can happen.*

> *The second one is that you start seeing that you're not who you think you are. The connection that you have with your identity, especially the good stuff, starts to dissolve. At times it can be nice when you see, "Oh, I'm not the garbage" but [what follows is] "Gee, if I'm not the garbage then I'm not the good stuff, and then WHO AM I? " That can be unnerving. It's like the rug being pulled out from underneath you. As that idea of self starts to dissolve, it can get very terrifying actually.*

The interesting thing is that the other side of seeing that you're not who you think you are is freedom.

51

When you see that you don't have to hold onto anything and be so caught-up in protecting and getting recognized and all these things, there's a tremendous letting go of stuff that allows you to really have connection, on a much deeper level, with other beings....

Another thing that often happens on retreat is that concentration can open up tremendous amounts of energy. That can be very terrifying. The system starts getting, seemingly, overloaded.

I remember one retreat, the first 3 month retreat I had. After doing the [meditation practice] for a couple of years I did a 3 month retreat. I started to feel like I was going to explode, literally explode. Just bursting...like I was a sun, about to explode. I didn't know where it was going to go and I got very frightened. Tears were running down my face and I went running up to the teacher and said; "Hey, I'm just watching my breath and all this stuff is going on. What's going on here?"

He said, "Oh, don't worry about it, just do this and do this ... and breath and a few different things."

It was awhile before I started seeing that you can become comfortable with that energy so that you can become a vessel for it. If can soften around it and be quite still and not anticipate the next thing, you open up your capacities to new levels of energy. But it can be quite fearful and overwhelming. In that state, if the mind trips out onto a thought of "What's next?" or "I don't know what's going on" you lose your center and it's difficult....

In addition to opening up to the energy, there's all sorts of psychic stuff that seems to happen at times, synchronistically. You start to experience things in a different reality than typically. Generally, if you report those things, the teacher says: "OK. Just notice them and let them go and keep on sitting."

[What he means is] ...It's not to get stuck in having any experience, it's just to watch it all coming and going.

(Baraz, 1985)

Leaving an intensive retreat also can be difficult because one needs to integrate newly discovered sensitivities into a life that is far more stressful and demanding than the quiet, supportive environment of the retreat.

After you've left that situation where you're wide open, where you have expanded to some extent, or to a large extent, coming back into the world is not so easy, especially the first few times you do it. That transition is really important. If you think of it in terms of...an energy system that's expansive . . .like a wide- open baby and this tender baby steps out on the highway and things are whizzing by... It can be jarring, to say the least. That sensory overload can be difficult to handle. The world is very fast. Your boundaries between yourself and the world are not as in place as they normally are....

53

I've gotten quite a few phone calls when people have left retreats, often from another particular style of practice where there's a lot of emphasis on body opening up and not much on transition. People have called up and said, "I'm having all these flashes and I don't know what to do."

Also, sometimes someone is stuck in a place where everything is dissolving and it still goes on after the retreat. Although it might be a very advanced space, it's still not very pleasant. Sometimes people don't even know what's going on.

(Baraz, 1985)

In this final quote Baraz provided an example of a spiritual teacher helping someone deal with psychic phenomena accompanying spiritual practice. One benefit of spiritual communities is that there is likely to be a teacher or priest who can provide guidance and support if a spiritual experience occurs during intense meditation or prayer.

The attitudes of the spiritual teachers/priests (and other community members in a church or community situation) have a broad impact on how a spiritual aspirant manages a spiritual experience. Teachers, gurus, and priests differ, however, in their capacity to deal with spiritual crisis. Some are able to defuse a crisis situation, but others have little understanding of or skill in dealing with the needs of someone in spiritual emergency.

Baraz gave suggestions for helping persons doing intensive spiritual practice so that their spiritual experiences do not take them into a state of crisis. He advocated compassionate understanding and a non-judgmental attitude toward the mental confusion and emotional upset that accompany spiritual emergence. This has also been the attitude of Buddhist teachers in the East.

Unfortunately, not all teachers, gurus, priests, or spiritual community members have such an attitude or the skills to work with disturbed people. Steindl-Rast made this point about monastic communities:

> *The communities in monasteries are made up of run-of-the-mill people from that particular culture. They share all the prejudices that other people in their culture share. So even though, on one level, they know...they have come to a place for spiritual emergence, and that is their path, they may also share, on another level that is closer to their reflective consciousness, all sorts of prejudice, even against mental diseases ....*
>
> *(Steindl-Rast, 1985)*

Even though the purpose of a monastic community is to support spiritual emergence, the members of the community do not necessarily teach skills in dealing with spiritual emergency (especially when emergency looks like mental disease). In their ignorance, these communities may unfortunately contribute to the disorientation and fear that can turn a spiritual experience into a spiritual emergency.

People's spiritual emergence may be overwhelming on a physical or emotional level. Offering a person a stable center, a grounding in the body and emotions, may be one of the most powerful contributions to spiritual emergence that monastic communities can offer their members (Steindl-Rast, 1985).

> *It seems to me that monasteries can and I think actually do perform a real function in this respect, precisely by what is often looked at negatively: namely the many people that leave, you see? I've always taken a very positive view of that and said, "Why worry about it?" ...I think **they** may be the ones who get as much out of it as the ones that stay! There's nothing wrong with it in many cases. Some people find nothing. Others find what they need, then leave. Still others stay, because they keep finding what they need. Those who find what they need, grow by the monastic experience. And that's what counts, whether or not they leave or stay.*
>
> *(ibid.)*

Different spiritual communities have different resources for helping their members through a spiritual emergency. Some communities have the capacity for supporting their members (for example, Naropa in Boulder, Colorado); however, other communities refer their members to psychiatrists and doctors expecting them to handle any emotional and physical disturbances. Chapter 5, Ongoing Support, presents suggestions for helping people who need support in spiritual emergency.

Physical Distress

Whether it be through an intensive physical workout, disease or injury, or giving birth, physical distress is one of the most provocative catalysts of spiritual experiences. These experiences push one to one's limits of physical endurance and bring one face to face with the boundaries of life and death. This is fertile ground for the occurrence of spiritual experience.

Athletes and Yogis

The practice of Hatha yoga is reputed for its ability to help people become flexible and relaxed. When practiced intensively, Hatha yoga is a way of purifying the body and precipitating spiritual emergence. In intensive practice, the yogi or yogini is constantly aware of pushing right to the limit of potential—to stretch, to remain balanced, and to retain concentration. To enhance their abilities, dedicated practitioners will also restrict themselves to a very simple diet and limit their sexual activities. The result of this regimen is a high-level wellness, where yogis of any age feel full of buoyant energy, at peace with themselves and the world, and consistently growing toward the transpersonal levels of their own development.

Athletes who are aerobically fit, and who push the levels of their physical endurance, also report experiences of ecstasy when they push through to a new level of energy, a second wind or when they complete a race in which they have gone "full out." These athletes, like the yogis, have usually led very disciplined lives, restricting their sexual activities and limiting their diet, so as to stay in shape.

> *A serious young runner named Jim Colvin has formulated it for himself: "To run to me means to practice a religion that reflects life in a microcosm, that cleanses the entire man--mind and body--and that allows an almost mystical communication with nature and meditation on existence...Running allows me to communicate with an inner being ... The successful runner achieves something of the transcendentalist's solitary status in which observation and imagination blend to span the schism between mind and matter. He extends himself toward something beyond common scrutiny, something almost indecipherable, something at once natural and cultivated. A contemporary psychiatrist, Alan McGlashan, has noted in The Savage and Beautiful Country: "For the profoundest questions the seeker himself is the essential instrument of the seeker." The runner, in the sensual euphoria of his inner soliloquy, discovers McGlashan's "central point within oneself the secret threshold where the world of the senses and the world of the psyche meet in mutual simultaneous recognition." For such a moment of illumination- - the eternal 'now' of the transcendentalist- - dichotomies such as mental-physical, inner-outer and pain-pleasure are suspended while "a man for a timeless moment discovers his own Center." The runner often wonders*

*whether or not he has brushed against, however
momentarily, the shadow of a fourth dimension.*
(Cusack, 1974)

Yogis have a body of literature and a community of fellow practitioners who accept spiritual emergence to help them integrate the unusual experiences borne out of intensive yoga practice. Athletes who have spiritual experiences might well ascribe them to good health, self-discipline, or concentration, and might never think about them in the context of spiritual emergence. No matter, both athletes and yogis reap the benefits of spiritual emergence in the above cases.

Near Death Experience

Near Death Experience (NDE) refers to the experience a person has when he has been clinically dead a short period of time and then revived. It appears that NDE often introduces people to transpersonal states of consciousness (Ring, 1984). It is not unusual for persons who have almost died to experience themselves as distinct from their bodies and to become aware of beings of higher intelligence and good will who are guiding them. The personality shifts that result from NDE typically follow a pattern, which may be described as follows:

1. Confirmation of the presence of God.
2. A sense of being a part of God.
3. An unusual ability to heal and demonstrate psychic abilities.

59

4. A sense of deep peace.

5. A desire to be of service to humankind.

(Ring, 1984)

These are the same kinds of shifts in personality that happen to people reaching transpersonal levels of development. They especially parallel what has been recorded about kundalini awakening:

> *However the actual process of kundalini arousal may be experienced, it is held that the energy it draws upon has the capacity to catapult the individual into a higher state of consciousness. In full awakenings, a state of cosmic consciousness can be attained and, under certain circumstances, maintained. The flow of energy is said to transform the nervous system and the brain to enable them to operate at an entirely new and higher level of functioning. Metaphorically speaking, kundalini appears to throw the nervous system into overdrive, activating its latent potentials and permitting the individual to experience the world and perform in it in an extraordinary fashion....*

> *In full kundalini awakenings, what is experienced is significantly similar to what many NDEr's report from their experiences. And more than that: The aftereffects of these deep kundalini awakenings seem to lead to individual transformations and personal world views essentially indistinguishable from those found in NDEr's. That these obvious parallels exist does not, of course, prove that they stem from a*

common cause, but it does at least suggest the pos-
sibility that there may be a general biological
process that underlies them both--as well as tran-
scendental experiences at large.

(Ring, 1984)

Surgery

Many people undergoing surgery have experiences similar
to a Near Death Experience as a result of their anesthetics
(Rogo, 1984). The anesthetic ketamine seems especially
effective for inducing spiritual experience. The aftereffects
of the anesthetic leave patients transformed in their thinking about death, life after death, and the nature of their
current life.

Following is the account of a doctor who had been anesthetized with ketamine before surgery:

He reported he heard odd buzzing sounds in his
ears. He fell unconscious, but then "gradually I
realized my mind existed and I could think, I had no
consciousness of existing in a body; I was mind sus-
pended in space." The doctor then found himself
floating in a void. "I was not afraid," he reported, "I
was more curious." He thought, "This is death. I am
a soul, and I am going to wherever I should go."

(Johnstone, 1973)

Reportedly, only 12% of those who are given ketamine in
medical settings experience phenomena similar to NDE
(Rogo, op.cit). Still it is a noticeable number.

Pregnancy and Childbirth

Pregnancy and birthing are especially stressful physical events that can also precipitate intense spiritual experiences and possible spiritual emergency. Miscarriage and abortion may have a similar powerful effect.

During pregnancy, birth and in the first few weeks of post-natal life, the spiritual energies surrounding a mother and child are especially intense. Clairvoyants have reported seeing beings of light surrounding the mother and child during this phase of life (Lievegoed, 1979). The hormonal changes during pregnancy, birth and lactation also bring psychological shifts that alter consciousness. Changes in sleep patterns and lack of dreaming time that accompany pregnancy and caring for an infant can also bring openings into transpersonal level experiences.

The sensitive attunement mothers have for their newborn children often expresses itself through a spontaneous knowing about the welfare of the child. Women awake in the middle of the night with the inner knowledge that the child will soon need to be fed—even when they are not keeping to a schedule other than the child's. Some women, without any outward signs, develop an uncanny knowing of when their child is in danger. These are psychic phenomena, manifestations of the transpersonal level of development.

Birthing is an experience in which many women have extraordinary experiences feeling they are close to death, and/ or that spiritual energies are protecting them and guiding them. Sometimes women have peak experiences of merging into "God's Light" while delivering a child. This may originate from a near-death experience in childbirth, or from the exhilaration of a normal birth.

Abortion and miscarriage can also precipitate major awakening experiences—either through a confrontation with death (because of a physical emergency such as hemorrhaging), or a confrontation with the child's death. Even a moral crisis can precipitate spiritual experience. A woman client was struggling with the dilemma of having an "unwanted" pregnancy. As she reflected on the situation, she realized that the child was functioning in her as a spiritual awakener—helping to bring forth in her new spiritual energies for which she had always longed. She also realized that it was appropriate for her to terminate the pregnancy. Her husband agreed. After the abortion she continued to have expanded perceptual abilities and stronger healing capacities—all characteristic of transpersonal level phenomena. She has continued to function well in her home and work life.

> *The child is potential future...the "child" paves the way for a future change of personality. In the individuation process it anticipates the figure that comes from the synthesis of conscious and unconscious elements in the personality. It is therefore a symbol which unites the opposites; a mediator; a bringer of healing; that is, one who makes whole.*
>
> *(C.G. Jung, 1968)*

Natural Disaster

Natural disasters such as earthquakes, floods, drought, and hurricanes precipitate a profound confrontation with the forces of nature. Many people are given to falling to their knees in supplication to God in response to any of these awe-inspiring acts of nature. In the face of natural disasters we are compelled to recognize ourselves as subject to forces far greater than ourselves. Powerful feelings erupt: hatred of God, mistrust in life, helplessness, awe, shock, profound gratitude for life, etc.

The house I lived in during the San Francisco quake of 1989 (7.2 on the Richter Scale) was a couple of miles from the epicenter in Aptos, California. My community was devastated by the quake. We rushed from house to house-- moving loved ones out of buildings which were near collapse. We were crying for the devastation of downtown Santa Cruz; we were standing in vigil at the places where people were killed inside buildings; we were wondering if a tidal wave might be expected to obliterate the nearby town of Capitola village as the radio station predicted. Adults spoke of horror being alone in a house while books and stereo receivers flew in unpredictable patterns across the room, while refrigerators hopped across the floor and plate-glass windows burst, shattering glass in all directions. Loved ones were separated from each other and telephones were not functioning. Hours and hours went by with people steeped in fear that loved ones may have been killed or badly hurt. TV and radio were incapable of offering a dependable representation of what was happening.

How did we tolerate the chaos? We told stories, embraced each other and fed the homeless in the midst of continuing aftershocks (2-5 points on the Richter scale which continued for weeks after the initial earthquake.) The quake actually drew out a rally of compassion within the community as neighbors helped neighbors and assistance came in from all around the country.

In the aftermath friends asked friends, "What is our defense against this kind of disaster? Should we move away from California?" We realized our only defense is our connection to information that can predict and prepare us for other disasters and our own sensitive connection to higher realms of inner knowing. We all had learned that in the midst of chaos, when mass media does not function consistently, one's personal connection to nature and transpersonal forces came to the foreground. Intuition, psychic phenomena, telepathy and synchronicities became more familiar to all of us as did intensification in our relationship with the Divine—all catalyzed by our confrontation with the forces of nature.

Emotional Distress

The moral choices, emotional adjustments, and life transitions associated with pregnancy, death, illness, or separation (from loved ones or loved jobs) are emotionally intense situations which often stimulate spiritual experiences. Intensive individual or group therapy produces emotional stress that can contribute to spiritual development. All of these experiences, including disasters, lead to confrontations about one's belief in God, a sense of what is real, and a sense of what is meaningful in life. During emotionally stressful situations, the power to create and destroy life and the power to pull ourselves toward or away from loving relationships and creative expression are more evident. We are also forced to acknowledge our vulnerability.

When we are vulnerable, psychological complexes that have been in the unconscious are more likely to rise to consciousness. Where there is an intense aversion to the complex, its birth to consciousness may provoke an overwhelming reaction (Sandner and Beebe, in Stein, 1984) — thereby catalyzing a spiritual emergency.

When emotional stress is most intense there is a turning point where a person reorients life toward continued growth, retrenches in the same life patterns and self-structure, or regresses. The inspiration to open to continued growth most frequently comes from a personal epiphany, a spiritual experience, or a deep sharing with another person—a deepening of love, of trust, and openness to life. This is most apt to happen when a helper, therapist, teacher, or compassionate friend is present.

Without the deep connection to a supportive source—personal or transpersonal—one who is in intense emotional distress typically feels isolated and overwhelmed. One may regress to lower levels of functioning, or rigidify one's identification with one's current level of development. In both cases, one is resisting transpersonal development.

Fragmentation

We live in a time when people feel fragmented (Metzner, 1985)—pushed by so many economic, personal, and social stressors that no stable sense of meaning or purpose exist. Many live isolated both from their own inner core and from other people. This fragmented state is reflected in hard rock music, where there is an overwhelming cacophony of sound that has no harmonic core.

The fragmentation is brought on, in part, by the breakdown of social institutions, and the speed at which people move from situation to situation—on the freeway, in elevators, in airplanes, in relocating to different communities. A sense of continuity with others and a sense of support from one's community are unlikely.

Emotional distress induced by the lifestyles we lead and the cultural mandates that we uphold may precipitate spiritual experience and spiritual emergency.

Emotional Deprivation

Under the stress of emotional deprivation some people fall to pieces, but others grow stronger. An example is the strong child in an alcoholic family who develops psychic abilities to survive the unpredictable and unsupportive nature of an alcoholic parent. Similarly, an individual on a vision quest—fasting from food, water and human contact—can envision true purpose in life, and realize the oneness of all life. Both the child and the questing person move

67

into transpersonal level experience—the one to survive, the other to intentionally stimulate spiritual growth. Each experiences deprivation and hardship, new insight and revelation.

Deprivation from human contact under circumstances where one is in emotional distress, creates a void from which can come a major spiritual awakening. When born out of an unstable, unpredictable life circumstance, however, deprivation from emotional support can be the stimulus to emotional paralysis and disease.

Intense Sexual Experience

Intense closeness with another person can also be a powerful trigger to transpersonal development. There are spiritual practices (such as Tantric sexual practices) that are done intentionally to stimulate spiritual experience. A person in sexual activity may have transpersonal experiences such as: clairvoyantly seeing the partner's past or knowing the partner's thoughts; clairsentiently feeling what the partner is feeling; becoming more sensitized to subtle energies; having visionary experiences activating the "central archetype"; feeling merged with the Divine; and feeling divine inspiration.

The sexual embrace models the archetype of divine union—where male and female energies are united, where those who are separate are one and there is the experience of wholeness. It is no wonder that our spiritual development can be stimulated by sexual union with a beloved.

Substance Use/Abuse

Aldous Huxley (1931) was one of the most public spokespersons for drug-induced spiritual experience.

> *The story of drug-taking constitutes one of the most curious and also, it seems to me, one of the most significant chapters in the natural history of human beings. Everywhere and at all times, men and women have sought, and duly found, the means of taking a holiday from the reality of their generally dull and often acutely unpleasant existence. A holiday out of space, out of time, in the eternity of sleep or ecstasy, in the heaven or the limbo of visionary phantasy. Anywhere, anywhere out of the world.*

> *Drug-taking, it is significant, plays an important part in almost every primitive religion. The Persians and, before them, the Greeks and probably the ancient Hindus used alcohol to produce religious ecstasy; the Mexicans procured the beatific vision by eating a poisonous cactus; a toadstool filled the Shamans of Siberia with enthusiasm and endowed them with the gift of tongues. And so on. The devotional exercises of the later mystics are all designed to produce the drug's miraculous effects by purely psychological means. How many of the current ideas of eternity, of heaven, or supernatural states are ultimately derived from the experiences of drug-takers?*

Primitive man explored the pharmaceutical avenues of escape from the world with a truly astonishing thoroughness. Our ancestors left almost no natural stimulant, or hallucinant, or stupefacient, undiscovered. Necessity is the mother of invention; primitive man, like his civilized descendent, felt so urgent a need to escape occasionally from reality, that the invention of drugs was fairly forced upon him.

All existing drugs are treacherous and harmful. The heaven into which they usher their victims soon turns into a hell of sickness and moral degradation. They kill, first the soul, then, in a few years, the body. What is the remedy? "Prohibition," answer all contemporary governments in chorus. But the results of prohibition are not encouraging. Men and women feel such an urgent need to take occasional holidays from reality, that they will do almost anything to procure the means of escape. The only justification for prohibition would be success; but it is not and, in the nature of things, cannot be successful. The way to prevent people from drinking too much alcohol, or becoming addicts to morphine or cocaine, is to give them an efficient but wholesome substitute for these delicious and (in the presently imperfect world) necessary poisons. The man who invents such a substance will be counted among the greatest benefactors of suffering humanity.

(A. Huxley, 1931)

Mind-altering substances have long been one answer to

human yearning for a more transcendent reality (Siegel, 1992). For many people, drugs have been the initiator into the transpersonal realms of experience, igniting their interest in further personal development (McKenna, T., 1992; Siegel, 1992). For others, drugs have been the initiator, as well, into the hell of addiction and moral degradation.

Which drugs facilitate spiritual emergence? Which drugs facilitate recovery from spiritual crisis? Which drugs block integration of spiritual experience? The May, 1985, SEN conference participants spent some time considering the effects of mind-altering substances (not including psychiatric or allopathic drugs) vis-a-vis spiritual emergence.

It appears that some drugs may legitimately be used to facilitate spiritual emergence *when used in the appropriate environment with appropriate guidance.* A few clinics in Europe are currently doing research on the therapeutic use of LSD and MDMA; however, more discussion and research is called for on this subject. There is still much to be learned about this field of substance use and abuse in relationship to spiritual growth.

The following paragraphs give a brief synopsis of the discussion of the 1985 SEN conference. They are included here for purposes of reflection and to stimulate further research. *They are not intended as an endorsement of drug use to stimulate spiritual experience.* Any experimental use of mind-altering substances must be managed with utmost care and respect for the current legal regulations as well as the psychological well-being of the client. Helpers in a position of assisting persons who have used mind-altering substances may find the following review useful.

Depressants- Alcohol
People attracted to the use of alcohol may be looking for spiritual experiences (Grof, C.,1993). Small amounts of alcohol can help "turn-off" the rational mind, and thus create an avenue of expression for previously suppressed emotions, thoughts, feelings and sensations. Where alcohol use may trigger a spiritual emergence process it may also inhibit the ability to maintain focus and/or the capacity to integrate the spiritual expreiences. Spiritual issues may arise out of a drying-out period after too much alcohol has been consumed.

Stimulants- Caffeine, Amphetamines, Chocolate, and Cocaine
These will not trigger spiritual emergence, nor facilitate integration of paranormal experiences. Stimulants, in fact, appear to block the integration of spiritual experiences. Amphetamines can, in some circumstances, precipitate psychotic episodes that may have spiritual aspects; however, they are not recommended for such a purpose.

Barbiturates
These have an effect very similar to alcohol vis-a-vis spiritual emergence. They do not catalyze spiritual experiences nor do they facilitate integration of spiritual experience. They are used, in some cases, for therapeutic purposes when sedation is important for a period of time.

Opiates- Heroine, Morphine, and Opium
Opiates can stimulate transpersonal level experiences in some people. The opiates stimulate imagination and fantasies, which can lead to out-of-body experiences and visions. When used wisely, opiates can help people in pain so that their minds are free to deal with spiritual issues and can thus help integrate spiritual experiences in special circumstances.

Marijuana
Marijuana is in a class between the opiates and psychedelics. It can produce new sensory experience, initiate a person to spiritual experience, and help integrate spiritual experiences. Its capacity to do this depends on the intent of the user, the dosage, the quality, the set and the setting.

Empathogens- MDMA (aka Adam, or Ecstasy)
This is a drug that can facilitate spiritual experiences. It often awakens the heart center, opening people to the here and now. It facilitates the integration of spiritual experience if used in the appropriate dosage and setting. Side effects are generally minimal and short-lived, although further research is now being conducted.

Psychedelics
Psychedelics can have a useful effect for promoting growth into higher levels of development when taken in the appropriate setting, with the intent for personal growth. Dosage levels must be monitored carefully, the environment must be especially peaceful, and follow-up procedures must be attended with care. Stan Grof (1980) discusses psychedelics used in a therapeutic setting.

The main objective of psychedelic therapy is to create optimal conditions for the subject to experience the ego death and the subsequent transcendence into the so-called psychedelic peak experience. It is an ecstatic state, characterized by the loss of boundaries between the subject and the objective world, with ensuing feelings of unity with other people, nature, the entire Universe, and God. In most instances this experience is contentless and is accompanied by visions of brilliant white or golden light, rainbow spectra or elaborate designs resembling peacock feathers. It can, however, be associated with archetypal figurative visions of deities or divine personages from various cultural frameworks. LSD subjects give various descriptions of this condition, based on their educational background and intellectual orientation. They speak about cosmic unity, unio mystica, mysterium tremendum, cosmic consciousness, union with God, Atman-Brahman union, Samadhi, satori, moksha, or the harmony of the spheres.

...In general, psychedelic therapy seems to be most effective in the treatment of alcoholics, narcotic drug addicts, depressed patients, and individuals dying of cancer. In patients with psychoneuroses, psychosomatic disorders, and character neuroses, major therapeutic changes usually cannot be achieved without systematically working through various levels of problems in serial LSD sessions.

(Grof, 1980)

74

The positive effects that are possible with psychedelics and empathogens are not commonly attained when drugs are taken in a recreational setting, without the intent for inner growth and without monitoring of set and setting by a trained guide. Nevertheless, it is possible for people to have spiritual experiences unintentionally through drug use, as drugs can be powerful catalysts for psychic and psychological phenomena.

Summary

Individual stressors press people toward change—to find new resources and to cope with change. Any of the stressors noted above (time of life, spiritual practice, physical distress, natural disasters, emotional distress, intense sexual experience, substance use/abuse) can catalyze spiritual emergence or spiritual problems. A person's ability to welcome change and expand his or her conceptual framework as well as open up his or her physical and emotional response patterns will determine the extent of the problem. Ideally, individuals can open gradually, integrating spiritual experiences at a comfortable pace.

Aside from intrinsic responses, the direction of the person's experience is affected strongly by the support people (friends, family, and professional counselors) involved. If support people are cognizant of spiritual emergence phenomena, they can support positive change in the distressed individual. When these support people are ignorant of spiritual emergence processes, the distressed individual will be less likely to resolve the spiritual problems in a positive way.

The next four chapters provide information on working with persons with spiritual problems.

Chapter 3 ─────────────────────────

Diagnosis

This chapter focuses on the criteria for distinguishing spiritual problems and spiritual emergency from pathological states. Both spiritual emergency and spiritual problems are conditions that are not attributable to a mental disorder; however, people with mental disorders may have spiritual experiences. Because some of the characteristic behavior patterns in spiritual emergency are similar to psychotic symptoms, it is critical to identify the differences so that an accurate diagnosis can be made. This discussion will clarify why spiritual emergency is also appropriately named an acute psychosis with a positive outcome (Dabrowski, 1964; Grof, 1985; Lukoff, 1985).

77

There are three ways in which people respond to spiritual experiences. One way is to gracefully integrate the experience into their lives, moving forward in their self development toward transpersonal levels. Another response is to be overwhelmed for a period of time, experiencing a spiritual emergency but eventually acknowledging and accepting the spiritual experience as a part of their reality. The third response is to fail to integrate the spiritual experience, and to deteriorate into a chronic state of fragmentation. As an example of the possible responses, imagine three persons who have an experience of unity with the Divine.

The first person, say a therapist, is initially immersed in a greatly expanded consciousness, totally absorbed in the experience of being God, and yet can flexibly shift to going on with her normal life—taking care of her clients and family, getting children to school on time, attending staff meetings, and the rest of life.

The second person, say a man, is so disturbed by the experience, he cannot function for several weeks. His partner assumes his household duties while he is taken care of by a support group. He needs time to rest and reflect. He feels disoriented. He can't be trusted to drive safely as he is self-absorbed and wants to move at a very slow pace. He avoids fast traffic, groups of people, intense sounds and bright lights. He prefers to be in a natural setting. At times, he is so energized he can't contain himself and talks on and on. He has realized he is God, and all other people are God, too. It's a big awakening. After a few weeks or months he is able to resume normal functioning, and chooses to participate in a group which supports spiritual emergence. This gives him a safe place to share his epiphanies and come to terms with the changes he feels drawn to make in his life. Within the year, he may well transform his relationship to his family and/or his occupation.

The third person, say a woman, is initially overwhelmed by the spiritual experience, and as time goes on she grows more confused and fragmented. At times, she believes she alone is the second coming of Christ, or the Angel Gabriel. At other times, she is a person paralyzed with infantile fear. Her identity is constantly shifting. As a result of unsuccessful ego development she lacks a stable core. Her attention span is poor. She is difficult to talk to. It is hard for her to relate to others. She loves her children, but is so self-absorbed that she cannot attend to her needs, let alone theirs.

A classically trained psychiatrist or psychotherapist following the standard diagnostic system, DSM-1V (1994), would probably categorize all three of these people as psychotic based on the **content** of their experiences. It could be construed that in the first two cases the criteria for "brief psychotic disorder" is present as there are so-called delusions, hallucinations, and highly unusual behavior or incoherent speech. Or, these two might be diagnosed as "psychotic disorder not otherwise specified" as it could be interpreted that there are persistent auditory hallucinations in the absence of any other features, persistent nonbizarre delusions with periods of overlapping mood episodes that have been present for a substantial portion of the delusional disturbance," or "psychoses with confusing clinical features that make a more specific diagnosis impossible." If other mood disorders are ruled out and there is no medical condition creating the symptoms, the third case would most likely be diagnosed as schizophrenic after the initial month of difficulty.

With notable exceptions, most psychiatrists and psychologists since Freud assume that hallucinations, dramatic experiences of uncontrolled energy, paranormal phenomenon, and feelings of unbounded unity are symptoms of mental pathology. Visions which absorb a person's waking awareness in a dramatic play of archetypal images are similarly discounted. Psychic phenomena are invalidated because they cannot be repeated or understood by means of Newtonian-Cartesian scientific principles. Freud felt that all these behaviors and perceptual experiences were symptoms of regressive tendencies. He did not consider that they might also be part of the initiation to higher developmental levels.

Many professionals in the field of psychology often hesitate to talk about their own transpersonal experiences for fear of being considered psychotic. Their ambivalence results in their being uncomfortable discussing similar experiences with their clients. They lack understanding or interest in transpersonal experiences, and may even be limited to consider mystical experiences only within the context of religion (Peck, 1993).

Jung and Assagioli (1981) were two notable exceptions who understood that some elements of the unconscious are transpersonal in nature, are superior to ego-consciousness, and contribute to optimal well-being. Contemporary theorists and clinicians following the lead of Jung and Assagioli have reconstrued the rigidly held negative image of acute psychoses; instead, they have seen in them the possibility of a phase of disintegration which, when complete, would contribute to psychological well-being (Boisen, 1962; Dabrowski, 1964; Laing, 1972; Grof, 1985).

Following is a table that illustrates the diversity of opinion and vocabulary among psychologists and psychiatrists regarding spiritual emergency. Dates refer to publications that illustrate the point of view of the author, listed by "Name." The column "Spiritual Emergency" refers to that author's recognition of episodes more recently defined as spiritual emergency. "Symptom" refers to the term the author used to classify patterns of spiritual experiences. "Treatment" refers to the author's preferred mode of caring for someone with symptoms of spiritual emergency.

Table 2

Name	Spiritual Emergency?	Symptom	Treatment
Freud (1924)	no	Regression and/or hallucinations.	Medically-oriented hospitalization and analysis
Jung (1932)	yes	Autonomous process arising out of the unconscious that uses client as its vehicle; evidence of complex previously split off.	Jungian analysis or psychotherapy; grounding with creative work and family activities
W. Reich (1949)	yes	Organism efforting towards unitary functioning and /or merging of organismic and cosmic orgone energy.	Vegetotherapy and character analysis; comprehension of cosmic and organismic orgone energy functions.
B.F. Skinner (1953)	no	Presence of negative conditioned response patterns	Conditioning techniques to change behavior and interpersonal aspects of client's life.
T. Szasz (1961)	yes	Behavior and perceptions which are not endorsed by mainstream ideas of reality.	A social environment which permits behavior and perceptions outside cultural norm.
Maslow (1971)	Yes	Phenomena related to evolutionary growth.	Permission for spontaneous expression and trust in the organism

Table 2: cont...

Name	Spiritual Emergency?	Symptom	Treatment
GAP* (1976)	no	A form of ego regression defending against internal or external stress	Medically-oriented hospitalization; analysis, therapy and /or psychiatric medication
J.W. Perry (1974)	yes	Psychological renewal; evolutionary step.	Empathic listening, supportive, egalitarian, informed companionship; 24 hour care in home-like atmosphere.
Mindell (1984)	yes	Individuals are channels for larger process taking place in the Universe	Process-oriented psychotherapy.
Lukoff (1985)	yes	Mystical experiences with psychotic features. (MEPF)	Same as Perry.
Grof (1986)	yes	Spiritual emergency.	Sympathetic and compassionate guidance from a helper; 24 hour care in home-like setting; holotropic therapy.

* Group for the Advancement of Psychiatry

Psychosis and the *DSM-IIIR*

According to the American Psychological Association's (APA) diagnostic manual of mental disorders, the *DSM-IIIR* (1987), symptoms of psychosis include the following:

1. Delusions.

2. Hallucinations.

3. Incoherence or loosening of associations.

4. Markedly illogical thinking.

5. Behavior that is grossly disorganized or catatonic.

As is evident, these criteria did not differentiate the delusions and hallucinations of the psychotic from the visions and psi phenomena of spiritual experience. They did not differentiate the 'word salad' characteristic of the psychotic from the jumbled speech of someone trying to articulate the noetic quality of a spiritual experience. They did not differentiate the catatonia of the psychotic with the need for solitude and quiet of the person in spiritual emergency. They did not differentiate the disorganized behavior of the psychotic and the bizarre behaviors of a kundalini experience. The *DSM-IV* still has not clarified these distinctions. Any of the six patterns of spiritual emergency described by the Grofs could be confused with symptoms of psychopathology as the following table suggests:

Table 3: Symptoms –
Spiritual Emergency vs. Psychopathology

FORM OF SPIRITUAL EMERGENCY	SIMILAR CRITERIA FOR MENTAL DISORDERS IN *DSM-IIIR*
1. Kundalini Awakening: Streaming energy, tremors, sensations of heat/cold, spasms and violent shaking, involuntary laughing/crying, unusual breathing patterns, and/or visions of light.	Autonomic hyperactivity associated with *generalized anxiety disorder.* Hyperactivity associated with *manic syndrome.* Alteration in physical function Symptom not under voluntary control & psychological factors judged etiologically evolved-associated with *conversion disorder.*
2. Shamanic Journey: Dreams/visions/sensing-evoking a special connection to animals and nature. Core psychic experience = death and rebirth.	Recurrent thoughts of death. Loss of interest or pleasure in ritual activities associated with *depression.* Somatic, grandiose, religious, nihilistic or other delusion without persecutory or jealous content associated with *psychotic disorders.*
3. Psychological Renewal Through Activation of the Central Archetype. Preoccupation with death, rebirth, and/or return to the beginnings of life. Focus on a clash of opposites and dramatic resolution of this opposition.	Bizarre delusions. Hallucinations associated with *psychotic disorders.* Recurrent thoughts of death associated with *depression.*

FORM OF SPIRITUAL EMERGENCY	SIMILAR CRITERIA FOR MENTAL DISORDERS IN *DSM-IIIR*
4. Psychic Opening: Experiences of extrasensory perception, including out-of-the-body experiences.	Delusions. Hallucinations associated with *psychotic disorders.*
5. Emergence of a Karmic Pattern: Experiencing dramatic sequences which seem to be occurring in a different temporal - spatial context.	Delusions. Hallucinations associated with psychotic disorders.
6. Possession States: Behavior, energetic or emotional expression may involuntarily take on character and/or habits of another entity. Somatic consequences may include disease, addiction or severe mental disturbance.	Delusions. Hallucinations associated with *psychotic disorders.* Symptom not under voluntary control. Loss of or alteration in physical functioning associated with *conversion disorder.* Behavior that is grossly disorganized associated with *psychosis.* Hyperactivity associated with *manic syndrome.*

It must be noted that it may be unusually difficult for a clinician to differentiate between spiritual emergency and psychopathology in persons who are highly dissociative. Those on the dissociative continuum routinely experience unusual body sensations, dramatic energy shifts, extraordinarily vivid dreams or visions, paranormal abilities, identity shifts, and both subtle and profound changes in temporal/spatial contexts. Accurate assessment of these clients requires an immense amount of clinical expertise as well as open-mindedness regarding the possibility of these phenomena being signs of spiritual emergence rather than simply psychopathology.

The difficulty in making these differentiations is that the content of the visions and sensory phenomena may be identical in psychosis and spiritual emergency. Thus, differentiating pathological psychosis from spiritual emergency must be based on other criteria that enable the clinician to make finer distinctions.

Criteria for Spiritual Emergence

Such criteria for identifying a person in spiritual emergence were defined by Grof and Grof (1986).

> 1. *Episodes of unusual experiences that involve changes in consciousness and in perceptual, emotional, cognitive, and psychosomatic functioning, in which there is a significant transpersonal emphasis in the process, such as dramatic death and (re)birth sequences, mythological and archetypal phenomena, past. incarnation memories, out-of-body experiences, incidence of synchronicities or extrasensory perception, intense energetic phenomena (Kundalini Awakening), states of mystical union, identification with cosmic consciousness.*

> 2. *The ability to see the condition as an inner psychological process and approach it in an internalized way; the capacity to form an adequate working relationship and maintain the spirit of cooperation. These criteria exclude people with severe paranoid states, persecutory delusions, and*

hallucinations, and those who consistently use the mechanism of projection, exterioriza-tion, and acting out.

(Grof and Grof, 1986)

Flexibility to adapt and accommodate to new areas of experience is part and parcel of the spiritual emergence process—in contrast to inflexibility, which characterizes deeply entrenched psychosis.

Criteria for Spiritual Problems

Such criteria for identifying a person with spiritual problems were defined by Grof and Grof (1986) as phenomena associated with spiritual emergence:

The criteria for a spiritual experience include:

1. Sense of newly-gained knowledge.
2. Perceptual alterations.
3. Unusual visual, auditory, olfactory or kinesthetic perceptions having themes related to mythology.
4. No conceptual disorganization (Metaphorical speech may be difficult to understand, but is comprehensible and should not be considered conceptually disorganized).

(revised from Lukoff, 1985)

If two out of the following four criteria are satisfied, a psychotic episode is likely to have a positive outcome:

1. Good *pre-episode functioning as evidenced by no previous history of psychotic episodes, maintenance of a social network of friends, intimate relationships with members of the opposite sex (or same sex, if homosexual), some success in vocation or school.*

2. *Acute onset of symptoms during a period of three months or less.*

3. *Stressful precipitants to the psychotic episode such as major life changes: a death in the family, divorce, loss of job (not related to onset of symptoms), financial problems, beginning a new academic program or job. Major life passages which result in identity crises, such as transition from adolescence to adulthood, should also be considered.*

4. *Positive exploratory attitude toward the experience as meaningful, revelatory, growthful. Research has found that a positive attitude toward the psychotic process facilitates integration of the experience into the person's post-psychotic life.*

(Lukoff 1985)

Following is a table which illustrates the determinants of spiritual emergency vis-a-vis brief reactive psychosis (a type of psychosis included in the *DSM-III R* (1987) which is most similar to spiritual emergency, in terms of professionally used terminology, and thus most often confused with spiritual emergency).

Table 4: Psychosis or Spiritual Emergency?

BRIEF REACTIVE PSYCHOSIS	SPIRITUAL EMERGENCY
Psychotic symptoms appear immediately following a recognizable psycho-social stressor.	Phenomena usually follow a recognizable psycho-social stressor; good pre-episode functioning. (Lukoff)
Emotional turmoil and at least one of the following: 1. Incoherence or loosening of associations. 2. Delusions. 3. Hallucinations. 4. Behavior that is grossly disorganized or catatonic.	All of the following: 1. Ecstatic mood. (Lukoff) 2. Sense of newly gained knowledge. (Lukoff) 3. Perceptual alterations. (Lukoff and Grof) 4. Delusions have themes related to mythology. (Lukoff and Grof) 5. No conceptual disorganization. (Lukoff) 6. Positive, exploratory attitude toward the experience as meaningful. (Lukoff and Grof) 7. Capacity to form and maintain an adequate working relationship. (Grof)
Symptoms last more than a few hours, but less than 2 weeks.	Symptoms last minutes, and up to months; acute onset during 3 months or less. (Lukoff)
An eventual return to the premorbid level of functioning.	Functioning enhanced after most intense period is complete. (Lukoff and Grof)

BRIEF REACTIVE PSYCHOSIS	SPIRITUAL EMERGENCY
No period of increasing psychopathology preceding the psycho-social stressor.	No period of increasing psychopathology preceding the psycho-social stressor. (Lukoff and Grof)
Disturbance is not due to any other mental disorder or organic disorder.	Disturbance is not due to any other mental disorder or organic disorder. (Grof)

COEX Systems

Growth to new developmental levels almost never happens in a direct linear course. As we develop past the normal ego levels, most of us need to work with and resolve issues left from earlier developmental levels, such as old griefs, angers, and obsolete patterns of thinking and feeling, before emerging into a transpersonal level of functioning and experiencing.

S. Grof's (1985) "COEX" system may be useful to describe why people regress to more primitive levels of functioning during their progression to transpersonal levels of consciousness. COEX stands for "systems of condensed experience" in the psyche. These are systems of traumatic experience at the primary level that are not fully metabolized on a primary level (such as those occurring while one is still in the womb or at birth), but which continue to exist in one's psychic structure as one matures, inhibiting full development. A regression to the primary level for the purpose of healing is necessary in order to dissipate the energy caught in the COEX system and to free the psyche. In this instance, the psyche regresses to a more primitive level in order to integrate past traumatic material. A person with a spiritual problem may, for a while, be in a more primitive and regressed state to resolve and integrate a COEX system before emerging to a higher level of integration. An episode of regression to pre-personal functioning may thus serve as a gateway to a transpersonal level of functioning. Wilber's spectrum of self development (Chapter 1) identifies the developmental levels but not the course of development itself.

As one approaches the transpersonal level, dysfunctional patterns of seeing and relating to the world from preceding developmental levels will be challenged. The nonlinear pattern of growth explains the emotional outbursts, dramatic physical sensations, even the phenomena of "emerging of a karmic pattern" or "kundalini rising." These may be the psyche—purging complexes left from previous developmental levels.

Multi-axial Evaluation

The DSM-IV includes a multi-axial evaluation system that allows mental health professionals to create a profile of an individual's health status at a particular time. This "promotes the application of the bio-psychosocial model in clinical, educational and research settings" (APA, 1994). This evaluation involves five categories, called axes, covering clinical syndromes (Axis I), personality disorders and other conditions that may be the focus of clinical attention (Axis II), general medical conditions (Axis III), psychosocial and environmental problems (Axis IV) and global assessment of functioning (Axis V).

This system pinpoints spiritual problems as a condition that is not attributable to a mental disorder that is the focus of attention or treatment. "Spiritual problems" belongs on Axis I in place, or alongside of clinical syndromes. If a multiple diagnosis for Axis I is made the principal diagnosis is indicated by listing it first. Spiritual problems could thus be listed at first or following the clinical syndrome(s) depending on the discretion of the diagnostician.

A diagnosis of "other conditions that may be a focus of clinical attention" will create an opportunity for people with spiritual problems to receive professional care but not be stigmatized with having a mental disorder. It will also create an opportunity for people with spiritual problems to be treated in a way that is most appropriate for their particular problem—avoiding mistakes in medicating and hospitalizing people inappropriately due to confusing spiritual problems with pathology. It will also relieve priests and spiritual directors from the sole responsibility of addressing the needs of people with spiritual problems. This is timely, as priests, spiritual directors, and pastoral counselors do not usually have the training to attend to the distressing emotional or physical symptoms that often accompany spiritual problems.

The possibility of diagnostic complication arises when individuals with clinical syndromes also have spiritual experiences. In this case, do the clinical syndromes belong as the primary focus of Axis I, or not? The placement of spiritual or religious problem as a primary focus of treatment would obviously have a dramatic impact on the treatment plan. This possibility needs to be the topic of further research.

With the new diagnostic category for spiritual problems, spiritual experiences should be identified as such and not assumed to be symptoms of a clinical disorder. For example, in the case of someone with a dissociative disorder, there may well be evidence of spiritual experiences. The treatment for the dissociative disorder would involve therapy that facilitates a person no longer being compelled to dissociate. Treatment for the spiritual problems in this case should include some form of individual or group therapy that involves validating spiritual experiences and nurturing spiritual emergence. Chapters Four and Five give suggestions for appropriate care for those trying to integrate spiritual experiences.

Summary

Learning how to distinguish between spiritual problems, spiritual emergency and mental disorder is essential in providing appropriate diagnosis and care. Persons misdiagnosed may be caught in treatment protocols that are inappropriate and even destructive to their growth. Hospitalization for 'disease' is not appropriate and may be devastating for a person in spiritual emergency.

The specific bundle of emotions, physical sensations, and extraordinary inner states that occur in spiritual emergency come from a combination of past developmental issues and present spiritual experiences. In a person with a relatively stable ego identity, past developmental issues can be largely resolved by giving appropriate emotional support which allows the client to clear inner conflicts and accommodate the newly emerging self-structure. The next several chapters describe how to give appropriate care to a client in spiritual emergency.

Chapter Four _____

Initial Interaction:
Client and Helper

What occurs in the initial meetings between a Helper and someone in spiritual emergency is critical. In the initial encounter a Helper must determine whether a person is in a spiritual emergence process or if he or she is experiencing a mental disorder, or both. This chapter explains eight steps to be used in the first interactions with a person who appears to be in spiritual emergency. They are:

1. Medical/psychiatric evaluation.
2. Discouraging use of psychiatric drugs, unless needed.
3. Providing a quiet and safe environment.
4. Providing compassionate and knowledge-able companionship.

5. Making a diagnosis.
6. Educating the client about spiritual experience and/or emergence.
7. Helping with grounding, centering, or catharsis.
8. Referring the client.

1. Medical/Psychiatric Evaluation

A person in spiritual emergency needs to be evaluated medically to determine if his or her symptoms are due to an organic imbalance or mental disorder. Alterations in perceptual, emotional, cognitive and somatic functioning could be caused by a gross brain disorder such as infection, tumor, cardiovascular problems or degenerative diseases of the brain. Psychological imbalance could result from physical diseases such as uremia, diabetes, toxic states, or cardiac disease (Grof, 1986).

A medical evaluation should also determine if the person is getting adequate rest, proper nutrition, and enough liquid to prevent dehydration. During a psychological crisis of any nature, many people fail to get enough rest, and/or adequate foods. Adequate intake of vitamins and minerals has a noticeable effect on psychological health. Simply giving a person time to rest and ensuring he or she receives proper nutrition can be a potent treatment for spiritual emergency.

Adequate exercise is also important to health and psychological well-being. A sedentary lifestyle can have a profoundly negative effect on psychological well-being.

2.   Minimal Use of Psychiatric Drugs

Psychiatric drugs should be used minimally because they tend to inhibit the natural processes which are occurring in spiritual emergency as the self-structure attempts to integrate a spiritual experience. These drugs can either slow down this natural process, or in some cases, curtail it.

Another significant reason for the minimal use of psychiatric drugs is to allow a person to be observed in his or her more natural state. This is essential for successful diagnosis. Psychiatric drugs often distort or render inaccessible a client's inner process when dealing with a spiritual emergency.

3.   Quiet and Safe Environment

A person in spiritual emergency is typically in a highly sensitized emotional and physical state. The person can be easily overstimulated by strong light or loud noise. Strangers such as unfamiliar physicians, psychiatrists, or nurses, can be very disturbing. Every caution should be taken to provide a quiet, pleasant environment.

The ideal environment for the first meeting with a client in spiritual emergency is a place with natural lighting, soothing colors, quiet music, and simple furnishings—an atmosphere that is more like a home than a hospital. Such an environment can help to allay the fears of persons in spiritual emergency and allows them to focus on their inner processes rather than on outside stimulation.

4. Compassionate and Knowledgeable Companion

A person in spiritual emergency needs the companionship of someone who truly understands this experience. Ideally, this companion will have personally experienced a spiritual emergency, or intense spiritual experiences. The companion can thereby have compassion for the client and understand the client's experience.

Ideally the companion should know about spiritual emergence processes and be able to educate the client on what is happening. The Helper is a companion and witness to the journey of the client, and tries to help the client understand and integrate his or her experiences. Chapter 6, "The Role of the Helper," gives a fuller description of qualifications for a Helper.

5. Diagnosis

The first interaction with a client is the time to determine if the client is in spiritual emergency. To do this, the Helper should identify the client's current psycho-social stressors and any COEX system that may be operative. Sometimes a full diagnosis cannot be made in the first interaction.

The Helper who is responsible for initial diagnosis needs to know about both psychological illness and spiritual emergency because of the possible confusion of spiritual emergency with other mental disorders. Fine distinctions must be assessed. For instance, borderline personality disorders can masquerade as spiritual emergency (Vaughan, 1985). Sometimes the confusion may be perpetuated by the client who prefers to see a disturbance in terms of spiritual emergence, which is more exciting and inspiring, than a stubborn personality disorder. Narcissistic individuals may enjoy the romance and specialness of seeing themselves involved in spiritual emergence. Hysterical personality types may be seeking permission to continue their neurotic behaviors under the guise of spiritual development.

The issue of diagnosis is complicated because the client may be experiencing both phenomena of spiritual emergence and symptoms of a personality disorder, organic mental disorder, or affective disorder. In such case, the diagnosis and treatment become very difficult even for the most qualified diagnostician. The diagnosis and treatment may be impossible for anyone not well-versed in both psychiatric differential diagnosis and spiritual emergence/emergencies. The qualifications (that is, knowledge, skill, and sensitivies) of the Helper are of utmost importance in the diagnostic phase.

Clients who are not in spiritual emergency but have had or are having an intense spiritual experience still need help to integrate this experience. The same eight steps appropriate for conducting an initial meeting with a person in spiritual emergency are also appropriate for these clients, although they may not need as much ongoing support. They need access to resources such as meditation groups, breathwork sessions, transpersonally-oriented therapists, and appropriate reading materials.

6. Educating about Spiritual Emergence Process

One of the most frightening aspects of spiritual emergency is that the client (and his or her family) often doesn't know what is happening. The client may be afraid of some energy that has taken hold, or afraid of newborn psychic abilities, healing abilities, or psychokinetic phenomena. Usually, the client feels like a victim of bizarre circumstances.

A Helper must provide a conceptual framework to structure the client's understanding of spiritual experiences and spiritual emergence. This allays fear and helps the client accept the emergency as positive. Educational materials, books, articles, and movies which help the client see that other people have undergone similar or identical experiences can be introduced at appropriate times. Wilber's developmental spectrum of consciousness is a useful framework for explaining spiritual development. A list of reading materials on spiritual emergence is provided in Appendix D.

Ideally, the companion or Helper can help bridge the intellectual understanding of spiritual experience gained from such resource materials with the phenomenological experience.

7. Help with Grounding, Centering, and/or Catharsis

When clients first come in for help, they are usually in disoriented and disorganized psychological states. Although full of emotional and physical sensation, the clients may try to control these sensations so as not to appear crazy. They may be completely absorbed in their inner worlds, not caring to communicate with other people. They may be excited, speaking as fast as possible, jubilant and expressive or they may be profoundly depressed. Persons in spiritual emergency may appear in any number of moods.

There is no one therapeutic approach to use with a person in spiritual emergency. Grounding, centering or stimulating catharsis, however, are commonly needed during the first encounter. It can be assumed that all those who come for therapeutic help are in need of some grounding. They need reassurance from others that they will be okay. They need some help to understand what is happening to them. A compassionate Helper acts as a container, holding all of the different parts of the person that are not yet integrated, and accepting the person's inner conflicts without demanding coherence. A compassionate Helper can allow the client to be a needy infant in Prepersonal consciousness one minute and a highly evolved being in transpersonal consciousness the next. The Helper's compassionate attitude is the most important resource needed by a person in spiritual emergency.

The clients may also need cathartic release. They need a place where it is absolutely okay to be physically out-of-control, to let go, to stop holding onto their feelings and sensations which need expression. Ideally, Helpers trained to enable cathartic release should be available at any time clients need their help. A Helper who sanctions and enables cathartic release in this way can speed the process of moving from spiritual emergency to emergence. Ideally, there would also be a safe space, cushioned and sound-proofed, for the client to do cathartic work at the appropriate times.

Spiritual emergency often manifests in very physical teens, for example, body tremors, flashes of heat, feeling healing energy in the hands, and so on. Touching the client—a hand on the shoulder, hand holding, a nonsexual hug—may reassure the client and have a grounding effect. More sophisticated bodywork such as massage, acupressure, or breathwork is also often helpful to a client in dealing with spiritual experience on the somatic level.

Stan Grof has innovated Holotropic Therapy, a group breathwork experience that helps people progress with spiritual emergence. The therapy is based on both cathartic work and grounding. Holotropic therapy is appropriate for clients in a moderate phase of spiritual emergency where they are not overstimulated, or severely under-bounded, and have the capacity to contain their inner experiences with minimal external assistance.

8. Referral

After the initial diagnosis of spiritual emergency has been made, the Helper may find it appropriate to refer a client to another Helper or group for support.

In the most intense phases of spiritual emergency, a client may need 24-hour attention by sympathetic, compassionate, and knowledgeable people. Because there are at the present time only a few places in the United States which provide this service (see Appendix D), Helpers may need to design 24-hour support systems in their community outside an institutional setting. This can be especially difficult in communities or with families with little or no understanding of spiritual emergence. Intentional communities and spiritual groups that share a common desire for psycho-spiritual growth seem best suited to provide 24-hour care for their members. Often, however, even these groups are not prepared to provide 24-hour care. There are alternatives that can be employed when such care is unavailable.

Case Study

What are the alternatives to 24-hour care? I will use an experience I had as an example. Bill, an accountant, had been practicing meditation outside of any formal religious group for a number of years. He was seeing me once a week for therapy to help him loosen muscle spasms in his throat which he felt were psychosomatic in origin. I had seen him for a year when he went into spiritual emergency. Bill was sleeping only 3-4 hours a night, talking to himself a lot, having emotional outbursts which were uncharacteristic of his former inhibited style, and seeing visions of the Virgin Mary. He remained grounded enough to drive safely and rework his schedule to accommodate more inner time. Bill himself was not frightened by the strange behaviors but his wife and family wanted to give him psychiatric medications immediately so he would "return to his old self." Bill wanted "refuge to go deeply into his experience" without the distractions of ordinary life and the fears of his family. He also wanted some companionship, perhaps "a priest, or someone who could understand the experiences he was having."

There was no place immediately available for Bill in the San Francisco Bay Area where he lived. As his Helper I did the following:

1. I made every attempt to educate the family about Bill's situation, and advised them about Bill's need to have permission to go through his experience without medication. I reassured them that Bill was not crazy but was going through a very intense period of growth that would probably last a matter of days or weeks.

2. I informed Bill's wife about what she could do to help him—walk with him outdoors so he could get fresh air and be nurtured and grounded by the beauty of nature, give him heavier foods like cheese and meat to eat, and not expect him to return to his "old self."

3. I made myself available as a support person for Bill's wife. I acknowledged the difficulty of her position, the fears she had, the strangeness of Bill's experiences and behaviors and how well she was doing in helping him. I told her to call me, or another support person, whenever she felt she or Bill needed support. I told her to call me if she noticed him being self-destructive, extremely disoriented, or fearful. I arranged for her to see a therapist for herself when she needed it.

4. I kept in contact with Bill. I called him at home on the days I did not see him in my office. I asked him consistently if he was having trouble, feeling afraid or feeling self-destructive. (I was alert to possible paranoia or suicidal ideation. If Bill had been paranoid, suicidal, or a threat to anyone, I would have modified his treatment plan to include more intensive care, even hospitalization.) I reassured him that his process, however strange, was valuable and good.

When I saw Bill for our sessions in the office, I asked him how he was and listened respectfully as he recounted his experiences. During his spiritual emergency, we did not work very much with the meaning of his experiences. Grounding work was more appropriate for Bill. After a period of talking, I recommended acupressure to balance and ground his energies and to give him physical reassurance through therapeutic human contact.

107

5. I contacted a psychiatrist at a local hospital with a good reputation for working with psychotics using minimal medication. I informed the psychiatrist about Bill so that, in the event Bill had to be hospitalized, I knew whom to call at a moment's notice. I wanted to be in agreement with the psychiatrist who would be treating Bill that it would be preferable if he were not given any drugs in the event of hospitalization. In the six weeks of Bill's spiritual emergency, he was never hospitalized. However, my knowing that the backup was there was reassuring for me.

Bill could afford to take time off work during his spiritual emergency. His wife was also in a position to come home at lunchtime, leave work early, and take some extra days off to be with him. Their relatively relaxed work schedules allowed Bill time to be with himself, and gave him meaningful and consistent contact with someone who cared for him.

During Bill's spiritual emergency his throat spasms disappeared. He gained understanding and clarity about his spiritual direction. After the crisis he had a surge of creative inspiration that he expressed through composing, playing, and recording music. He deepened his spiritual connection with his wife. He committed himself more deeply to his own development (I think this was inspired by our work together and by his reading books I referred to him about spiritual emergence.) He learned how to set limits with his in-laws around their involvement in his personal life. He gained confidence that he could manage a spiritual emergency if it happened to him again. Furthermore, Bill's wife started to become more actively involved in her own inner development.

Bill's case also affected my professional life. I was working at the Transpersonal Counseling Center at the time Bill was my client. My peer counselors offered me support and facilitated my referral to the psychiatrist at the local hospital. My supervisor, a psychiatrist, supported me in advising Bill not to take any medications. The psychiatrist at the hospital supported my assessment of Bill's situation and the concept of using no psychiatric drugs. In summation, I realized I had a network of community support and a number of Bay Area resources for helping people in spiritual emergency.

A Helper's referral network is an important resource. No single individual can be as effective in spiritual emergency as a group of persons who can provide different kinds of support 24 hours a day. Being a Helper to a person in spiritual emergency is an intensely demanding service. Thus, the Helper's support network is valuable for both the Helper and the client in order to manage the spiritual emergency as well as possible.

Chapter Five _____

Ongoing Support

After a person in spiritual emergency has been diagnosed and given initial assistance, it is necessary to provide ongoing support by:

1. Providing a safe environment.
2. Facilitating grounding.
3. Restructuring response patterns to increase energy levels ("getting unstuck").
4. Supporting spiritual emergence.

This chapter describes each of these ongoing steps in detail.

A person in spiritual emergency is typically in a highly sensitized state — overwhelmed, over-stimulated, frightened, disoriented, self-absorbed, sometimes out of touch with other people and incapable of self-care. Such a person may be experiencing new capabilities — reading other people's thoughts, perceiving archetypal themes of life, seeing and palpably feeling auras, or experiencing several episodes in time simultaneously.

A person in spiritual emergency needs emotional reassurance, insight into the nature of the experience, and perhaps physical support. Above all, the person needs to have someone confirm that the novel inner experiences are valid and valuable.

A person in spiritual emergency needs a particular kind of environment and a particular kind of personal help to integrate visions, insights and kinesthetic experiences into ongoing life. The person needs help both to undo inhibiting emotional and physiological response patterns and be able to contain and use expanded sensitivities, new awareness and energy that come with spiritual experience. Ongoing treatment of each individual must be tailored to the person's developmental stage of growth, and the resources of the community.

Providing a Safe Environment

A safe environment is one in which the inner processes of the person can proceed without interruption and one in which the companions of the person provide support. Specifically, a safe environment includes:

1. A quiet, home-like setting with access to nature, that makes few demands on the client so that the client has the time and opportunity to explore and express his or her inner experience.

2. Companionship that supports the client's inner work and further understanding of spiritual emergence.

The Setting

Metzner (May,1985) reported a case in which a client admitted to a psychiatric ward was overwhelmed with constant voices in his head and unusual visions in front of his eyes which prohibited him from verbal interaction. The man was put in a small, soundproofed room where he was asked to lie down on a mattress. The lights were dimmed to almost total darkness. There was nothing else in the room except the man and the cot.

Metzner told the man that he would be on the other side of the wall and instructed the man to signal him by way of an intercom whenever the man saw visions or heard voices. To Metzner's surprise, he heard very little from his patient for 25 minutes. Finally, Metzner interrupted the man, "What are you experiencing?" His patient answered lucidly, "Finally—peace."

From this experience, and his subsequent interactions with the man on the ward, Metzner deduced that the man had such a high sensitivity to outside stimuli that he became quickly overwhelmed in an environment of bright light, noise, or people moving around. When he was emotionally supported and looked after in an environment of minimal stimulation he became centered and no longer felt victimized, frightened, or out of control. At that point he gained perspective about what was happening to him and learned to manage it.

An innovative kind of environment for people with schizophrenic symptoms is described in an article in Appendix C of this manual. It is entitled "Soteria: An Alternative to Hospitalization for Schizophrenics." It illustrates the kind of work that has been initiated by a few psychiatrists to explore alternative therapeutic environments.

Learning how to manage one's expanding sensitivities is the most important aspect of growing into higher developmental levels. The environment that is most suitable to this task is a place of quiet, with low light, either no noise or soothing music, access to a natural setting, and access to a safe space for catharsis. An aesthetic arrangement of furniture that pleases the eye and sense of touch has a dramatic effect on subduing an over-stimulated psyche.

This environment is much closer to a monastic setting that feels like a home for normal people than a psychiatric ward for sick people. But, similar to a psychiatric ward, it is an environment where a person can be totally supported physically, if need be, and reassured emotionally within a humanistic context that does not rigidly hold to the formal rules of any particular religion.

The Companions

There should be few social demands placed on a person in spiritual emergency. A demanding child or a needy friend is not an appropriate companion, whereas a supportive friend who is interested in personal development is.

Sogyal (1985) described the qualities of the interpersonal environment most appropriate for someone in spiritual emergency. He referred to the culture of Tibet:

> *People know about it (spiritual emergency) before they get it so that when it happens, generally speaking, rather than panicking, they have something to refer to, they're not alone. Actually the opening is a further clarification of what their whole education had already been illuminating for them: that the material world reflects only a small part of reality....*
>
> *There are cases when they do kind of freak out. Then it is the environment that helps a person through. Such an environment includes compassion, understanding, the confidence that inspires, warmth, and humor. (For the Tibetans, cultivating the quality of kindness is of uppermost importance.)*
>
> *...for such people (in spiritual emergency) environment is more important than anything else, because, when you reach to that level, you begin to have a problem relating to the environment, to the world. So creating some kind of environment which*

115

is stabilizing (is extremely important). Nature is very wonderful since we are very much related. This is the place of natural growth and this is the place where you can grow.

...when these people break through, like in a death experience and also a new birth experience, they become like little children. The loving environment is a very important aspect. We have to think in terms of creating an environment for them that is loving, understanding and stable. They also need some basic kind of support system.

Environment is more important than analyzing what is wrong or using a technique. Often we may make mistakes in our analysis when we start analyzing things (chuckle).

(Sogyal, 1985)

When Anne Armstrong, now famous as a psychic counselor, was going through her initial spiritual awakening she was at first very frightened. She had out-of-body experiences and past-life recalls that changed her perspective of reality. Armstrong acknowledged the critical importance of people who supported her and encouraged her to explore the experiences and to trust them.

The first time around I turned it off because I felt I couldn't cope with it, I didn't understand it, I didn't know anything about this area. I wasn't even aware that there might be a way of negotiating with this other part of myself I felt that it was out to get me,

*to manipulate me. Instead it was out to give me
an expanded awareness, a higher level of consciousness. The experiences were probably
brought about by my meditation practice, but at
that time I didn't know that. A lot of people will
have a tendency to squelch it as soon as it happens, because frequently it comes in very
bizarre ways. I don't really feel that it means to
frighten you or to manipulate you, but we're all
making so much "head noise" that it's very difficult for that part of the self to speak to us.
Usually it speaks in a very gentle or a very
quiet voice, but, if we don't listen to it, it may do
something bizarre to get our attention.*

(Armstrong, 1985)

Fourteen years later Armstrong began to work with hypnotherapy, seeking relief from migraine headaches she had
had since being a young girl. Fortunately, she was at a time
in her life where she could take 2-3 hours a day for therapy and meditation. Anne's husband became an active partner in her process and worked with her using hypnotherapy to help her find a way to understand her evolution into
higher consciousness. Armstrong wrote that it was the
loving acceptance others gave to her, and her study of
diverse religious texts which helped her integrate her
extraordinary experiences.

*Through hypnosis I found the way into that
opening again. The second time around, thank
God, I was a little more knowledgeable
and felt in control, which I feel was the major
difference between the first time I had the
opening, and fourteen years later. The second*

117

time, I felt totally in charge. I felt that no matter what happened, there was some part of me that in some sense was 'minding the store,' and that I didn't have to worry about it. There needs to be some way to communicate this to a client who is having spontaneous out-of-body experiences, hallucinations and other related phenomenon, as I was. They need to be assured that there is a part of the self, that I call the Witness or the Monitor, that is always "on guard," that is always looking out for your best interests. Once you learn to trust this Monitor, you lose the feeling of being a victim. So I went from feeling victimized by the energy to saying, "What is this energy and what can I do with it?" I made friends with it.

Also, another thing that was very helpful was that I had a therapist who understood exactly what was happening to me. Fortunately, the universe brought these kinds of people in to me. And I also had a very supportive husband, who was fascinated by the process. So, instead of saying "You're crazy!" he'd say, "Now, what's going on? What else can we do with this new tool that we have?" Fortunately, I was in very good hands. And I feel that it's very important for the therapist to understand that there can be spontaneous emergence of these other levels of consciousness, that it can manifest as past life recall, as hallucinations, and various kinds of paranoid feelings and actions. The therapist needs to be supportive, no matter what the client comes up with. My therapist and my husband treated my fears and

118

past life recall as if they were real. Whether or not they were real is irrelevant. The important thing is that that part of my self was being given expression and I was getting more and more trust in myself and my process. So let me say it again, the supportive environment was very important.

(Armstrong, 1985)

Facilitating Grounding

An important strategy for integrating transpersonal experience is to 'ground' oneself, that is, to come back to earth and to oneself after being in a 'space' that seems "out of this world."

To be grounded is another way of saying that a person has his feet on the ground. It can also be extended to mean that a person knows where he stands and therefore that he knows who he is. Being grounded, a person has "standing", that is, he is "somebody". In a broader sense grounding represents an individual's contact with the basic realities of his existence. He (or she) is rooted in the earth, identified with his body, aware of his sexuality, and oriented toward pleasure. These qualities are lacking in the person who is "up in the air" or in his head instead of in his feet.

(Lowen and Lowen, 1977)

Paradoxically, spiritual experiences often take people outside the context of their religious affiliation. It is difficult or impossible to find words or scriptures that

119

describe the experience adequately. A spiritual experience is totally unique, and at the same time universal—connecting one to all of life. One of the most liberating and, at the same time, frightening qualities of these experiences is that they are beyond words, beyond normal reality and normal expression.

The following list of techniques can be helpful to ground clients when they are "spaced out" and feel disconnected to people and the physical world. It is also important to teach clients in spiritual emergence how to ground themselves, and to recognize when they need grounding.

1. Stay in contact.
2. Stay in the present moment.
3. Affirm boundaries.
4. Support creative expression.
5. Affirm connection to people and nature.
6. Eat grounding foods.
7. Do simple rhythmic activity.
8. Do grounding visualizations.
9. Read books on spiritual emergence.
10. Minimize the use of psychiatric drugs.
11. Create meaningful rituals.

1. Stay in Contact

Be available to talk to persons in spiritual emergency in a way that is engaging. Maintain eye contact. Touch them lightly (always non-sexually) if appropriate. Affirm their experience by putting it in a positive framework. Be trustworthy.

2. Stay in the Present Moment

Ask the clients to tell you what sensations they are having in their bodies. Ask them to tell you what they perceive in the room in a concrete way, for example, "I see the plants in the corner. They have long, droopy leaves about 2 feet long. They are next to the door that is painted blue. The rug is beige. There are 10 pillows lined up against the wall." This helps people orient to their surroundings and differentiate who they are from what is around them. This is especially useful when a person is feeling frightened by a unitary experience or is under-bounded for other reasons.

Share emotions and your bond to the client. For example, "I support you, I want to be with you, I feel honored you are sharing your experience with me." Do not relate emotions that can be interpreted as divisive. For example, "I hope that never happens to me." Ask the persons to tell you what they want. For example, "I want to eat some pudding...I want to have a back rub...I want you to hold my hand and not talk."

3. Affirming Boundaries

All people have a strong sense of personal space around their bodies with which they identify. Persons in spiritual emergency may be highly sensitive to other people entering their personal space. Affirm that you are aware of their personal space and you do not want to violate that space by forcing intimacy or 'support' on them.

Kathlyn Hendricks (1985), a dance therapist, author and teacher, suggests asking persons to identify their personal space by pressing against the imaginary line of their boundaries with their hands. Doing this all around the body can give them a stronger sense of their own identity and help them communicate to another person how they experience their personal space.

Resting and bathing can also help them ground and identify with their own sense of space.

4. Creative Expression

Supporting persons to express the nature of their spiritual experiences through expressive dance, artwork, sand tray, clay, music, or poetry also helps them find a means to communicate to others and reconnect with their world. Artistic expression is a language of symbol and metaphor that can help people bridge the spiritual experience with ordinary consciousness. Gay Hendricks (1985), a teacher, author and clinical psychologist, tells people to "give it away. Experience all of what is happening to you—then give it away." How one can share one's emotional response to a spiritual experience might be through a hug, a dance, or any other creative expression.

5. Affirm Connection to People and the Natural World

When a person in spiritual emergency has difficulty relating to other people, a walk in nature can provide a stabilizing source of connection to the earth and the physical world. Just taking a walk in an area where there are trees and growing things is a powerful reminder of the earthy simplicity of life, that each thing that grows has its own individual pattern of growth. Pets can also provide grounding.

Grounding can be greatly facilitated by connecting to a few people or a group who are all involved with spiritual emergence. It is especially important that all in the group identify with their own development to transpersonal levels and thereby affirm their own and others' experiences. All forms of sharing can also help ground—holding hands, singing, chanting, telling one's story, or any creative expression of one's spiritual experience. Groups engender a sense of belonging and provide a context where one is seen for one's extraordinariness, as well as accepted for one's part in the larger whole.

Stanislav and Christina Grof ask people in their groups to draw mandalas depicting their experience after experiential therapy. Each person is then given the opportunity to show his or her work to the group. The picture itself communicates something of the nature of their experiences often more clearly than the person's verbal description. Gathering in a circle to share experiences of this nature is preferable to gathering in a way where people cannot see each other's faces. The circle includes everyone as equals. Each person faces the group. No one person stands out as leader, or authority, or outsider.

6.   Grounding Foods

What we choose to eat has a lot to do with how we feel. A light diet of mainly fruits, vegetables and grains can help people to stay slim and feel light. Vegetarianism may help people to attune to the more subtle energies of life, which are the gateways and guideposts of the transpersonal realms. Denser foods such as meat and dairy products have the effect of helping people identify more with the grosser energies of the physical world. The denser foods are more difficult to digest and therefore demand more vital energies in the process of digestion and assimilation.

A person in spiritual emergency may benefit by a diet heavier in meat and dairy products as it will help bring the person down to earth. On the other hand, if a person is in a spiritual emergency coping with unpredictable rushes of energy, the person's system may be too imbalanced to be able to handle much, or any, food at all. There are many differing opinions about diet and it is not within the scope of this handbook to cover diet in any depth. Certainly, when a person is in crisis the body is usually in a highly sensitized state and will benefit from a simple diet devoid of food additives and preservatives. Fresh air is also a boon to anyone in this state.

7.   Simple Rhythmic Activity

Walking, housecleaning, baking bread, sweeping the floor, raking leaves, weeding, swimming, and other easy-paced activities which have some repetitive rhythmic movement in which the whole body comes into coordinated motion are all excellent for grounding.

8.   Grounding Visualizations

Persons in spiritual emergency are identified more with the world of extraordinary phenomena than with the earth and its relatively slow rhythms. Visualizations can be used to foster a reconnecting with the earth. Ask these persons to feel their feet on the ground, to feel the support of the earth underneath them, or to imagine a line going from the base of their spine and anchoring to a spot in the core of the earth. The shorter and simpler the instruction the better because persons in crisis will often not have long attention spans. They may also be suffering from feeling lost in their own inner world, and a visualization which takes them further into their own inner world could be negative.

It may be wise for persons who meditate to decrease the amount of time they spend in meditation while they are experiencing a spiritual crisis. It may be better for them to stop meditating altogether for a time, rather than amplifying the inner world drama by continued meditation. This decision must be made on an individual basis because some meditations can serve as powerful grounding devices whereas others are designed to disconnect persons from their habitual grounding.

9.   Books to Read

Books about people who have experienced spiritual emergence / emergency in a positive way provide models for people attempting to make sense out of their own disturbing spiritual experiences. Reading about someone else's experience can be reassuring, and often inspiring.

Refer to a list of reading material useful (see Appendix D) for understanding the phenomenon of spiritual emergence.

10. Minimize Psychiatric Drugs

Most psychiatric drugs inhibit the process of spiritual emergence by preventing potentially therapeutic catharsis, dulling inner awareness and unbalancing the body's own homeostatic process. The side effects of many psychiatric drugs take energy away from the process of moving into a higher level of awareness or from the process of grounding. Some psychiatric drugs increase disorientation, and inhibit personal contact that is so crucial to a person in spiritual emergency.

One of the participants at the SEN conference (1985) had been institutionalized because he could not carry out his duties in the military. At the time he was very involved in his inner process. In the psychiatric hospital he was given phenothiazine and thorazine. He described these drugs as "debilitating, and (preventing him) from staying present with what was happening." He inferred they interfered with his journey of awakening to higher levels of self-development.

In Appendix C is a report of a study on people hospitalized for schizophrenia who were treated without phenothiazines. The results indicated that some schizophrenics have a better chance of recovery when left to work through their processes in a non-drugged state.

Some institutions have established settings for people in

psychological crises where psychiatric drugs are not preferred treatment (Telles, Perry and Price, 1985). Diabasis
and Soteria were institutions for the care of first-break psychotics in San Francisco. A ward of Agnews State Hospital
in California also functioned for a time with minimized
drug use. Both of these treatment facilities attempted to
provide safe environments and both reported positive outcomes from their clientele. Unfortunately, both facilities
folded for lack of funding. The research on Soteria (See
Appendix C) indicates the cost of treatment per client was
less than in traditional facilities and fewer clients were
institutionalized again. This may be significant to recognize during our current period of health care reform.

11. Ritual

Ritual focuses attention and can be particularly useful with
people who are distracted or overwhelmed and are trying
to regain a sense of stability.

Universally, ceremony and ritual have been used to evoke
elevated feeling and to remind people of the presence of
spiritual forces. As people develop towards the transpersonal level they become more palpably aware of the presence of universal energies. Participating in ceremony
which formalizes reception of higher wisdom can help persons who are overwhelmed by spiritual emergency.

Some of the common rituals are ceremonial dance, listening to music, watching a fire or candlelight, spiritual

singing and chanting, prayer and meditation. Community participation accentuates the power of any ritual, although a private ceremony done alone or with a few people can also serve well to focus spiritual energies.

Prayer is especially powerful for anyone confronting possession as the right prayer evokes empowerment and protection, a shield against invading forces. Mantra, a repeated set of syllables or words that bring a person into harmony with a higher force, may be quite conducive to healing. At the very least it is a positive replacement for a negative obsessive thought: "I can't. I can't. I can't." With a mantra, a person can begin to take responsibility for the contents of their thought process and empower themselves to move into dynamic union with a source of wisdom which is higher than their own ego. Prayers which punctuate the day at certain ritual times like meals also serve this same function. The most important aspect in prayer is to recollect that there is a compassionate, wise force that is accessible to give nurturing, guidance and protection.

The grounding effect of ritual is that it gives definition to energies that are not visible and are seemingly out-of-control and unpredictable. The symbols used in religious rituals represent spiritual energies in visible form. For example, the blood of Christ is imagined in the communion wine. When we drink the wine, we symbolically take in the spirit of Christ. Tibetan Buddhist Thangkas (religious paintings) are symbolic renditions of the energies of the Divine, which are used in meditations to evoke higher spiritual energies in the meditator.

Creating a place which is sacred and used only for ritual can be very important for grounding. A corner of the living room for a small altar and book of prayer can provide a sacred place in one's home to stimulate one's awareness of spiritual energies. Religious objects can also be used as a focus. Giving a person in spiritual emergency a religious object, for example, a crucifix for a Catholic, or a small statue of Kuan Yin for a Chinese Buddhist, can be especially helpful.

Assisting those in spiritual emergency to find a religious ceremony or symbol that has particular meaning for them and to which they can create a bond is a powerful way to help. Formal religious ceremony has usually served this role; however, there are more and more people who develop their spiritual awareness outside of any religious institutions.

It may be appropriate for a Helper to introduce a symbol from a different culture that can enhance spiritual understanding for those in spiritual emergency. For example, the Hindus have a goddess called Kali who embodies energies very different from any feminine religious symbol known in the West. Kali is an awesome creature with a necklace of skulls adorning her neck, her tongue dangling out of her mouth, her eyes bulging out of her head, and her long black hair blowing wildly. She symbolizes the energies of chaos, death and change. She affirms that change is part of life, that ignorance dies and wisdom is born in change. Knowing Kali as a religious symbol can assist a person undergoing spiritual emergency to recognize the value of chaos and change as an opportunity to grow into higher realms of knowledge.

129

A ritual which combines prayer and visualization is especially impactful. The following is used with 'spirit releasement,' and de-possession:

Every morning before starting your day call upon the sacred power which represents the most enlightened force in the universe for you.

Say: "By the name and through the power of (Jesus Christ, Buddha, etc.) I cleanse and purify the energy centers of my body." Visualize a stream of white light coming from the higher source into the energy centers of your body, entering in like water fills a vessel, cleansing and filling the centers with the light of higher power.

Say: "By the name and through the power of (the highest power you have selected), I seal the doors (of my energy centers)." Visualize a cross, or symbol which represents the power of higher force, across the front and back of the energy centers.

Finally, visualize yourself in a stream of light. It circulates around your body like water, covering every inch of you- your head, your neck, your torso, your arms and legs, all the way down to your toes. Let this energy that represents the highest, flow in and around every detail of your body and then let it flow out filling your aura to a distance an arm's length out from your body. See yourself and feel yourself surrounded by this holy, powerful light.

At any time during the day, if you feel you need protection or empowerment, visualize the light circulating all around you, forming a protective shield.

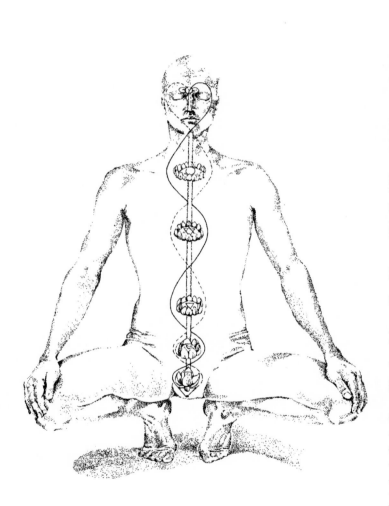

Illustration by Sunita Alyson King from Ashtange Yoga Primer published by Sri Rama Publishing/Hanuman Fellowship.

Ritual and symbol create boundaries and structure for unbounded and unstructured experience. They are a way to integrate spiritual experience with worldly experience, and to focus on growth toward higher levels of development.

Getting Unstuck

Letting go of old emotional patterns and physical tensions that limit range of movement and growth is part of the process of spiritual emergency. A Helper must be able to facilitate clients' changing response patterns, help them to intensify their connection with their inner process, and help expand their awareness of their new level of consciousness. Each demands some training, but does not require a graduate degree in psychology. It is recommended that properly credentialed practitioners be employed.

Establishing Therapeutic Rapport

Therapeutic rapport will provide the foundation for any supervised inner work. The full attention of a Helper who is both empathic and respectful of the inner experience of an individual in spiritual emergency is a powerful healing force. It encourages the individual to give significance to his or her own inner process. Furthermore, the intensified awareness of the inner process helps these individuals process the emotional response to their spiritual experience.

This 'therapeutic' rapport with another seems to provide a containing framework for the individual, within which the process can be experienced in its fullest intensity and yet in some measure of security. It does not seem particularly important that the person in the 'therapist' position be able to make 'interpretations' according to any psychological theory; an empathetic participation with the individual in the inner experience seems to be sufficient.

(Perry, 1974)

Thus, empathic participation helps clients to be fully in their inner process.

The Helper does not need to have any special training to be able to give full attention to individuals in spiritual emergency. Simply employing principles of active listening is sufficient (Speeth, 1982; Young, 1983). However, a Helper may need to have experienced altered states of consciousness many times in order to be present with the client without being worried or feeling pressure to make the client conform to expectations of normalcy (Perry, 1974).

There is little need to interpret and analyze the clients' inner experience until the spiritual crisis is over and the clients are in the process of integrating the experience. At that time, helping clients interpret the experience is a vital part of the therapeutic process.

Establishing rapport with clients involves forming a

relationship which has some depth of intimacy. The Helper must function as a close friend and guide, caring, giving without expectation of return, respectful of the inner life of the client, providing safety, and yet simultaneously, allowing the client's full experience and expression of his or her inner process.

Education: Active listening skills and empathy have been developed in some people through family life and normal life situations. Some have developed these skills by participating in grassroots self-help movements such as 12-step programs and Co-counseling. Formal programs training counselors and health professionals include training in establishing therapeutic rapport or a positive "bedside manner" as this is essential to any successful counseling relationship.

The following adjunctive therapies, Regression Therapy, Breathwork and Energy Balancing are especially potent in opening the doors to the unconscious. Each one can catalyze catharsis, insight and/or integration when supervised by appropriately trained practitioners.

Regression Therapy

Regression therapy is a supervised procedure taking a client into an altered state where the individual is detached from the normal limitations of the ego and in greater contact with what is usually below consciousness, accessing repressed memories. Current research indicates that hypnosis allows a person to enter into brain-wave patterns that are slower than the normal

Beta frequency, producing more and more focused attention, yet simultaneously retaining Beta, enabling communication with the therapist and integration. Under skillful supervision, this multi-dimensional attention can be pointed to areas that are conducive to healing. "It is possible to shift from experiencing a past life to observing it, then to processing it, then to observing it again, and weave back and forth" (Lucas, 1993). The purpose of this therapy is to enhance connection with inner wisdom and repressed feelings to catalyze healing and personal growth. A belief in reincarnation is not essential for effective work in regression therapy.

The process of moving an individual into an altered state can be accomplished in many ways: shamanic drumming, hypnosis, guided meditation, guided relaxation induction, concentration on a particular image, music and ritual. Particular places, in themselves, may induce an altered state such as churches or areas where important rituals have been performed, i.e., Stonehenge, the Parthenon, Delphi. Some recreational drugs produce altered states that open access to resources of intuitive knowing and feelings. However, the potential value of using these recreational drugs is obscured by the lack of adequate supervision in their use, and the fact that these drugs are generally illegal.

The most commonly used induction device in regression therapy is hypnosis. Ideally, the therapist will induce a hypnotic state that is deep enough to enter Delta but not so deep as to lose Beta. When a subject loses Beta he loses his ability to remember what has taken place. This can impede integration.

Before the induction a goal is set, i.e., to get to the root of a chronic physical pain or obsession, or shed light on a particular life issue. Once the goal is set and the induction is complete, the client is focused on paying attention to material brought to consciousness. The therapist may suggest that new material come in a certain form, such as a vision of a past life, but everything that comes to consciousness is regarded as having some value. During the process, dialogue goes on between therapist and client. The client reports what is being seen and experienced in the past life. The therapist serves as guide, suggesting to the client where to place his or her attention in order to get the most information and/or healing experience.

The client is focused on the inner world, similar to the dream world where extraordinary things happen which can not happen in the everyday time-space continuum. The therapist can suggest that the client change perspective on any scene at any time. For example, one can move to a safe space outside the body in a threatening situation, or move ahead in time or behind in time, or locate a particular time when the individual was especially lucid. Consciousness can be moved, like a video player, going to one scene, or fast-forward to the end of the movie (life), or rewind to the beginning. In the case of past-life regression, all the lives are on one video, including what happened in between each life, in the "inter-life."

Winafred Lucas, Ph.D., author of *Regression Therapy: A Handbook for Professionals* (1993), believes that taking a client into the "inter-life" experience is potentially the most healing experience of all. In an "inter-life" the individual can actually experience the joy, the light, the peace, the reunion with loved ones and the connection to Divine energies which are so hard to come by in normal life experience. There is a kind of rest and revitalizing which is possible in an inter-life episode under hypnosis which can not be gleaned in any normal life experience. There is phenomenological evidence that this kind of inter-life episode, may contribute to the same kind of personal transformation that is reported by people who have a Near Death Experience.

Other uses of hypnosis that serve transpersonal growth and may be helpful to someone in spiritual emergency are exploring prenatal trauma, birth, child abuse, dialogue with the unborn soul, the death experience, future life progression, and release of negative entity attachment. An individual under hypnosis can gain perspective on past experiences and liberate him or herself from fixations that have a profound impact on a current situation. Beyond the particular problem, clients in regression therapy are also exploring the idea that life on earth is for learning, that every experience and lifetime is contributing valuable lessons, and the lessons ultimately serve a transpersonal goal: to become whole and realize the transpersonal realms of consciousness.

Education: Proper use of regression therapy is a skill that can be learned in training programs with certified hypnotherapists. Excellent trainings are offered by the Hypnotherapy Academy in Santa Fe, New Mexico: http://www.hypnotherapyacademy.com/. Explore the International Association for Regression Research and Therapies, for its many resources: http://www.iarrt.org/.

They offer training, certification, conferences, continuing education, and publications.

Transpersonal Breathwork

Transpersonal breathwork is a natural physical and psychic stimulant useful when clients need a catalyst for self-expression. As breathwork raises energy in all systems of the body, it increases the possibility of breaking through inhibiting response patterns to increased levels of energy. Results range from having spiritual experiences, to remembering forgotten important life events, to creating deep energetic or emotional experiences, to learning how to manage higher levels of energetic expression.

Breathwork is not advised for people who are at a stage in their spiritual emergence when they are overstimulated and need grounding. It is also contraindicated for pregnant women and people who are recently out of surgery, have a heart condition or epilepsy.

It is advised for people in phases of spiritual emergence when they are relatively grounded and need to be more closely aligned with their emotional and bio-energetic life. Jacquelyn Small (1985) finds breathwork highly effective with drug addicts and alcoholics in recovery. It is also very effective in training Helpers because it can lead to experiences of altered states of consciousness.

People in spiritual emergency usually dissociate to some

degree, and separate from their emotional response to their spiritual experience. This happens because they have not yet learned how to contain or manage the larger amounts of energy that come with spiritual experience. Thus, they need special help to connect fully to their inner process and learn new patterns of response to heightened energy levels, to express and contain rather than repress or dissociate. This connecting reduces their fear of what is happening to them, because it gives them the feeling of being at one with themselves. This helps clients trust the process of spiritual emergence as positive.

Doing breathwork stimulates the body's own homeostatic processes. If persons need to let go chaotically in order to come into balance within themselves, the breathwork will move them closer to a chaotic letting-go. If persons need to have visions to assist them in their evolution, they will be likely to have a vision. If persons need deep peace, they will be likely to have that experience. Personal volition, desires originating from the ego, and the voluntary nervous system are less influential during breathwork than the autonomic nervous system—which is in charge of homeo-static processes both in the body and mind.

"Breathers" may have any number of inner experiences during a session. Chronic muscular tension becomes more apparent and may heighten and then spontaneously release. Emotional catharsis can also occur. The release of muscular tension may stimulate insight into emotional complexes and COEX systems. "Breathers" may review physical trauma, feeling and expressing the emotions that were not expressed at the time of the trauma. They may experience enlivening energy streaming in their bodies and they may have visions or subtle sense perceptions characteristic of transpersonal states.

Transpersonal breathwork should always take place in an environment which is private, protected, and supportive. In a breathwork session, the therapist allows anything to happen *excepting sexual acts and actions that could hurt someone.* The breathers are encouraged to trust their inner knowing, to surrender to what is deeply felt, and to stay in touch with their own inner process. A significant aspect of this work is that it provides a social context which supports this open way of being. The context in the breathwork demonstrates to people that there is a place in life where it is appropriate to totally let go, to connect fully with inner process, to express fully, to surrender to the unknown.

At the end of breathwork sessions, which last 1-2 hours, participants in a group are asked to gather together and share their experiences. Similarly, in an individual session, a breather reports to the therapist and thus, grounds his or her experience, verbally reinforcing the learning and gaining objectivity.

Breathwork comes out of the shamanic and ancient yogic traditions, which use breathing techniques and evocative music to catalyze spiritual experiences, and from Reichian therapy, which uses breathing techniques and deep tissue massage to catalyze emotional catharsis and psychological integration.

Breathwork has been criticized as a mystification of hyperventilation because people often feel dizzy and /or get muscular spasms around their mouths, hands and feet which are characteristic of hyperventilation. It is now, however, well established by breathwork therapists (Cucuruto, 1977; Jackson, 1984; G. Hendricks, 1985 and K. Hendricks, 1985; Grof, 1985) who have seen thousands of people in hundreds of sessions, that dizziness and muscular spasms subside as a person accommodates higher levels of energy in the body. Dizziness and spasms appear to be linked to chronic patterns of muscular tension that interfere with natural energetic flow and muscular holding characteristic of people who are holding down their energetic capacities.

I believe it is important for people to have individualized attention from a trained breathwork therapist during most of their breathwork sessions. By doing specific body manipulations the trained therapist will assist the breather in re-educating his or her body to find a new pattern of containing high energy and expressing it in an integrated way—a way in which the body maintains alignment and balance, and the person knows when it is appropriate to express and when to contain expression. Without individualized assistance, breathers will still break into areas of themselves that have been repressed because of the increased energy charge of the breathwork activity itself and they will have the characteristic experience of peacefulness after the session, but, they will not necessarily retrain themselves to manage increased energy smoothly.

Proper training to facilitate breathwork with an individual or a group is important. Breathwork can stimulate powerful experiences on any level—physical, emotional, or spiritual. A Helper facilitating breathwork needs to have a strong background in being both a 'breather' and a 'sitter,' a companion to the one who is breathing. 'Sitting' with anyone in deep emotional states like rage, grief, fear, and love can train Helpers to stay centered in high stress situations such as spiritual emergency. A breathwork facilitator also needs training in how to release energy blocks which are painful and sometimes occur in a session, for example, muscular spasms in the throat or chest which inhibit breathing, severe tension in the shoulders, or cramping in the stomach or legs. The breathwork facilitator must also educate the clients about what to expect from breathwork and how to manage the phenomena which arise both during and after the session. The facilitator also needs to be skilled in identifying when people are dissociating and in helping them become grounded.

Education: The two oldest forms of breathwork used for healing and transpersonal exploration: *Radiance Breathwork and Holotropic Breathwork*. Training for facilitating Radiance Breathwork is known as "The Hendricks Method of Body-Centered Transformation Using Radiance Breathwork" was conceived by Drs. Kathlyn and Gay Hendricks and is now taught through the Hendricks Institute: **http://www.hendricks.com/**. Holotropic Breathwork originated with Christina and Dr. Stanislav Grof, **http://www.breathwork.com/**. Certified trainees of both forms can be found in many parts of the world.

Energy Balancing

Evolution has a biological basis, and every transition in human development has its somatic expression. Infants are enabled to differentiate from their parents as young children when they gain the capacity to walk out of sight of their parents. Young people are enabled to differentiate more fully from their families when they make sexual bonds with a mate and establish their own families. The bridge between the egoic levels and the transpersonal realms is possible when a person can consciously use large amounts of energy in a balanced way.

> *All the systems of Yoga and all religious disciplines are designed to bring about those psychosomatic changes in the body which are essential for the metamorphosis of consciousness. A new center—presently dormant in the average man and woman—has to be activated, and a more powerful stream of psychic energy must rise into the head from the base of the spine to enable human consciousness to transcend the normal limits. This is the final phase of the present evolutionary impulse in man. The cerebrospinal system of man has to undergo a radical change, enabling consciousness to attain a dimension which transcends the limits of the highest intellect. Here, reason yields to intuition and revelation appears to guide the steps of humankind.*
>
> *(Gopi Krishna, in White, 1984)*

The energy system of a person in spiritual emergency

143

needs to be considered when the Helper is creating a treatment plan. Bodywork designed to align and balance a person with his or her natural flow of energy is helpful in spiritual crisis. Examples of energy balancing techniques include accupressure, acupuncture, Lomi, cranio-sacral, Polarity, Network Chiropractic, Rosen Work and Motion Quest®. These forms of bodywork are less active and more structured than transpersonal breathwork. They are advisable for people in spiritual emergency who are too ungrounded for breathwork or in a vulnerable physical condition. Hatha Yoga is appropriate for people who can focus and be active for periods of time.

The Spiritual Competency Resource Center, http://www.virtualcs.com/ offers a wealth of information and referrals.

Education: Becoming a bodyworker skilled in energy balancing involves a long-term program of study. There are many institutes available throughout the world which concentrate on various forms of energy balancing techniques. The "Yoga Journal", published bi-monthly in Berkeley, Ca., has an annual listing of yoga programs located around the USA. Local advertisers are available in New Age/Metaphysical bookstores which promote a wide variety of bodywork programs. I recommend Process Accupressure, conceived by Aminah Raheem, Ph.D., who teaches how to facilitate processing psychological and spiritual issues while doing hands on energy balancing. Visit: http://www.processaccupressure.com.

Supporting Spiritual Emergence

After a client has had a spiritual emergency, how does a Helper assist the client's subsequent growth? This section explores three basic elements necessary to support development into transpersonal levels:

1. Maintain a positive attitude.
2. Identify a map of the journey.
3. Invite new ways of being.

Maintain a Positive Attitude

Maintaining a positive attitude toward development into transpersonal levels is an essential support to a client's growth. Such development can be a difficult process because it requires that we disidentify with our familiar ego state and explore unknown perceptions and awarenesses. The journey into new realms can be frightening, just as it can be ecstatic.

Buddhists believe that the mainstay of support in the journey of transpersonal development is "taking refuge in the Triple Gem." The Triple Gem refers to Buddha, Dharma and Sangha.

> *To take refuge in the Buddha means acknowledging the seed of enlightenment that is within ourselves, the possibility of freedom. It also means taking refuge in those qualities which the Buddha embodies, qualities like fearlessness, wisdom, love and compassion. Taking refuge in the Dharma means taking refuge in the law, in the way things are; it is*

145

> *acknowledging our surrender to the truth,*
> *allowing the Dharma to unfold within us.*
> *Taking refuge in the Sangha means taking sup-*
> *port in the community, in all of us helping one*
> *another towards enlightenment and freedom.*
>
> *(Goldstein, 1976)*

This Buddhist wisdom applies to anyone in any religion. It is a universal truth that the seeds of our highest potential are within us. We need only to nourish those seeds and be with people who support us in this growth.

Finding a community of friends who will support one's process of spiritual emergence is a blessing. Such friends can be people inside or outside an institutionalized religion who recognize that human growth proceeds past ego development to levels of wisdom, compassion, and creativity which are extraordinary. The friends might be a group who meet to meditate together or to discuss writing about the transpersonal realms.

All people who value the states of mind associated with transpersonal realms and want to experience them, and there are many, can be considered supportive friends for someone in spiritual emergence. Many groups have evolved to support their members within a group context. The most consistent support for self development will come from the group with whom one shares the most in common—a similar meditation practice, a common living place, or the same spiritual guide.

Physical places can serve to support one's spiritual emergence. A church, the birthplace of a spiritual leader, a mountain retreat, a ritual mound built on top of a ley line are all places which serve to stabilize and inspire one in the intention to grow to higher levels.

Support for spiritual development can also be received from things, animate or inanimate, which reflect to us our deepest nature. This may be a figure from our dream lives, a person who comes to us in meditation, a flower, a candle flame, a child, a dog, anything that serves to guide our own unfolding.

Some people who have progressed into transpersonal levels of development believe they have communicated with and felt support from the spirits of people who have passed away. Da Free John communicated with Shakti (the Divine Cosmic and Manifesting Energy) and the spirit of his teacher, Swami Nityananda, who had passed on:

> *Then, one day, to his great surprise and immense good humor, the Shakti manifested Itself to him in visible form as the Virgin Mary. She began to guide his spiritual practice. Eventually, she told him to go on a pilgrimage of the major Christian holy places in Jerusalem and Europe. Master Da related these experiences to Bhagawan Nityananda, who appeared to him in a vision. Nityananda told him that he belonged to the Mother Shakti now and that She (The Divine Spirit-Presence, In Person) would be his Guru or Guide. With Nityananda's Blessings, Master Da left India to carry out the Mother's*

instructions. In the course of his pilgrimage, Master Da was released of his remaining emotional ties to Christianity. Indeed, he was released from the total past, and he emerged simply in Love with his "Blessed Companion."
                                                    (Da Free John, 1985)

Identifying a Map of the Journey

Maps of the journey to the transpersonal realms of development can be found in three places: one's inner psyche, a teacher (or teachers) who models the way, and belief systems which literally map the path and give instructions for specific spiritual practices.

One's own inner psyche often points the way through dreams or visions. Jung's story of his life in *Memories, Dreams and Reflections* (1961) is an example of this. Jung was not drawn to the Eastern way of working with a spiritual teacher and also felt alienated from his father's church and the religious institutions of his community. It was through his dreams and inner reflections that Jung became aware of his longing for the experience of the Divine. This led him into a journey of intensive study, research, writing and retreat, where he went more and more deeply into his experiences of the Divine.

Sometimes psychic pressure produces a vision which becomes a beacon and guides us towards transpersonal reality. According to Bolen (1984), the heroine in classic folk stories (meaning the woman who will discover the transpersonal truths and bring them back to society) frequently feels alienated from her family as a child, and feels that her parents are not her real parents. She develops a vision of meeting her 'real family' later on in life after she has accomplished some of the necessary tasks of her own growth. The 'real family' is the group who will acknowledge her higher transpersonal self, relating to her with deep love, compassion, and wisdom. This vision then inspires the girl to live with patience, perseverance, and to maintain her awareness of higher reality.

The map of the journey can come from a spiritual teacher who models the path to higher development by his or her own lifestyle, inner attainment, and teachings. In this context, a spiritual teacher is anyone who has attained the transpersonal levels of development. This person is then in a position to teach other people about spiritual emergence by sharing experiences of his or her own journey and teaching them techniques used to catalyze transpersonal growth.

Spiritual teachers have not necessarily qualified themselves to teach through a particular course of study, or a specific discipline aimed at self-development. Many people who have experienced the transpersonal realms (for example, through a Near Death Experience) have the ability to transmit their wisdom. These people are spiritual teachers because they have the ability to transmit the quality of the experience and thus be guides to some extent.

The ideal spiritual teacher has integrated his or her own spiritual experiences, and is geographically accessible, perhaps a yoga teacher, a meditation teacher, a member of the Native American Church, a minister or priest. Each serves to support growth toward transpersonal levels of self-development. The best spiritual teacher has attained transpersonal levels of development. How does one recognize a person who has reached the highest level of development?

In the traditions of yoga certain guidelines are given to help distinguish one who is advanced from one who isn't. In the Bhagavad Gita, Arjuna asks his teacher how can one identify a man who is firmly established and absorbed in the highest consciousness. He is told that such a person is "not shaken by adversity," that he is "free from fear, free from anger" (Bhagavad Gita, Ch.2). The way the teacher sits is carefully scrutinized. He who is restless with poor posture betrays his lack of control over the body and reveals a dissipated, unfocused mind. The way he walks is observed; whether it indicated hurriedness, a sense of being torn and pressured, a posture of defensiveness, or whether, on the other hand, it reflects confidence, ease and self-control. Speech is also evaluated. Is one distracted, wandering, rambling, losing the thread of the conversation? Is he critical and negative in his comments about others? Does he tend to focus on the negative aspects of everything around him, and do his own actions tend toward destructiveness? Does he become angry for no apparent reason, misinterpreting what others say and do, distorting them so that they fit his own ideas?

150

One need not ask the customary question about hallucinations, bizarre ideas, etc. to distinguish such a person from the mystic who despite his "strange ideas" presents a vastly different picture. The traditional observations amount to a pragmatic sort of descriptive psychiatry. The authentic mystic reflects an inner discipline despite the fact that his ideas and behavior may be difficult to understand. However baffling his speech or actions, he nevertheless reflects an inner peace through a relaxed body and harmonious coordination, and through patience, confidence, clear thinking and an unselfish attention to the needs of others.

(Rama, et al., 1976)

The support of such a person helps point the way to inner peace, compassion, and energetic creativity.

Many types of literature can serve to guide one in spiritual emergence. Personal accounts, ancient texts and scriptures, or instruction books on how to perform specific exercises all give a map of the journey. *The Autobiography of a Yogi* (1946), the story of Yogananda, an East Indian who came to the United States to teach about Yogic principles as well as Christian philosophy, is one of the most widely read stories of personal evolution.

Poetry, music, and various art forms including architecture and dance can also serve to evoke in people a feeling for higher levels of consciousness. The ecstatic poetry of Kabir, a 15th-century Indian influenced by the Sufis and Hindus, spoke directly of the inner knowledge which comes in the transpersonal levels:

Are you looking for me? I am in the next seat.
My shoulder is against yours.
You will not find me in stupas, not in Indian
shrine rooms,
nor in synagogues, nor in cathedrals:
not in masses, nor kirtans, not in legs winding
around your own neck, nor in eating nothing
but vegetables.
When you really look for me, you will see me
instantly—
you will find me in the tiniest house of time.
Kabir says: Student, tell me, what is God? He
is the breath inside the breath.

(translated by Bly, 1971)

Judith Whitman-Small's contemporary poetry is similarly inspiring:

The sacred space expands
in all directions
making the whole world
an altar for worship.
Light the incense of devotion
to all life
and watch its healing smoke
spiral past
the boundaries of the mind.
(Small, 1985)

These two poems point to the experience of God, to that which is sacred outside the limitations of a specific religion. They point to an experience that may be found anywhere, · by anyone.

152

Most of the literature we have pertaining to higher levels of consciousness is contained in particular religious writings, which seems to imply that the higher states are accessible only to people who follow a particular religious path. In fact, the higher states of consciousness are available to anyone, inside or outside a formal religious setting. Literature which illumines this is liberating for people seeking spiritual development.

Exploring new belief systems is a way of opening the door to increased self-awareness and profound new perspective. For example, astrology has been studied for thousands of years in the West and in the East. Although it is frequently dumbed down in overly simplistic newspaper horoscopes, an in-depth study of astrology may provide a key to understanding human personality and karma *(Astrology, Karma and Transformation,* Stephen Arroyo, 1978). Richard Tarnas, astrologer and author of *The Passion of the Western Mind* (1991), has found a distinct correlation between spiritual crises and particular planetary movements in an individual's astrological chart. Seeing our spiritual crises from the perspective of astrology may help us see our personal problems in the context of much larger natural cycles which lends a sense of profound connectedness between our own small existence and the movement of the planets, our earth and sun. The study of astrology can be understood as the study of archetypal energies in the context of deepening a connection to the earth itself. Other belief systems which can enhance attunement to larger, universal cycles are *The I Ching,* the *Tarot,* and the *Native American Medicine Wheel.*

153

Inviting New Ways of Being

Spiritual teachings and transpersonal therapies are designed to evoke new ways of being which are less
cen¬tered on egoic consciousness and more attuned to
transpersonal consciousness. The individual who wants to
grow into these higher levels must seek out the teachings
and therapies appropriate for himself or herself.

Shirley MacLaine began to explore transpersonal realms
after she reached 40. She wrote a book of her experiences
that was made into a movie, "*Out on a Limb*" (1987), for
national television. She sought friends to teach her about
expanded states of consciousness, read transpersonal literature, and went to psychic mediums who guided her development. She had no other impetus except her own deep desire
to learn more. Her support community consisted of one
friend who helped her maintain a positive attitude, showed
her a map of the journey, and helped her explore new ways
of being.

MacLaine's story (1984, 1987) is one well-publicized
model of a path which has been independent of the more
traditional ways of inviting new ways of being. In the past,
people seeking transpersonal levels of development would
commit themselves to monastic life, and divest themselves
of their former identities. In monastic life they would do
spiritual exercises designed to guide them toward spiritual
experiences and transpersonal development. This system
was hierarchical. A teacher or abbot had authority over the
monastic's life.

Other ways of inviting new ways of being include group seminars such as the Forum and Avatar. Both courses, offered internationally, are designed to enable people to realize deeper parts of their nature in a more social context. The Forum (**http://landmarkeducation.com/**) has innovated many types of programs to help people expand self-concept and find a way to make a contribution to the world. Avatar (**http://www.avatarepc.com**) is a speedily effective course which brings participants into the experience of operating free of any belief system, at one with transpersonal levels of consciousness. Avatar provides a safe gradient approach to spiritual emergence, appropriate for people of any age and any background. During the course participants explore their own belief system and are given tools to modify aspects of life which they wish to change. Participants who want to maintain the levels of consciousness they reach in these group intensives need to continue to work with the tools they acquire on the courses.

Therapy which is transpersonally oriented is designed to help people develop and experience new possibilities for themselves in all aspects of their lives. It is oriented towards increased well-being. It invites clients to adventure, to explore new ways of being in the world which would increase satisfaction.

Community Resources

The community resources available to you as a Helper are an important part of your professional care of clients in spiritual emergency. In Appendix 'A' of this manual are

a questionnaire and discussion guide of community resources. Reading and responding to this will help you
identify community resources for referral.

Summary

Supporting people in spiritual emergency is a humanistic
art based on compassion and kindness mixed with the
technologies of clinical psychology and theology. As we
become more aware of the needs of people entering into
this critical phase, we will be better prepared to care for
them. At this point, we have identified basic elements most
necessary to address: a safe environment, grounding,
restructuring inhibiting response patterns, and supporting
spiritual emergence. Next is a discussion on the role of
the Helper.

Chapter Six ———————————————

The Role of The Helper

This chapter is designed to assist you to identify your competencies as a Helper. A list of competencies is given, followed by a description of the qualities listed. At the end of the chapter, questions are asked to help you review.

Because the list of competencies in an ideal Helper is long, it would be highly unusual to find all qualifications in one person. As you read the following list, keep in mind that the ideal helper is likely to be a team of people, not just one person.

Competencies of a Helper

1. An open heart and deep compassion.
2. Experience of opening to the Divine.
3. Clinical experience with people having symptoms of psychosis.
4. Substantial experience with one's own unconscious, including the transpersonal levels.
5. Groundedness.
6. Stability within oneself.
7. Knowledge and skill in working with body-mind aspects of spiritual emergency.
8. Commitment to excellence in one's work.
9. Access to excellent supervision.
10. Knowledge of literature on spiritual emergence.
11. Ability to teach someone about spiritual emergence.
12. Knowledge of one's own skills and the ability to recognize when to make referrals.
13. Knowledge of caring for one's own needs.

An Open Heart

An open heart, which creates the ability to be present with compassion, is the most important qualification for a Helper of someone in spiritual emergency. More than anything else, it is the open-heartedness of the Helper that is essential to facilitating healing or balancing.

The Experience of Opening to the Divine

A person who has already had a spiritual experience can give reassurance to a person in spiritual crisis. People who have had an opening to the Divine embody a knowingness of the Divine. This deep personal knowledge and the ability to reassure clients about spiritual experience are important characteristics of a Helper.

Clinical Experience

Clinical experience with psychotic clients is essential for the Helper who carries the responsibility of making a correct diagnosis. This experience gives a Helper the skills to work with someone in a psychotic state.

A person with this clinical experience can determine how much and what kind of assistance a client needs, if and when it's safe to leave a client alone, and if the client is sufficiently grounded to get along without assistance.

Experience With One's Own Unconscious

Having a familiarity with the unconscious implies that a Helper has "confronted his [or her] own demons and become conscious of the psychic and astral levels within himself [or herself]" (S. Grof, 1985). With this familiarity comes a respect for the unconscious and, relatively speaking, less fear in dealing with it. A Helper who has worked with the unconscious is able to provide a client in spiritual emergency with a workable strategy, a model, for relating to unconscious material as it arises.

159

A Helper who has a deep familiarity with his or her own unconscious is less likely to become destabilized by the eruptions that may come from the unconscious of a client. In helping someone in spiritual emergency, an ability to work with the dark, or shadow side of transpersonal experiences is just as important as the ability to accept and work with the transpersonal or higher aspects of the unconscious.

> *My experience as a trainer of counselors is that a lot of people have had religious awakenings but sometimes they haven't been connected with any aspect of the shadow side of life. The tendency with a therapist is to only give what one understands, and with therapies of the heart, the therapist is the frame that we have. If a person starts to confront their dark side, especially in some dramatic way, where there is movement happening and some sort of a reaction occurring, counselors tend to stop that process, unless they've been willing to go through it themselves. Sometimes they don't stop it consciously, because they know they've been trained not to, yet you will pick up a vibration from them, like "Well, that's enough, now." You'll notice they'll start manipulating the body, sometimes doing bodywork techniques or moving in with an intervention that may accomplish a therapeutic goal for the person at the time, but it has stopped their process.*
>
> *(Small, 1985)*

Another benefit of a Helper who is intimately familiar with the unconscious is that the Helper may have greater familiarity with dreams, archetypal themes, and sym-

160

bols. This knowledge may be of help to a client in interpreting a dream, creating a meaningful ritual, or sharing a vision. A Helper who is deeply aware of his or her own (and others') unconscious material can contribute in a number of meaningful ways to a client developing a strategy for dealing with the unconscious.

Groundedness

A Helper needs to recognize whether he or she is grounded and, if not, how to become grounded. Without such knowledge, the Helper cannot be a stabilizing influence in a spiritual emergency, nor a dependable member of a team of Helpers.

It is not necessary to be grounded all the time. To become close to someone in spiritual emergency, a Helper may need to become relatively ungrounded for a time to match the client. This empathic matching can be reassuring for the client. However, the Helper in this situation must be able to recognize when he or she is ungrounded and be able to become grounded at will. The client also needs to learn how to move from grounded to ungroundedness and back. The Helper is a model and teacher for this.

Stability Within Oneself

Being stable within oneself means having a stable self-structure, a stable identity. A stable person can withstand being challenged physically, emotionally, and intellectually and not "go to pieces." This does not imply that he or she is "together" all the time, invulnerable or emotionally unavailable.

161

One of the most important aspects of being stable is recognizing when you are unstable. Each us is in the process of growing all the time. Although Helpers need to have achieved a level of mature ego development (using Wilber's model in Chapter One), there will be times when the Helper is relatively unstable as part of normal growth. It is essential that the Helper recognize these periods and receive stabilizing support.

A stabilizing force in my life was weekly staff meetings at the Counseling Centers where I worked from 1984 -1989. In addition to helping with client-related problems, these meetings served to provide support for each of us in our personal lives. We taught each other about the difficulty of being therapists—of having to maintain a supporter role for clients when we, as therapists, may be feeling at sea. We taught each other ways to tolerate these periods and provide support to one another in hard times. It eased the weight of the role of Helper to acknowledge that we were together in this process of growth.

Knowledge and Skill in Bodywork

A skilled bodyworker is an important member on a team of people helping those in spiritual emergency. The purpose of bodywork is not important—whether for grounding, catalyzing emotional catharsis, or balancing subtle energies. Most important is the ability of such a Helper to articulate the somatic aspects of psychological disturbance.

Recognizing somatic manifestations of spiritual emergency is helpful for diagnosis as well as planning for treatment. For example, many of my clients have transpersonal experiences but have trouble staying grounded. These people lose their sense of priorities; they have trouble steadily working toward a goal; they have difficulty standing up for themselves when challenged. The somatic manifestations of these psychological problems are weak ankles, tight shoulders and neck, and a retracted pelvis. When I see this pattern in the body, I already know that person under stress loses a sense of boundaries and self definition and becomes uncertain or hypersensitive in relationship to others. I know he or she likes spiritual experiences and needs grounding. I also know that as the person gains flexibility in the neck and pelvic areas and strength in the ankles through process-oriented body work, he or she will become more grounded and more able to integrate ongoing spiritual experiences. This kind of information is useful to both clients and other Helpers who are not as familiar with somatic therapies.

Commitment to Excellence

If I were in spiritual emergency, I would want to be with a Helper who was committed to excellence. When I choose a team to work with, I choose people who are committed to excellence. I learn from them. I can depend on them. I am inspired by them. Isn't that so for all of us?

Access to Excellent Supervision
A good supervisor is an inspiring model as a Helper and can be a lifesaver. A good supervisor both helps us in our

own personal growth and watches to see if we are appropriately caring for our clients.

Novice Helpers might overlook some very important aspect of their client's lives—especially in times of spiritual crisis. For instance, a novice Helper might be far more involved with some fantastic transpersonal experience than a suicidal idea that may be presented by a client. The Helper might find it easier to talk to the client about God than to ask him if he has any thoughts of suicide. The supervisor's role is to see that the Helper is working with the suicidal ideation as well as the uplifting images of God, and to modify treatment to address both symptoms of depression as well as spiritual emergency.

Knowledge of the Literature of Spiritual Emergence

The Helper who has a good intellectual understanding of spiritual emergence is a valuable advisor to a clinician struggling with diagnosis. Also, this Helper can be a reassuring advisor to clients in spiritual emergency who are looking for an understanding of what is happening to them.

Ability to Teach About Spiritual Emergence

The transpersonal level of experience is difficult to talk about because it involves phenomena that can not be adequately described in words. In addition, many people are highly skeptical about spiritual experiences and are not receptive to learning about something which might challenge their ideas.

A client who holds a traditional scientific perspective of reality may be petrified with fear that he or she is crazy. The Helper must be able to teach the client a positive conceptual framework for his or her experiences.

Sometimes the family of a client in spiritual emergency is determined not to accept the authenticity of spiritual experiences. The ability to teach this family to respect the value of spiritual emergence may be the ingredient that convinces them not to hospitalize their family member for schizophrenia, but to explore an alterative diagnostic and treatment procedure. In this example, the Helper who can teach about spiritual emergence is of critical importance.

The Helper who teaches about spiritual emergence is also important in interfacing with doctors, priests, and other support members in the community who may have an impact on a client's life.

Knowledge of One's Own Skills and When to Make Referrals

> *"It's important to know what you know and it's even more important to know what you don't know."*
>
> *(Roberts, 1973)*

A Helper needs to know his or her skills and limitations so that referrals to others can be made, as necessary, for the comprehensive care of the client. For example, a Helper trained in verbal therapy may want to bring a body-worker in to assist with a client. A Helper who is a bodyworker may need to cooperate with a medical doctor about a client's care, and so on.

Knowing How to Care for One's Own Needs

Perhaps the most important skill of the Helper is providing for his or her own well-being. Helpers, as well as clients, need ongoing support for their personal growth and well-being.

Helpers need to identify their own needs for rest and retreat, for play, physical exercise, and proper nourishment, close contact with friends and family, and activities in which other interests are pursued. Helpers need to also have cultivated their own connections with a community, a network of friends, a religious institution or teacher that support their spiritual unfolding. Helpers serve as models of well-being to their clients in spiritual emergency. The Helper's ability to provide for his own wellbeing thus serves not only himself but his clients.

Assess Your Competencies

Following is a list of questions you can use to assess your competence in helping people in spiritual emergency. You may find it helpful to reflect on these by yourself, and subsequently in discussion with your peer group.

1. Do I want to be a Helper? Do I feel compassion for and interest in people in spiritual emergency?

2. What kind of experiences have I had in the transpersonal levels? What kind of support am I

capable of giving to another person opening up in this area?

3. What clinical experience have I had? Have I worked with people who are clinically psychotic? Can I recognize people who are in spiritual emergency?

4. What are my skills in doing experiential body-work with people? How much experience have I had? At what point would I refer a client to someone else in transpersonal bodywork or breathwork?

5. How comfortable do I feel with my own shadow, with the dark elements of myself? Have I met my grief, my rage, my fear, my sexuality, my ecstasy, my power? Have I been around paranormal events? Have I seen visions? Have I experienced kundalini? Have I experienced other forms of spiritual emergency?

6. Do I feel grounded at this time in my life? Do I know how to get grounded when I feel out of balance? What do I do to get grounded? What can I teach other people to do? Can I perform well in highly stressful situations? Do I know when to say "No" and how to care for my own personal needs?

7. Do I feel a strong sense of connection with energies larger than my own ego, which are positive and universal?

8. Do I have support/supervision which will back me up in my work as a Helper? Who are these people?

9. What is my knowledge of psychological literature to help me differentiate between psychological disturbance and spiritual emergency? What is my knowledge of spiritual texts? Can this knowledge be applied to other's spiritual experiences?

10. Whom am I most suited to help?

11. What do I know of other people who are working in this area as Helpers? What do I know of their work? Do I feel comfortable referring clients to them? What self-help groups and spiritually oriented communities do I know? What do I know of their work? Can I refer people to them? Do I feel comfortable with referring people to them?

References for Helpers

Following is a list of books that I have found to be helpful in exploring the role of a Helper:

Da Free John, *The Dawn Horse Testament*. San Rafael, CA.: Dawn Horse Press, 1985.

Guggenbuhl-Craig, A., *Power and the Helping Professions,* Irving, Texas: Spring, 1971.

Grof, S., *Beyond the Brain,* Albany, New York: State University of New York, 1985.

Hendricks, G. and Weinhold, B., *Transpersonal Approaches to Counseling and Psychotherapy,* Denver, Colorado: Love, 1982.

Kopp, S., *Back to One,* Palo Alto, California: Science and Behavior Books, 1977.

Lucas, W., *Regression Therapy: A Handbook for Professionals,* Vol 1 & 2, Crest Park, CA: Deep Forest Press, 1993.

Mindell, A., *City Shadows: Psychological Interventions in Psychiatry,* NY: Routledge, Chapman and Hall, Inc., 1988

Perry, J.W., *The Far Side of Madness,* New Jersey: Prentice Hall, 1974.

Podvoll, E., *The Seduction of Madness,* NY: Harper Collins, 1990.

Ram Dass and Gorman, P., *How Can I Help?,* New York: Knopf, 1985.

Schaef, A.W., *Beyond Therapy, Beyond Science: A New Model for Healing the Whole Person,* San Francisco: Harper Collins, 1992.

Small, J., *Transformers: The Therapists of the Future,* California: De Vorss & Co., 1982.

Speeth, K.R., *On Psychotherapeutic Attention. The Journal of Transpersonal Psychology,* 1982, 14(2), pp. 141-160.

Weiss, B., *Many Lives, Many Masters,* NY: Simon & Schuster, 1988.

Wilber, K., *No Boundary,* Boulder, Colorado: Shambhala, 1981.

Zukav, G. *The Seat of the Soul,* NY: Simon & Schuster, 1989.

Emma Bragdon, PhD. is available as a coach assisting people in spiritual emergence processes as of 2006. **http://www.emmabragdon.com/coaching.html**

Coaching usually takes place on the telephone. Client calls in at an appointed time previously agreed upon with Dr. Bragdon.

Session length: from 50 minutes to 65 minutes.

Fees: payable by credit card or check in advance of session.

Our office is not set up to manage insurance payments. We can offer some sliding scale sessions on request.

To schedule an appointment: please email Dr. Bragdon directly at **mailto:EBragdon@aol.com**

Chapter Seven ————————————————————

A Case Study

The following case study is the story of my mother, age 56, and me, age 24, as we went through a period of intense spiritual experiences in 1971.

My mother, Marjorie, was living alone in a small Vermont town, working as a visiting nurse, and practicing Zen Buddhist meditation 6-8 hours a day. She had no affiliation with a church at that time, although previously she had been Unitarian. She had separated from my father in 1964, 7 years prior, and he lived several hundreds of miles away as did all of her three children, including me.

My mother had experienced periods of depression during her life and had occasional heart palpitations that at times inhibited her activities. She resisted any form of medication or psychotherapy although she inwardly feared she might have inherited her mother's manic-depressive disorder. Marjorie paid attention to her diet and exercise and was basically in good health.

I was not aware of any particular psycho-social stressors other than the normal anxieties of middle age. Although we were not particularly close, she was planning to visit me to help with the birth of my first child, expected in a couple of months.

Her immediate personal support came from the local general practitioner and a few companions who lived close by, none of whom were involved in Zen Buddhism. The two people she regarded as spiritual teachers lived hundreds of miles from her home.

Her closest friend became alarmed because Marjorie began to sequester herself for such long periods of time in meditation, and seemed to be more emotional than was typical for her. This woman had called my brother about her concern, and was trying to do what she could to bring Marjorie back from her new behaviors.

One day Marjorie went up into the woods alone. She was reading a passage from *Zen Mind, Beginner's Mind* (Suzuki, 1970), which compares enlightenment to physical death. When Marjorie was found, she still had her finger marking the page. She had cut her wrist and throat, and passed on.

Her suicide was a great shock to our family and friends. It was totally unexpected. We had all assumed she was getting along quite well, despite some depression and spending a great deal of time alone. She had been taking trips and she was very active in her work.

How did I find out? My husband walked into the house in the middle of the day and told me he had heard some bad news. I was in the midst of doing relaxation exercises in preparation for childbirth. When he told me my mother was dead (not knowing the reason at first), the shock catapulted me into an intense period of spiritual and psychological experiences which were simultaneously confusing, overwhelming and enlightening.

Fortunately, the Zen Center community, of which I had been a member for several years and Suzuki Roshi himself served as Helpers for me. Suzuki was deeply compassionate, present, and non-judgmental. He was also willing to extend himself on my behalf. He flew with my husband and me to Vermont to lead the traditional Buddhist funeral ceremony at my mother's home. My brother and sister felt this was appropriate. Two of my dearest friends in the Zen community joined us. Their support helped me come to terms with the profound issues surrounding my mother's suicide.

The love and compassion I experienced buffered me from the abysmal loneliness and fear typically felt by people in spiritual emergency. The philosophical understanding I received from Buddhist writings, my spiritual teacher,

Suzuki Roshi, and ritual gave me a structure to help comprehend my mother's death, and my own transpersonal experiences.

The transpersonal experiences began when my husband, who knew none of the details of her death, told me my mother had died. I sobbed in grief for a few minutes. Then, a tremendous peace came over me. Starting at my toes, I felt liquid light fill my body, up through the top of my head accompanied by a sense of ecstatic release. I felt sure, at the time, that I was experiencing what my mother had gone through. In a flash, I realized that she was fine and that her passing had been a great relief for her. I realized those of us who were left behind would go through a period of darkness, of doubt, missing her, and wondering if we were at fault in any way. But, I knew in that moment, in every cell of my body, that there was no need to blame anyone, and that she was 'happy'. Then, my consciousness returned to grieving and feeling her loss, but I retained the inner knowingness of her happiness. I felt I had in some way experienced her passing with her.

The experience of feeling her presence did not continue with the same intensity; however, I still felt unusually close to what I sensed was happening with her. I felt a quality of bliss and release I had never before experienced in my life. I sensed she had become one with all things, and, at the same time, although bodily gone, was still present as herself, her Soul.

My subjective experience of her passing was confirmed by her friend who found her. She told me that mother had a smile lighting her face, even at death.

After the funeral, when my family and friends sat with Suzuki Roshi in conversation, someone asked, "Where did Marjorie go when she died?" He said, " She did not go anywhere. She is a part of the grass, the trees, the sky, the brook. She is here with us and, she is everywhere."

After the funeral I became preoccupied with my own questions. How did I know that she was happy? How did I retain the sense of where she was? How could I know these things so certainly? Was I deluding myself because of the stress of the experience? My inner preoccupation continued for weeks. I wondered if I was a bit crazy. Finally, when I had gone 10 days past my delivery date, I began to worry that something was wrong. I went to my garden to pray and made an internal commitment to stop questioning myself about my mother for now and until two months after the birth. Within an hour, the contractions started and eight hours later my son was born. Two months later, I saw a spiritual teacher who validated my experience of knowing what was happening with my mother. She told me that I was having a series of transpersonal level experiences (although she didn't use those terms). She confirmed that I wasn't crazy. She encouraged me to continue to be receptive to these experiences.

There were many sources of support during that period when I thought I was going crazy...rituals, friends, family, and the beauty of the Vermont countryside. Suzuki Roshi performed a succession of rituals around the death which lasted several days and included prayers to guide my mother's soul into her next life. My friends and family shared these rituals. One included a procession to the funeral at the top of the hill, to a place we had gathered for picnics. I sounded a bell every few steps. My husband carried the ashes in a ceramic pot I had made.

It was a very touching ceremony that we created. At one point during the funeral, I dissolved in tears. Sadness, anger, confusion, and doubts had overwhelmed me. I wondered what was real, I felt confused about my becoming a mother when my mother had just suicided. Even though I had the deep knowingness in the background that she had transmitted her bliss to me, I wondered, like a child, where she was. I let myself feel all the instinctual feelings that are part of deep grief. My friends and family did not intrude, or withdraw. They allowed me my grieving, for which I am deeply grateful.

The beauty of the Vermont countryside also helped me. It seemed to absorb my pain and reaffirm my faith that life would be abundant and peace would return.

All these resources—my Zen community, Suzuki Roshi, the rituals, my friends and family, and Vermont's natural beauty, prevented my period of grief from becoming an unbearable crisis. Additionally, I had developed an ability to deal with deep emotional and spiritual experiences through my own spiritual practice and Reichian therapy.

My experience might not have been so positive had I not understood intellectually what was going on, had I no philosophical background to guide my understanding, had I no person who was compassionate or understood what was happening to me, had I felt alone or felt afraid of the overpowering spiritual, emotional, and physical experiences, or had I felt unsupported in expressing myself emotionally or creatively.

My mother had not benefited from support as I had. My belief is that she took her life in a misunderstanding that physical death would bring her the enlightenment experience for which she yearned. If a spiritual teacher or a competent Helper had been close by, she most likely would not have fallen into this illusion. She may have been, instead, guided into some inner work that would have been life-affirming, empowering her spiritual emergence in life.

Although both my mother and I had spiritual experiences that resulted in spiritual emergency, only I received the excellent support required to integrate the experience in a life-affirming way. This story is a dramatic illustration of the value of Helpers.

Nirvana, the Waterfall:

Our life and death are the same thing. When we realize this fact, we have no fear of death anymore, nor actual difficulty in our life...When the water returns to its original oneness with the river, it no longer has any individual feeling to it; it resumes its own nature, and finds composure. How very glad the water must be to come back to the original river!

...That is why we say, "To attain Nirvana is to pass away." "To pass away" is not a very adequate expression. Perhaps "to pass on," or "to go on," or "to join" would be better. Will you try to find some better expression for death?
(Suzuki, 1970)

Chapter Eight _____

Global Trends
Catalyzing Spiritual Emergence

This chapter describes major social, scientific and technological changes that are compelling people all over the
world to reflect deeply on the nature of their lives and to
actively participate in the evolution of life on earth. In
essence, we are being forced to grow to higher levels of
consciousness, to become more mature in order to handle
the responsibilities demanded by the times. Increased
tempo of change and increased self-awareness are two
catalysts for spiritual emergence on a global scale.

Increased Tempo of Change

*Never before has a product of evolution partic-
ipated so actively in accelerating the evolutionary process. Here are just a few
examples...within the last decades biologists
have learned how to modify the genes in a cell,
opening the door to the creation of completely
new species. Now new life-forms can be
designed consciously and created rapidly...with
the advent of particle accelerators,
scientists...are now able to change some elements into others, or even create completely
new elements, by bombarding the nucleus with
atomic particles and thereby changing its structure...we have created a fundamentally new
way of directly harnessing the sun's energy: the
solar cell. This invention represents an evolutionary development as significant as that of
photosynthesis 3.5 billion years ago.*

(Russell, 1983)

*Jumps by so many orders of magnitude, in so
many areas, with the unprecedented coinci-
dence of several jumps at the same time,
and these unique disturbances of the planet,
surely indicate that we are not passing
through a smooth cyclical or acceleration
process similar to those in the historical
past. Anyone who is willing to admit that
there have been sudden jumps in evolution
or human history, such as the invention of
agriculture or the Industrial Revolution, must
conclude from this evidence that we are passing through another such jump far more*

concentrated and more intense than these, and of far greater evolutionary importance.
(John Platt, "The Futurist"
as cited in Russell, 1983)

Two of the most important innovations in science and technology are improved communications and increased mobility, both of which have accelerated the growth of knowledge around the world. In this century we have moved from cars travelling 15 miles per hour to supersonic rockets travelling at 25,000 miles per hour. We have progressed from radio broadcasting to television satellite linkups—increasing significantly the quantity, quality, and availability of information.

Sharing knowledge among nations has greatly increased, with dramatic consequences. This has led to better health care, increased production, higher standards of living, and more efficient land-use factors enabling the population to grow faster. In fact, the human population is now growing at a superexponential rate; in the 1960's, it was already doubling every 35 years (Russell, 1983). Increasingly more people share a high standard of living with time to reflect on themselves and to network with people all over the world.

International communications have allowed for a cross-fertilization of ideas, attitudes, and values affecting the quality of our inner lives just as international monetary trade and technology exchange have affected the quality of our outer lives. Increasingly more people, even those formerly our adversaries, reveal they are just as desirous of international peace as the North Americans are. As we learn about the variety of religious practices, medical practices, and cultural patterns in the world, we come to realize that we have far more in common with others than we have differences.

Above all, the longing for peace and well-being in the world in the face of terrorism and nuclear meltdowns has created a deep bond amongst many people, a bond felt all the more strongly as more people comprehend that human beings now have the power to destroy all life on this planet in a matter of minutes by the explosion of nuclear warheads.

Not only is there accelerated growth in communication, travel, and population but some of our most stable social institutions are breaking down. As Harman (1985) pointed out, Americans have put more and more energy into stabilizing our economic and defense systems, and have, ironically, produced unwieldy deficits, and incalculable risks to our security because of nuclear warheads which must be managed faultlessly or else lead to global destruction. The institutions of finance and defense in the United States are no longer a witness, guard, or even symbol of our stability as a nation. The social order of Caucasian male domination is being dismantled by the civil rights and women's movements. This is the state, as Tofler put it, of "future shock."

One of the most dynamic changes in our perception of reality has been suggested by physicists—especially those who study particle physics. Just as Ptolemy initiated the Copernican revolution by suggesting that the earth rotated around the sun, so today some physicists have initiated a crisis by proving that the observer has a dynamic relationship to the observed, that is, the observer modifies the thing observed by his or her expectations and attitudes. Thus, it is now possible to say with some proof that what we study is inseparable from who we are. Some physicists have thus demonstrated in physical terms the content of a transpersonal experience—the inseparableness of all things, the unity of all things, that life is determined by consciousness itself, which cannot be seen, observed objectively, or quantified. These thoughts go beyond all mainstream collective attitudes about the nature of our world.

This new understanding of the nature of reality, the acceleration of information and technological change, and the simultaneous breakdown of our most powerful social institutions is bringing on a crisis of momentous proportions—especially in the population of high technology cultures (Harman,1985). And, because our world has grown into a hierarchical structure with the rich and powerful commanding the most resources and making decisions which determine the quality of life of the not-so-rich, the most well-educated people are the first to experience this crisis. What we do will have a major impact on the rest of the world. So, what do we do?

Those people who hang on to the old perspective, that reality is only that which can be seen and measured, and those people who hang onto the old social institutions for stability may find it increasingly difficult to understand their world. Those people who choose to become conscious of and accepting of a new reality are the ones emerging into a "global consciousness" (Harman, 1985). Global consciousness is integral to spiritual emergence in that it is founded on the unitary nature of all things. People caught in the middle of the new and the old realities may find themselves in spiritual emergency, and feel incapable of integrating the new perspective. Their old realities are shattering and they are attempting to make way for the new reality which demands more self awareness and a deepening sense of one's true nature.

Television, radio and newspapers constantly bombard us with pictures and stories of events and people around the world and force a wider awareness on anyone who listens. People who listen to the news become aware of the starvation of whole nations in Africa, earthquakes in Mexico, the carnage of political civil wars in South America, ethnic cleansing in Yugoslavia and so on. This awareness of the chaotic state of our world creates a catalyst toward spiritual emergence as educated and sensitive people feel the need to respond on an ever more highly conscious level to the world situation (Cappadonna, 1985; Lindberg, 1955).

This impulse toward global consciousness is beautifully expressed in a song recorded by a group of celebrities in 1985:

> *We are the world,*
> *We are the children.*
> *We are the ones who make a brighter day*

So let's start giving.
There's a choice we're making -
We're saving our own lives.
It's true we'll make a better day
just you and me.
        (United Support of Artists for Africa, 1985)

Greater communication and mobility has also brought a new level of awareness supplementing the Western Christian-Judeo perspective.

Cross-Fertilization of Religious Practices

In the west we have generally accepted the con-cretization of the world. We see it as really something solid and permanent. This has been built on since the development of sciences and Cartesianism. The contradiction of the inner realization of the dreamlike quality of reality to the outer world's belief system is an enormous conflict to live with. Without a supportive phi-losophy and supportive friends, persons under-going the awakening in the West might well assume they are going crazy as they have noth-ing to support their experience as real and pos-itive. This realization is not as difficult for a tra-ditional Buddhist to accept because he has rec-ognized this as truth from the time he first heard the Buddhist teachings.

                                        (Sogyal, 1985)

As Buddhist and other Eastern practices become more available in the West, some Westerners have found them supportive in transforming their experience of reality to include "global consciousness" and transpersonal states of consciousness.

The Tibetans' evacuation from their country and subsequent absorption into other areas of the world has made Tibetan Buddhism accessible to many cultures. Sogyal Rinpoche is one of the Eastern religious leaders who has helped introduce Eastern religious ideas in the West. Sogyal is an incarnate Lama, a scholar, the author of *The Tibetan Book of Living and Dying* (1992), and a meditation master. He was born in Tibet, the son of one of the greatest Buddhist masters of this century. Sogyal left Tibet when it was invaded by China in the 1950's. He studied at Cambridge University and has lived in the West teaching about Buddhism since the 1970's.

Other non-western religions have also moved into the stream of Western culture in the last century as a result of political shifts and increased mobility. Although Eastern mystics and religious leaders had been introduced in the West before the latter half of the 1900's (for example, Yogananda, Alice Bailey, Krishnamurti, and Graf von Durkheim) it wasn't until the baby-boomers born after World War II became teens in the 1960's, that Eastern religions and religious practices (Transcendental Meditation and Zen especially) were popularized. Today, evidence that the realities proposed by Eastern religions are becoming integrated with Western perspectives can be seen in Western literature, e.g. *Zen and the Art of Motorcycle Maintenance,* Pirsig, 1974), movies (The Karate Kid, I and II), spiritual teachers like Brother David

Steindl-Rast who incorporate Eastern meditation techniques into devotional Catholic monastic life, and the popularity of the practice of martial arts, Hatha Yoga, and T'ai Chi for relaxation, exercise and spiritual development.

As religions change to accommodate new points of view about vitalizing the life of the spirit, dynamic change occurs in religious communities. The Pope, once perceived as the ultimate authority on earth, is challenged to change his stand on birth control in light of the fact that the earth cannot sustain overpopulation. Nuns and monks are choosing to integrate into society in a new way, as they let go of traditional robes and habits or leave the religious communities and the celibate life in favor of becoming householders, husbands and wives. These individuals are forced to confront the breaking of the marriage vow each made to Christ and the consequent catapult into profound crises of re-evaluation for which there is little support in their communities.

One of the most provocative changes in religion has been the advent of mind technologies purported to bring about the enlightenment experience, heretofore thought of as religious. Some of these technologies are seminars which combine interactive exercises developed in Western Psychology with meditation practices from ancient spiritual practices. For example, the Avatar Course, an 9-day intensive program that blends Eastern and Western techniques for exploration and enlightenment, is now translated into 9 languages and is being taught in 36 countries. Without a guru or priesthood or any religious rites or symbols, the Avatar course brings a person into the living experience of enlightenment, of unity consciousness. Their main office is located in Florida (800) 589-3767, http://www.avatarepc.com/.

Clinical laboratories are also experimenting with direct stimulation to brain centers to bring on the enlightenment experience independent of any experiential learning, psychological development, spiritual practice, or moral training. *Omni* magazine's article in October, 1993, titled "Finding God in the Three Pound Universe: The Neuroscience of Transcendence" by David Porush, synthesizes the current brain research on the synthetic stimulation of unity consciousness. Michael Persinger, head of the neuroscience lab at Laurentian University of Sudbury in Ontario, has replicated paranormal experiences, including out-of-body and near-death experiences and the presence of Higher Power in subjects by direct stimulation of the temporal lobe. Devices which stimulate the auditory and visual apparatuses with special sound and light and purport to open up resources of accelerated learning and deep peace are also available now through mass marketing.

Cross-Fertilization of Medical Practices

Like religious practices, Eastern medical technologies which substantiate the new reality have also had a widespread effect on Western culture. Bill Moyers' PBS Special, "Healing and the Mind," first aired in February, 1993, and now distributed on video, is a profound contribution to the integration of Eastern and Western medical practices.

Eastern medical approaches, such as Chinese acupuncture and Tibetan Ayurvedic medicine, see the body as a dance of universal energies, constantly in flux, constantly influencing the energetic balance of each organ system. Eastern medical perspectives diagnose imbalances in the body by taking into account both concrete, physical events as well as non-physical processes.

> *Tibetan medicine looks very much into what is called prana, the wind, the inner wind...when the wind goes through different channels it creates different experiences. When the wind goes into the heart area then it begins to create some kind of very (spiritually powerful opening) experiences....*
>
> *(Sogyal, 1985)*

"Prana" is a spiritual force that comes from what Westerners might call 'the Universe'. It is an energy which, combined with the heart, can uplift and purify the emotional nature of any person. Thus, it is a force that can create profound experience.

In diagnosing and treating people who are involved in spiritual emergency it is particularly important to look at the way subtle energies are moving in their bodies (Raheem, 1985). Movement toward greater awareness in the mind creates a shift in the energies of the body. Balancing of energy must be done by someone who understands both the physical body processes as well as subtle energies. These techniques are not taught in the medical schools of the West but come through the

189

traditions associated with Chinese medicine, including Chinese herbal medicine, Ayurvedic medicine, and some of the practices coming from the ancient Yogic traditions of India.

These ancient systems of looking at the body, diagnosing illness, and treating imbalance have an inherent belief that human beings are expressions of the elemental forces that are part of all nature. These systems teach the value of attuning to subtle energies in the body so as to feel more palpably akin to life and more able to sense our connection with the highest energy, the Divine.

Heidegger, the German philosopher, stated this concept of what it is to be a human being in the following way: "A person is neither a thing nor a process, but an opening or a clearing through which the Absolute can manifest."

This point of view, prevalent in the medical practices of the East, is increasingly more often having a profound effect on Western health practitioners. The number of people turning to the holistic health movement in the West is also a sign of the success and acceptance of the Eastern approaches to health maintenance.

The addictions field has also turned to Eastern religious philosophy to take a new look at helping people overcome alcohol abuse. Buddhism's Four Noble Truths state that suffering is caused through desires (addictions) and there is a way to end suffering. The Buddhist way is to meditate so as to transcend desires. This has influenced thought in the addictions field so that addiction is conceptualized as a potential stepping stone to a more conscious path of spiritual emergence and "bottoming out," the nadir of alcohol abuse, is perceived as a spiritual emergency, a desperate and ill-informed attempt to find spiritual ecstasy. From this viewpoint, alcohol abuse is lifted up out of the realms of disease and moral weakness, into the more respectable arena of a very human and spiritual problem.

Increased Self-Awareness
Through the Use of Drugs

Recreational drug use has been a dual-edged sword for our society; at the same time as it has been the catalyst for destruction for some, it has opened a world of new perspective and increased meaning for others.

Drug use has been epidemic in the West since the late 1960's. This is a by-product of our increased international trade, mobility and more sophisticated technology. Drugs come to us from all over the world, including our own well-equipped laboratories.

The fact that the irresponsible use of drugs has thrown users into lives of ill health and self-destruction is well known; less recognized are the potentially positive aspects of the so-called "recreational drugs" which can catalyze self-healing and spiritual experience, as discussed previously.

Ideally, we could decide to create a time when:

> *abuse (of drugs) apparently was fairly rare,*
> *perhaps because careful cultural, religious,*
> *and social proscriptions determined a uniform*
> *manner in which these substances were used*
> *and the experiences one was expected to have*
> *as a result of their use.*
>
> *(A. Weil, 1972)*

The opportunity to explore the potential benefits of these drugs that have often been misused by an uneducated and unprepared public will be affected by research monies and political opinion.

Fanaticism

In the midst of the progress that comes with increased communication around the world, there are fanatic groups who are rigidly attached to the old order of religion, national authority, family and ancestral rights. They will fight for the authority to say: "my God is best," "my religion is best," "my country is best," "your ancestors hurt my ancestors and you owe me something for it now," and "you have no right to see things differently from me." These people can take advantage of the ease of commerce to terrorize others who are looking to establish a new order based on equality, cooperation and peace.

As I write Tibet is still being terrorized by China. Ireland is still a nation at war with itself over religious differences. Yugoslavia is crumbling under the weight of religious and ethnic war. In our own country, pro-lifers wage war on pro-choice advocates regarding abortion rights, people who smoke marijuana are being imprisoned by people who drink alcohol because alcohol is legal but recreational drugs have no redeeming value in the eyes of the law. On every continent war is still fought in a murderous attempt to determine who is right and who is wrong.

Collective rigidity, in the form of fanaticism and terrorism, undermines the ability of a collective to open to cooperation and trust between diverse groups just as rigidity undermines an individual's capacity to easily integrate spiritual experiences. At the same time we look at unity consciousness as the highest state of evolution of an individual, we might consider maintaining world peace as the highest state of evolution for the nations of the world.

The possibility of nations cooperating to serve world peace becomes more and more a reality each day. Evidence of this is the destruction of the Berlin Wall, the enduring attempts to negotiate peace in the mid-East, efforts to ban nuclear arms and the USA coming to the assistance of the new states that were the USSR. There is a message gaining strength in the collective consciousness: "Unity and an appreciation of differences is more important than cold war and separation." As a global collective we are straining to pass into a higher state of evolution, even as some parts must hold us back to take care of old wounds.

Summary

Alternative medice protocols are challenging the authority of our mainstream medical institutions; and the new physics is challenging the authority of conventional science. Global consciousness is challenging nationalism. Altered states of consciousness brought on through drugs or meditation practices are giving people new perceptions of their identity. The political authority of the world leaders is challenged by violent assassinations and political scandal. This is the evidence that we are involved in a collective Dark Night of the Ego, a deep identity crisis brought on by tumultuous change.

This time of upheaval has intensified self-inquiry by many individuals and nations. It has made many people push against the limits of their own developmental level. Under the stress of meeting a constantly accelerating change in reality, some of these people (and countries) will break into pieces in their own kind of spiritual emergency and others will move more flexibly into accelerating developmental processes.

Individuals and nations grow; there is a collective global growth process, too. All people on this globe may be in the process of expanding to a level of self-structure beyond the ordinary bounds of ego, or national identity. This level may have more to do with self-actualized spirit than the ordinary kinds of self-centered organizations that have heretofore made up our identity structures.

The end point could possibly parallel an individual's transpersonal level of consciousness on a larger scale—a global community that has found a way to live in harmony, sharing material well-being, radiating peace, creativity and joy. This has been suggested by visionaries like Willis Harman, and channeled Masters, eg. The Prophecies of the Tibetan by DK.

Appendix A

Identifying Community Resources for Helping People in Spiritual Emergency

I suggest first answering the following questions by yourself and then discussing them with other people to get ideas about additional community resources you may not have recognized. You might make notes for your own referral system for future use.

I. Joe

You become aware of a man, Joe, who is very upset and is not functioning in his job. He is having visions. He says they are visions of God. He is also afraid he might be going crazy because no one seems to be able to understand him. Joe has no religious context to understand the visions either. He is spending time by himself, and seems to be feeling more and more alienated by people. Joe is also suffering from migraine headaches.

What are your community's resources for helping this person? Consider the following questions:

1. Is there a doctor, psychologist, or paraprofessional who could identify whether Joe is in spiritual emergency and/or whether he needs psychiatric care?

2. Is there a health-care worker who can evaluate the appropriateness of using drugs to help Joe?

3. Is there a retreat where Joe could go to get intensive care and support if he is unable to care for himself? Where is this?

4. Is there a person in the community who can help Joe deal with the energy in the migraine headache, to diagnose its physical cause and/or free the energy blockage? Are there persons in the community skilled in transpersonal

bodywork and/or breathwork? Who are they? Where are they located?

5. Is Joe a member of a religious group? Does this group have the resources to give him guidance? If there is no one in the community of ministers who can help, are there other persons who might be able to give guidance as needed? Who are they? Where are they located? Are they available?

6. What resources are there outside the community to help in any of the above?

II. Ginny

You become aware of a woman, Ginny, who is reaching out to make friends, and wants to talk about her experience living in an ashram for 4 years. She feels her life has been enriched by the experience, but she now needs to be more in contact with other kinds of people. She is experiencing dreams and paranormal phenomena which lead her to feel as if she has made a mistake in leaving the ashram. Ginny's old friends at the ashram are pressuring her to return; they threaten that if she doesn't return she will lose her only chance at becoming enlightened. Ginny often feels depressed, scared and lonely.

1. What are your community's resources for helping Ginny? Consider her religious background, her current social situation, and her moods. Refer to the numbered questions in case #1 for help in reflecting.

III. Jim

A mother calls you to talk about her 13-year-old son, Jim, who has "turned into a different person since being turned on to drugs." When he was younger he used to play alone with his "imaginary friends" but he "got over" that. He became more outgoing and played with other kids. Now, she is worried that Jim won't develop the discipline to get along in life. He's lost interest in school. She doesn't know how to talk to him. She doesn't know anything about what drugs he is taking. Jim is withdrawing more and more from the family. He likes to sit quietly by himself and paint.

1. Who in the community is most prepared to help Jim and Jim's family? Why?

2. Is this just a drug problem? Are there other issues related to Jim's personal development? Who is in the best position to answer this question?

3. What would be the best way to help Jim in his personal development at this stage in his life?

IV. Lyn

Lyn, a woman of 42, calls you. She has been reading Dancing in the Light by Shirley MacLaine. She wants to know community resources for learning about her past lives. Her marriage is breaking up. Lyn has just had a hysterectomy and has been hospitalized with a pelvic infection which caused high fevers for several weeks. She said she had some "bizarre experiences" while she was sick. She felt she was "leaving her body." She wants to understand what is happening to her. She feels lonely and afraid. She feels she can't talk to her doctor or her minister about any of this. Her husband calls her "crazy." Lyn has a passion to find out more about these inexplicable phenomena. "I just have to understand what's happening to me!"

1. Who in your community could help Lyn with her interest in past lives? Is the approach useful for Lynn? What kind of help does she need?

2. Who in the community could help her understand what happened to her when she was sick?

3. Does this woman need continued support? If so, what kind, or kinds.

Your Community's Resources

After reflecting on the above situations, list the answers to the following questions regarding your community resources.

1. Who would be skilled at diagnosis that differentiates between spiritual emergency and psychopathology? What are their specialties?

2. Who offers retreat settings or therapeutic communities to support people who need intensive care or adequate supervision for their religious practices?

3. Who is most knowledgeable about psychiatric drugs and mind-altering drugs? What are their opinions about psychiatric drugs, recreational drugs, or the therapeutic use of drugs?

4. Is there a body worker in our community who can help a person work with energy blockages? If not, where can you locate one?

5. Who would you trust to help you if you were in a spiritual emergency? Why?

Appendix B _____

Evaluating Your Knowledge
of Spiritual Problems

Following is a list of questions to help you reflect on what
you have read in the sourcebook.

    1. What is a spiritual problem?

    2. What is spiritual emergence and spiritual
       emergency?

    3. Identify the signs of spiritual emergence.

    4. Identify the symptoms of psychosis.

5. How do you distinguish between psychosis and spiritual emergence/emergency.

6. Identify six forms of spiritual emergency.

7. Briefly define the transpersonal levels of human development. Why is it called transpersonal?

8. Do people grow from one developmental level to the next in an orderly progression?

9. Why does progress to transpersonal levels include deeply regressed states?

10. Identify six personal circumstances that can catalyze spiritual emergence.

11. Identify seven social circumstances that may be catalyzing people towards spiritual emergence on a global scale.

12. Identify five elements of giving ongoing support to a person in spiritual emergency.

13. Identify three themes vital to helping someone in spiritual emergence.

14. How many people in the USA have had deep experiences of a transpersonal nature? Why do many people hesitate to talk about their transpersonal experiences?

15. If you were to be a Helper with people in spiritual emergence, how do you imagine yourself working?

After completing these questions, you may want to review parts of the sourcebook for further clarification or to note some of your own reflections on spiritual problems and spiritual emergence/emergency.

Appendix C _____

Articles of Interest

Forms of Spiritual Emergency

Dr. Stanislav Grof and Christina Grof.
This seminal article was first published in 1985 in
the Spiritual Emergence Network Newsletter.

All forms of transpersonal crisis can be seen as dynamic exteriorizations of deep unconscious and super-conscious realms of the human psyche, which represents one indivisible, multidimensional continuum without any clear boundaries. It is, therefore, obvious that sharp demarcation of various types of spiritual emergency is in practice not possible.

However, we feel on the basis of our work with individuals in spiritual crisis and the study of relevant literature that it is possible and useful to distinguish several major experiential patterns which are particularly frequent. Although they often overlap, each of them has certain characteristic features of its own that differentiate it from others.

I.   Awakening of the Serpent Power (Kundalini)

Although the concept of Kundalini found its most articulate expression in the Indian Tantric tests of Hinduism, Buddhism, Jainism, and in the Tibetan Vajrayana, important parallels can be found in Christian Mysticism, Sufism, Taoist Yoga, Korean Zen, in the Freemasonic tradition, among the North American tribes, and the Kung Bushmen of the African Kalihari Desert to name just a few. In a sense, the awakening of Kundalini can be seen as a central mechanism underlying many types of transpersonal crises.

The ascent of Kundalini as described in the Indian literature can be accompanied by dramatic physical and psychological manifestations called Kriyas. The most striking among these are powerful sensations of heat and energy streaming up the spine, associated with tremors, spasms, violent shaking, and complex twisting movements.

Quite common is involuntary laughing or crying, chanting of mantras or songs, talking in tongues, emitting of vocal noises and animal sounds, and assuming spontaneous yogic gestures (mudras) and postures (asanas). As the Kundalini is freeing physical blockages, the individual can experience intense pain in various parts of the body.

The process of Kundalini awakening can simulate many psychiatric disorders, particularly schizophrenia or other types of psychosis. The presence of characteristic energy phenomena, intense sensations of heat, unusual breathing patterns, pains in characteristic blocking sites for which there is no organic basis, visions of light, and the typical trajectory of the process are among the signs that distinguish the Kundalini syndrome from psychosis.

The individuals involved are also typically much more objective about their condition, communicate and cooperate well, show interest in sharing their experiences with open-minded people, and seldom act out. Although hearing of various sounds is quite common, intruding persecutory voices do not belong to the phenomenology of Kundalini awakening.

II.   Shamanic Journey

Transpersonal crises of this type bear a deep resemblance to what the anthropologists have described as the "shamanic" or "initiatory illness." It is a dramatic episode of a non-ordinary state of consciousness that marks the beginning of the career of many shamans. The core experience of the shamanic journey is a profound encounter with death and subsequent rebirth. Initiatory dreams and visions portray a descent into the underworld and exposure to unimaginable tortures.

In the experiences of individuals whose transpersonal crises have strong shamanic features, there is an emphasis on physical suffering and encounter with death followed by rebirth and elements of ascent or magical flight. They typically sense special connection with the elements of nature and experience communication with animals or animal spirits. It is also not unusual to feel an upsurge of special powers and impulses to heal.

Shamanism is practically universal; its varieties can be found in Siberia and other parts of Asia, in North and South America, Australia, Oceania, Africa, and Europe. The individuals whose spiritual crises follow this pattern are thus involved in an ancient process that touches the deepest foundations of the psyche.

III.   Psychological Renewal Through Activation of the Central Archetype.

This type of transpersonal crisis has been explored and described by the California psychiatrist and Jungian analyst, John Weir Perry. In his clinical work with young psychotic patients, twelve of whom he saw in systematic intensive psychotherapy over long periods of time, he recognized to his surprise that the psychotic process was far from being an absurd and erratic product of pathological processes in the brain.

If sensitive support was provided, the nature of the psychopathological development was drastically transformed and what resulted was emotional healing, psychological renewal and deep transformation of the patients' personalities. Moreover, John Perry discovered in this work that the majority of his patients manifested certain standard experiential patterns and characteristic stages if their process was not suppressed by routine psycho-pharmaceutical treatment.

The individuals in this type of crisis experience themselves as being in the middle of the world process, as being the center of all things, which Perry attributes to the activation of what he calls the 'central archetype'. They are preoccupied with death and the themes of ritual killing, martyrdom, crucifixion, and afterlife. Another important theme is return to the beginnings of the world, to creation, the original paradisiacal state, or the first ancestor.

The experiences typically focus on some cataclysmic clash of opposite forces on a global, or even cosmic level that has the quality of a sacred combat. The more mundane form of these experiences stage as protagonists, capitalists and communists, Americans and Russians, the white and yellow race, secret societies against the rest of the world, and the like. The archetypal form of this conflict involves the forces of light and darkness, Christ and Antichrist or the Devil, Armageddon, and the Apocalypse.

A characteristic element of this process is preoccupation with the reversal of opposites—cultural, ethical, political or religious beliefs, values, and attitudes. This is expressed particularly strongly in the sexual area. It in volves intense misgiving in regard to the opposite sex, homosexual wishes or panic, and fear of the other sex or gender reversal. These problems find their resolution typically in the theme of the union of opposites, particularly the Sacred Marriage (hierosgamos). It is a union of a mythological nature, an archetypal fusion of the feminine and masculine aspects of one's personality. Here belongs the belief of being selected as spouse for a god or goddess, becoming a bride to Christ, being visited by the Holy Spirit as the Virgin Mary, identification with Adam and Eve, marriage of the Sun and the Moon, King and Queen, or Prince and Princess.

This process culminates in an apotheosis, an experience of being raised to a highly exalted status, either above all humans, or above the human condition altogether – becoming a world savior or messiah, a king, a president, emperor of the world or even lord of the universe. This is often associated with a sense of new birth or rebirth, the other side of the all-important theme of death. Women more frequently experience giving birth to some extraordinary child-savior, redeemer, or messiah, while men more commonly experience being born themselves. The birth of the divine child is often seen as the product of the sacred marriage.

During the time of final integration, individuals tend to draw diagrams representing the quadrated world, in which the number four plays an important role - four cardinal points, four quadrants, four rivers, or a quadrated circle. They can also create a drama, in which four kings, four countries, or four political parties play a crucial role.

In his later books, *Far Side of Madness* and *Roots of Renewal in Myth and Madness*, Perry was able to show many uncanny parallels between the ritual drama of renewal associated with sacral kingship and the sequences in the renewal process observed in acute psychotic episodes. What existed during the archaic times of sacral kingship as externalized social forms, was thus later internalized and has become inner images and processes of contemporary individuals.

IV.   Psychic Opening

Transpersonal crisis of this type is characterized by striking accumulation of instances of extrasensory perception (ESP) and other parapsychological manifestations. In acute episodes of such a crisis, the individual can be literally flooded by extraordinary paranormal experiences. Among these are various forms of out-of-body phenomena (OOB); one can experience detaching from the body and observing oneself from a distance or from above. It is not uncommon to accurately witness in an OOB state events happening in another room of the building or in a remote location. This phenomenon has been repeatedly described by thanatologists in individuals facing death (Raymond Moody, Kenneth Ring, Michael Sabom), but here it occurs without the element of vital threat.

Many mystical schools and spiritual traditions describe emergence of paranormal abilities as a common and particularly tricky stage of consciousness evolution. It is considered essential not to become fascinated by the new abilities and interpret them in terms of one's own unique-ness. The danger of what Jung called "inflation of the ego" is probably greater here than with any other type of spiritual crisis.

V.   Emergence of a Karmic Pattern

In a fully developed form of this type of transpersonal crisis, the individual experiences dramatic sequences that seem to be occurring in a different temporal or spatial context in another historical period and another country. These experiences can be quite realistic and are accompanied by strong negative or positive emotions and intense physical sensations. The person typically has a conviction of retrieving these events from memory – reliving episodes from his or her own previous incarnations. In addition, specific aspects of such sequences suddenly seem to throw new light on various emotional, psychosomatic, and inter-personal problems of the person's present life, which were previously obscure and incomprehensible.

Karmic experiences of this kind seem to be frequently connected with simultaneous or alternately reliving of biological birth. This occurs with characteristic patterning; birth sequences involving certain specific emotions and physical sensations tend to be linked with past-life themes with the same or similar elements.

When the individual's resistance against the emerging karmic material is strong which is common in a culture for whom the concept of reincarnation is alien it is possible to experience a variety of strange emotions, physical sensations, and distortions in interpersonal relations without confronting and recognizing the karmic pattern that underlies them. We have encountered in our workshops a number of people who relived and resolved in an experiential session with breathing, music, and body work a karmic pattern, the elements of which had been plaguing them for months in everyday life.

Full experience and good integration of past-life sequences has typically dramatic therapeutic effects. Emotional, psychosomatic and interpersonal problems can be drastically alleviated or disappear after a powerful karmic experience. For this reason, therapists should recognize this phenomenon and utilize it, irrespective of their own belief system or the historical truth of such sequences.

VI.   Possession States

This transpersonal crisis can occur in the context of experiential psychotherapy, a psychedelic session, or as a spontaneous development in the life of an individual. It happens that during experiential work with or without drugs, the nature of the process suddenly changes dramatically. The face of the client can become cramped and takes the form of a mask of evil, the eyes assume a wild expression, the hands and the body show bizarre contortions, and the voice has an uncanny quality. When this condition is allowed to develop fully, the session can bear a striking resemblance to exorcist seances in primitive cultures or medieval exorcisms of the Christian church.

The resolution of this problem requires support from people who are not afraid of the uncanny nature of the experiences involved and who can facilitate full emergence and exteriorization of the archetypal pattern. The resolution often happens after dramatic sequences of choking, projectile vomiting, or frantic motor behavior with temporary loss of control. With good support, experiences of this kind can be extremely liberating and therapeutic.

Being an initial attempt at classification in a complex territory which has not been given adequate attention in the West, the above outline is rough and sketchy. However, we hope that even in this form it will be of use to individuals undergoing transpersonal crisis and to those interested in offering assistance.

In conclusion, we would like to recommend good sources of information about specific types of transpersonal crisis for those readers who would like to explore them in greater depth. Please contact SEN for a bibliography.

The following article was first published in 1979 in New Directions for Mental Health Services. *"The Final Progress Report" was presented at the American Psychiatric Association Conference in 1993. An abstract of the final report is reprinted at the end of the article.*

Soteria: An Alternative to Hospitalization For Schizophrenics

L. Mosher, M.D. and A. Menn, A.C.S.W.

Difficulties that we encounter with the treatment of psychosis in hospital settings provided a major impetus for the establishment of Soteria, a home where schizophrenics who would otherwise have been hospitalized live through their psychosis with a nonprofessional staff.

Background

Hospitals—even well-staffed "progressive" ones— invariably have institutional characteristics that create barriers to establishing the types of relationships which could maximally facilitate the process of recovery from psychosis. The "barrier" characteristics to which we refer (present to varying degrees in different settings) are of four kinds.

Theoretical Model – Although a variety of other models may be mixed in, or explicitly avowed, most psychiatric wards function primarily within a medical model. Doctors have final authority and decision-making powers; medications are accorded primary therapeutic value and used extensively; the person is seen as having a disease, with attendant disability and dysfunction that are to be "treated" and "cured"; and labeling and its consequences, objectification and stigmatization, are almost inevitable.

In contrast, at Soteria (from the Greek, salvation or deliverance) the primary focus is on growth, development, and learning. The staff are to "be with" the patients, or "residents" as we call them, to facilitate these processes insofar as they can. They share decision-making powers and responsibility with residents. They are not there either to treat or to cure the residents. Medications are infrequently used. Although we have no quarrel with the demonstrated heuristic value of the medical model, we do believe its application to psychiatric disorders can have unfortunate (and unintended) consequences for individual patients. We are not proposing an alternative model, however, because we know of none that encompasses enough of what we know about schizophrenia. We do propose an alternative attitude or stance. Basically, we advocate a phenomenological approach to schizophrenia—that is, an attempt to understand and share the psychotic person's experience without judging, labeling, or derogating it.

Size - Most psychiatric hospital wards have at least 20 patients. Thus, the staff-plus-patient group is apt to be 40 to 60. But for severely disorganized persons, a social reference group of no more than 12 to 15 persons is especially important. We believe a group of this size, when combined with a homelike atmosphere, maximizes the possibility of the disorganized person's getting to know and trust a new environment and to find a surrogate family in it. At the same time, it minimizes the labeling and stigmatization process. This number is, interestingly, about the maximum number of persons in one extended-family household, or in a single commune, and is also the upper limit for members in small task groups for group therapy and experimental psychology. Thus, rather than being a 20-bed ward, Soteria is a home that sleeps 8 to 10 comfortably, with six beds occupied by residents and two by staff.

Social Structure – Social structure interacts closely with size. To function effectively, every organization, large or small, needs structure; and generally speaking, the larger the organization, the greater the structure. Unfortunately, more elaborate structures have aspects that impinge negatively on persons undergoing psychotic disorganization—inflexibility, reliance on authority, institutionalization of roles, and decision-making power that resides in the hierarchy, outside patient's purview. Those at the bottom of the hierarchy feel relatively powerless, irresponsible, and dependent. Because of these negative aspects, at Soteria we attempt to be as un-structured as is commensurate with adequate function. Structure that develops to meet functional needs is dissolved if the need is not a continuing one. There is no institutionalized method of dealing with a particular occurrence. For example, overt aggressive acts are dealt with in a variety of ways, including strict limit-setting, depending on a myriad of variables which affect the situation. In most settings, in contrast, aggression is dealt with, almost automatically, by medication.

Medication – We live in an overmedicated, too frequently drug-dependent culture despite ambivalence which is resolved by creating two categories of drugs: good ones like alcohol and bad ones like LSD. Our society is basically pro-drug. Psychiatry's attitude is no different from that of the wider social context; we are all looking for the magical answer from a pill. The antipsychotic drugs have provided psychiatrists with real substance for their magical-cure fantasy applied to schizophrenia. But, as is the case with most such exaggerated expectations, the fantasy is better than the reality. After two decades, it is now clear that the phenothiazines do not cure schizophrenia. It is also clear that they have serious, sometimes irreversible toxicities[4] that recovery may be impaired by them in at least some schizophrenics,[6,17] and that they have little effect on long term psychosocial adjustment.[15] These criticisms do not deny their extraordinary helpfulness in reducing and controlling symptoms, shortening hospital stays, and revitalizing interest in schizophrenia. One aim of the Soteria project is to seek a viable informed alternative to the overuse of these drugs and excessive reliance on them, often to the exclusion of psychosocial measures. We use them infrequently and when prescribed they are kept primarily under the individual resident's (patient's) control; that is, the patient is asked to monitor his or her responses to the drug very carefully, to give us feedback so we can adjust dosage, and after a trial period of two weeks he or she is given a major role in determining whether or not the drug will continue to be used.

Soteria is a reaction to criticisms of existing facilities in each of the four areas mentioned above. Much of what is involved in the program, however, is based on the positive contributions of a variety of other researchers, clinicians, and theorists. In fact, we have come to recognize that no single element of the Soteria program is new; their combination in one setting is what we believe unique. Some of Soteria's roots are to be found in: the era of moral treatment in American psychiatry[2], the tradition of intensive interpersonal intervention in schizophrenia,[5,20] the therapists who have described growth from psychosis,[11, 16] the current group of psychiatric heretics[10,21] and descriptions of the development of psychiatric disorder in response to life crisis.[1,9]

Research Design

Although our research design is not the primary focus of this paper, a brief outline of it is necessary to understand the findings to be cited here. The basic design is a comparative-outcome study of two matched cohorts of first-admission, unmarried, carefully diagnosed schizophrenic patients between 16 and 30 years of age, deemed in need of hospitalization and followed for two years after admission. Both experimental and control patients are obtained from a large screening facility (600 new patients a month) that is part of a community mental health center. Patients who meet the research criteria are assigned on a consecutively admitted, space-available basis to either the experimental group or the control group.

The selection criteria are designed to provide us with a relatively homogeneous sample of individuals diagnosed schizophrenic, "at risk" for prolonged hospitalization and/or chronic disability (early onset and being unmarried both predispose to chronic care).[19] In addition to its value in homogenizing our sample, our elimination of individuals with extensive previous hospitalization reflects our wish not to deal with the learned patient role before actually involving the person as him or herself in the Soteria program. We recognize that these criteria limit our study's generalizability, but we feel that the advantages of relative homogeneity outweigh the disadvantage of more limited generalizability when it is possible to study only a relatively small number of subjects.

Control patients are admitted to the wards of the community mental health center where they receive "usual" treatment. Experimental patients, on the other hand, are treated at Soteria House. A battery of tests is used to assess both patient groups from a variety of points of view; psychiatric (diagnosis, type of onset, paranoid/nonparanoid status, symptom pattern), ward and house staff (behavior and improvement ratings), family (perception of behavior and personality characteristics), and self-rating (social and work functioning, attitude toward illness, and the like). Patients are followed at 6-month intervals for 2 years through psychiatric, family, and self ratings. All psychiatric assessments (baseline, discharge, and follow-up) are conducted by an independent evaluation team. Because the experimental treatment program is specifically designed to enhance psychosocial functioning, our postdischarge assessments address this area in particular. Because of the very different use of neuroleptics, we did not expect symptomatology (or readmission rates) to be preferentially affected by the experimental program. The rationale and methodology of the research design has been published in detail elsewhere.[12]

The Program

Soteria is a 1915-vintage 12-room house located on a busy street in a "transitional" neighborhood of a city in the San Francisco Bay area. Bordering Soteria on one side is a nursing home and on the other a two-family home. The neighborhood has a mixture of businesses, medical facilities (a general hospital is one block away), single-family homes, and small apartments (usually homes that have been remodeled for this purpose). It is a designated poverty area inhabited by a mixture of college students, lower-income families, and former state hospital patients. Some 15-20 percent of residents in the area are Mexican-American, and there is a sprinkling of blacks.

Primarily because of licensing laws, the house may accommodate only 6 residents at one time, although as many as 10 persons can sleep there comfortably. There are 6 paid nonprofessional staff plus the project director and a quarter-time project psychiatrist. One or two new residents are admitted each month. In general, two of our specially trained nonprofessional regular staff, a man and a woman, are on duty at any one time. In addition, one or more volunteers are usually present, especially in the evening. Most staff work 36-48 hour shifts to provide themselves the opportunity to relate continuously to "spaced-out" (their term) residents over a relatively long period of time. Staff and residents share responsibility for household maintenance, meal preparation, and cleanup. Persons who are not "together" are not expected to do an equal share of the work. Over the long term, staff do more than their share and will step in to assume responsibility if a resident cannot do a task to which he has agreed. The project director acts as friend, counselor, supervisor, and object for displaced angry feelings by staff, whereas our part-time project psychiatrist supervises the staff and is seen as a stable, reassuring presence (in addition to his formal medicolegal responsibilities).

Although staff vary somewhat in how they see their roles, they generally view what psychiatry labels a "schizophrenic reaction" as an altered state of consciousness in an individual who is experiencing a crisis in living. Simply put, the altered state involves personality fragmentation, with the loss of a sense of self. In this state "beyond reason," modalities of experience merge, the inner and outer worlds become difficult to distinguish, and mystical sensations are experienced. Often the individual's terror at their altered state is reinforced by the intense fear he or she arouses in others, whose own sanity is challenged by his or her seemingly inexplicable behavior.

Few clinicians would disagree with a description of the evolution of psychosis as a process of fragmentation and disintegration. But at Soteria House, the disruptive psychotic experience is also believed to have unique potential for reintegration and reconstitution if it is not prematurely aborted or forced into some psychologically straitjacketing compromise. Our view of schizophrenia implies a number of therapeutic attitudes. All facets of the psychotic experience are taken by Soteria House staff members as "real." They view the experiential and behavioral attitudes associated with the psychosis—the clinical symptoms, including irrationality, terror, and mystical experience—as extremes of basic human qualities. Because "irrational" behavior and mystical beliefs are regarded as valid and as capable of being understood, Soteria staff try to provide an atmosphere that will facilitate integration of the psychosis into the continuity of the individual's life. Thus, psychotic persons are not to be considered nonhumans, nor are they to be related to in a depersonalized way, for such an attitude would invalidate the experience. Too often, systematic and pervasive invalidation of the psychotic person's experience by his or her family and associates appears to have contributed to the development of madness in the first place.

Any truly therapeutic program should therefore minimize invalidation. When the fragmentation process is seen as valid and as having potential for psychological growth, the individual experiencing the schizophrenic reaction can be tolerated, lived with, related to, and validated, but not "treated," or used to fulfill staff needs. Limits are set if the person is clearly a danger to themself or others, rather than merely because others are unable to tolerate his or her madness. The psychotic experience is considered intelligible in terms of the nature and characteristics of the psychosocial matrix in which it developed. That premise forms part of the basis for our orientation to the patients and their families and for the goal of developing sympathetic, understanding relationships in Soteria House.

Soteria House staff members have been selected because

they seem to have the potential ability to tune in to the resident's altered state of consciousness and because they have no "theory of schizophrenia" into which he or she is to be fitted, procrustean fashion.

During the acute phase of psychosis, staff members form special one-to-one or two-to-one relationships with the disorganized resident, performing a role similar to that of the LSD-trip guide. The psychotic experience is shared and reflected, so long as both residents and staff member do not experience intolerable levels of fear and anxiety. The "guide" is someone for the resident to be with, and their intense, dyadic relationship is the program's primary interpersonal unit and source of control. Phenothiazines are ordinarily not used for 6 weeks. If the resident shows no change at that time and is either paranoid or has an insidious onset, chlorpromazine (300 mg per day or more) is given. Thus far only 10 percent of Soteria residents have required a therapeutic course of phenothiazines. As residents become less psychotic, they become more active participants in the family-commune scene with its attendant problems—sibling rivalry, fairness in division of work, failures to perform as expected, and the like. These problems are worked out at the level at which they occur, ranging from between two individuals to involving the entire staff-resident group.

There is minimal organized structure. Meal preparation (including menus, cooking, and cleanup) is planned and tasks assigned at the beginning of each week. All eat together between 6 and 8 each evening and there is usually one meeting of the entire staff-resident group

226

each week. These are the only regularly organized activities. However, everyone is free to pursue other activities like pottery, painting, yoga, and independent study, and usually does. Residents do not ordinarily use any outside mental health resources while staying at Soteria.

Authority lines and roles are flexibly defined, depending on the functions to be served; for example, there are no staff-only meetings, anyone can shop for groceries, and staff are not seen as having "the answer." They are expected to be in step with residents rather than one step ahead. There is the explicit expectation that Soteria will be transitional (for staff as well), thus setting up positive expectations that residents will eventually "get it together" and leave.

Discharge is effected by informal group consensus when residents see themselves and are seen by others as "together." Reluctance to leave is dealt with directly and firmly and is almost always accompanied by an offer to help with the process. After discharge, relationships between residents and staff are maintained if the individuals concerned are interested and agreeable.

Readers of this chapter are apt to wonder what can be derived from a program like ours, assuming it is not to be duplicated in all respects for theirs. We have come to see seven ingredients of the Soteria program as critical, and would advise others to implement all of these, or as many as possible, to facilitate the treatment of newly admitted psychotic persons. They are (1) positive expectations of learning from psychosis; (2) flexibility of roles, relationships, and responses; (3) sufficient time in residence for imitation and identification with staff to occur; (4) acceptance of the psychotic person's experience of himself as valid; (5) staff's primary responsibility to "be with" the disorganized resident, and specific acknowledgment that he need not do anything; (6) great tolerance for unusual ("crazy") behavior without anxiety or a need to control it; and (7) normalization of the experience of psychosis.

Staff

We believe that relatively untrained, psychologically unsophisticated persons can assume a phenomenological stance toward psychosis more easily than can such highly trained persons as M.D.'s or Ph.D.'s because the untrained have learned no theory of schizophrenia, whether psychodynamic, organic, or a combination of both. The unsophistication allows them freedom to be themselves, to follow their visceral responses, and to be "persons" with the psychotic individuals. Highly trained mental health professionals tend to lose this freedom in favor of a more cognitive, theory-based, learned response that may invalidate a patient's experience of him—or herself if the professional's theory based behavior is not congruent with the patient's felt needs. Professionals may also use their theoretical knowledge defensively when confronted, in an unstructured setting, with anxiety-provoking behaviors of acute psychotics. This pattern of response is not so readily available to our unsophisticated nonprofessional therapists, nor is it reinforced by a professional degree with its status and power.

We believe the ingredients critical to the success or failure of Soteria are the characteristics and attitudes of its staff and the types of relationships developed between staff and residents. New staff are selected from a pool of candidates by the current staff-resident group in consultation with the project director. The candidates comprise persons who have heard, usually by word of mouth, about Soteria and who come because they want an opportunity to relate to unmedicated, "spaced out" individuals. Serious candidates are asked to work first as volunteers; some move into Soteria House to live, while others spend a day or more in the house each week. This process accomplishes two objectives: First, the candidate learns the principles of "being with" a resident by apprenticeship to an experienced staff person. Second, it allows the staff-resident group to get to know him well. Over time, these allow both the candidate and the house members to select each other based on experience.

The kinds of people who choose to work at Soteria are those who want neither to become part of the 9-5 business world nor to drop out and became part of the hippie scene. They are young and bright; most have attended college, but few have formal education in psychology. They can be characterized as having led intense lives in relatively few years, and as being individuals who are tough but tolerant, hard-working, energetic, and well integrated. The degree of their toughness and integration (ego strength) came as a surprise to us, because fewer than we had expected reported having experienced crises of psychotic proportions. None of the crises they did experience were labeled and treated. We also expected that many would have had extensive experience with psychedelic drugs, but that was not the case. Like most Californian youth, they have tried various drugs, but did not adopt drugs as a lifestyle. Their current use of intoxicants of any type is minimal.

In exploring the reasons for these two unexpected findings, we found a very interesting pattern; all but one of their families of origin were "problem" families. Psychiatrists reading the staff's autobiographies might well predict serious psychological problems for many of them. Instead, our staff seem to be examples of invulnerable children raised in difficult situations.

In attempting to discern the reasons for their invulnerability, we found that they had not been so intimately entwined with the psychopathologic parent as was a sibling, usually older. (Significantly, none of our staff are first-born or only children.) Although our data are incomplete on this point, the siblings of several staff members appear to be significantly psychologically impaired. Interestingly, the role most often played by our staff members in their problem families was that of a somewhat neutral caretaker for the parent. That experience may have something to do with their having chosen to work at Soteria, since a comparable pattern of family life has been noted by Henry[7] for healers and by Burton[3] for psychotherapists. Stone[18] has also noted similar phenomena in psychotherapists who had unusual success with schizophrenic patients. We have published elsewhere our complete staff data and compared them with staffs of typical hospital wards.[8,14]

Results

Sample

A total of 37 experimental and 42 control subjects met study admission criteria and were treated in the respective facilities. By the time of this analysis, 30 experimental and 33 control subjects were eligible for 2-year follow-up. By the 2-year follow-up, 4 experimental and 10 control subjects were either lost to follow-up or refused further participation in the study. Thus, 2-year psychopathological and psychosocial data are reported from 26 experimental and 23 control subjects. Data are reported as percentages (with sample sizes at the top of each table) because we were not able to obtain 2-year data from every subject not lost to follow-up.

Baseline Assessment

There are no significant differences between the experimental and control groups on a total of 24 demographic, psychopathologic, and psychosocial variables examined on admission.

Resource Utilization

Initial Residential Care – Experimental subjects stayed significantly longer on their initial admission and less often received antipsychotic medications (Table 1). During the initial 6 weeks, no Soteria patient received antipsychotic drugs. Three subjects received them later in their stays. All control subjects received neuroleptics while hospitalized; doses averaged 730 mg per day of chlorpromazine equivalents.

Readmissions – Over the 2-year follow-up, control subjects had more readmissions (67 vs. 53%) but the differences do not quite reach the .05 level of significance.

Table 1

Initial Residential Care

	Experimental	**Control**
Length of Stay: Mean ± S.D.	166 ± 142	28 + 48
Median	142 days	15 days
Neuroleptic Drug Treatmeant †	8% ††	100%
Average dose in clhorpromazine equivalents	660mg/day	730 mg/ day

†   Two weeks or more of antipsychotic medication at a level >300 mg/day

††   No experimental subjects received neuroleptic drugs during their initial six weeks

Table 2

Resource Utilization After Discharge

	Exper. (%)	Control (%)	Exact Prob. †
Neuroleptic drug Treatment: Cumulative to 2 years after admission	(N=23)	(N=21)	.00001
Continuous	4	43	
Intermittent ††	30	52	
Occasional	9	4	
None	57		
Other mental health contact: Cumulative to 2 years	(N=22)	(N=22)	
Any contact	59	100	.0007
Outpatient therapy	45	100	.0001
Day/night care ‡	19	41	.04
Total days /nights ‡	110	1.251	

†   Exact probability for a 2x2 contingency table.

‡   Includes readmissions to original treatment facilities as well as other psychiatric hospitals.

†† At least two weeks of continuous medication.

Outpatient Care After Initial Discharge

Neuroleptics. As may be seen in Table 2, over the 2-year period there were striking differences in neuroleptic drug use in the two groups. More than 50 percent of experimental subjects never received any psychotropic drugs while 43 percent of the control subjects were maintained on them.

Other outpatient care. – Table 2 indicates that control subjects more often used and consumed many more days of day or night care and outpatient therapy. Interestingly, about 40 percent of experimental subjects had no contact whatever with the regular mental health system.

Two-Year Outcome Data

Psychopathology – Although not a major focus of this paper, at 2 years overall levels and profiles of psychopathology, as rated by the Inpatient Multidimensional Psychiatric Scale (IMPS), were not significantly different between the groups. Both groups showed significant and comparable reduction in psychopathology over the 2-year period.

Psychosocial Adjustment –

Employment (Table 3). – Two aspects of working are reported: overall occupational level as rated on a three-point scale (2 = fallen, 3 = same, 4 = risen) and amount of time working. There are no significant intergroup differences between the groups in percent of subjects working full- or part-time at 2 years after admission. Experimental subjects, however, had significantly higher occupational levels.

Table 3

Psychosocial Adjustment: Employment

	Exper. (%)	Control (%)	Exact Prob. †
Prior to admission	(N=36)	(N=28)	
Full-time ††	64	64	
Part-time	19	21	1.0
Not working	17	14	
Two years after admission	(N=20)	(N=19)	0.64
Full-time ††	35	21	
Part-time	45	58	
Not working	20	21	
Occupational Level ‡	2.71± .56	2.33 ± .49	

† Exact probability for RxC contingency table (that is, the probability of obtaining a table as probable as, or less than, the given table).

†† Full-time category includes patients attending school on a full-time basis.

‡ Significant intergroup difference p > .05.

Living arrangements and friendships (Table 4). – Many more experimental subjects were living alone or with peers (that is, not at home with their families) at 2 years after admission, accounting for overall differences found. A four-point scale is used to rate how many friends patients have and how often they are seen (0 = no friends and social membership, 3= many friends and social memberships). There is a consistent nonsignificant trend favoring the experimental group on this variable.

Table 4

Psychosocial Adjustment: Living Arrangements

	Exper. (%)	Control (%)	Exact Prob. †
Prior to admission	(N=37)	(N=39)	
W/parents/relatives	68	62	.81
Independently ††	30	36	
Board and Care, etc.	3	3	
Two years after admission	(N=20)	(N=23)	
W/parents/relatives	28	52	.03
Independently ††	60	30	
Board and Care, etc.			
Soteria/hospital			
readmission	12	4	
Friendships	1.95± .59	1.56± .92	

† Exact probability for RxC contingency table (that is, the probability of obtaining a table as probable as, or less probable than, the given table).

†† Includes living alone, with peers, or with spouse and/or children.

One other preliminary result is of interest. The cost of the initial six months of care in both systems (Soteria and the "usual" state -and county-financed one) is almost exactly the same – $4,400.[13]

Summary

In summary, although considerable caution should be exercised in view of the relatively small numbers of subjects studied and lack of random assignments, our data indicate that first-break schizophrenics deemed in need of hospitalization can be treated successfully by a nonprofessional staff, usually without medication, at no greater cost, in a home in the community. We have no data concerning the efficacy of this approach for longterm schizophrenics or other types of patients. It does appear, as hypothesized, that the experimental program is more effective than competent "usual" care in preserving and enhancing psychosocial adjustment in the group of subjects "at risk" for chronicity.

References

1. Birley, J.L.T, Brown G.W.: "Crisis and life changes preceding the onset or relapse of acute schizophrenia: Clinical aspects." *British. Journal of Psychiatry* 116:327-333, 1970.
2. Bockoven, J: *Moral Treatment in American Psychiatry.* New York, Springer, 1963.
3. Burton, A: "The adoration of the patient and its disillusionment." *American Journal of Psychoanalysis* 29:194-204, 1969.
4. Crane, G.E: "Clinical psychopharmacology in its twentieth year." *Science* 181(4095): 124-128, 1973.
5. Fromm-Richmann, F: "Notes on the development of treatment of schizophrenia by psychoanalytic psychotherapy." *Psychiatry* 11:263-273, 1948.
6. Goldstein, M.J: "Premorbid adjustment paranoid status and patterns of responses to phenothiazine in acute schizophrenia." *Schizophrenia Bulletin* 3:24-37, 1970.
7. Henry, W.E: "Some observations on the lives of healers." *Human Development* 9:47-56, 1966.

8. Hirschfeld, R. et al: "Being with madness: Personality characteristics of three treatment staffs." *Hospital Community Psychiatry* 28(4): 267-273, 1977

9. Holmes, T.H., Rahe, R: "The social readjustment rating scale." *Journal of Psychosomatic Research* 11: 213-218, 1967

10. Laing, R.D: *The Politics of Experience.* New York: Ballantine Books, 1967.

11. Menninger, K: *Psychiatrist's World: The Selected Papers of Karl Menninger,* Hall BH (ed), New York: Viking Press, 1959.

12. Mosher, L: "Research design to evaluate psychosocial treatments of schizophrenia." *Hospital and Community Psychiatry* 23:229-234, 1972.

13. Mosher L., Menn A., Mathews S.: Soteria: "Evaluation of a home-based treatment for schizophrenia." *American Journal of Orthopsychiatry* 45(3):455-467, 1975.

14. Mosher L., Reitman A, Menn A: "Characteristics of nonprofessionals serving as primary therapists for acute schizophrenics," *Hospital & Community Psychiatry* 24(6):391-396, 1973

15. Niskanen, P., Achte, K.A: "The Course and Prognosis of Schizophrenic Psychoses in Helsinki: A Comparative Study of First Admissions in 1950, 1960 and 1965." *Monograph No. 4.* Helsinki, Finland, Psychiatric Clinic, Helsinki University Central Hospital, 1972.

16. Perry, J.W: "Reconstitutive process in the psychopathology of the self." *Annual New York Academy of Science* 96:853-876, 1962

17. Rappaport, M. et al: "Are there schizophrenics for whom drugs may be unnecessary or contraindicated?" International. *Pharmacopsychiatry* 13:100-111, 1978

18. Stone, M.H: "Therapists' personality and unexpected success with schizophrenic patients." *American Journal of Psychotherapy* 25:543-552, 1971

19. Strauss, J. et al: "Premorbid adjustment in schizophrenia: Concepts, measures, and implications." *Schizophrenia Bulletin* 3(2):182- 244, 1977

20. Sullivan, H.S: *Schizophrenia as a Human Process.* New York: Norton, 1962

21. Szasz, T: *The Myth of Mental Illness: Foundations of a Theory of Personal Conduct.* New York: Hoeber-Harper, 1961

Soteria Final Progress Report Summary
by L. Mosher

This report details the findings from Phase II of the Soteria Project, covering 1976-1981. During this period 45 experimental (Soteria or Emanon) and 55 controls (Valley or Chope Hospital psychiatric wards) who met all research criteria were randomly assigned and followed for 2 years. The two groups were comparable on all 29 admission variables. At six weeks both groups had improved significantly, and similarly, despite minimal neuroleptic drug use with the Soteria and Emanon treated subjects. Thus, the two experimental milieus were as effective as hospital based neuroleptic drug treatment in reduction of acute psychotic symptomatology in the short term. This finding replicated what we reported earlier for subjects treated between 1971 and 76 at Soteria.

Two year outcome differences in this sample were infrequent, although in no instance did the experimental subjects do worse. The lack of replication of Phase Its (1971-76) psychosocial adjustment findings clearly favoring the experimental group was thought to be due to the lack of immediately available peer based social networks on discharge. These networks dissolved in 1979-81 (after being in place since 1973) as it became clear the project would end and the clinical facilities would close. Among these newly diagnosed DSM-II schizophrenics 2 year "good" outcomes were predicted for both experimental and control subjects by better pre-illness levels of psychosocial competence.

The following is a review of an article entitled "Schizophrenics for Whom Phenothiazines Are Contraindicated or Unnecessary" by M. Rappaport, K. Hopkins, K. Hall, T. Belleza, and J. Silverman. The article summarized some of the results of a three year research program with psychiatric patients with schizophrenia as diagnosed before DSM-III (At that time an acute psychotic episode and an acute schizophrenic episode were synonymous). Designed by Drs. Julian Silverman and Maurice Rappaport, the project was carried out on a specially created experimental ward of Agnews State Hospital in San Jose, California.

Schizophrenics for Whom Phenothiazines are Contraindicated or Unnecessary
Esalen Institute, 1985

One hundred twenty-seven young male schizophrenics were examined after the onset of an acute psychotic episode and also for up to three years after discharge from the hospital study. (Female patients were not included in the study; changes in females' sensory functioning are known to occur in different phases of the menstrual cycle. This fact was presumed to make it impossible to differentiate between sensory-physiological changes due to the acute schizophrenic episode and those due to menstrual cycle changes. The results of the neurophysiological research will not be summarized in this review.) Follow-up information was obtained on 108 patients for up to thirty-six months after discharge from the project. Of this number, 55% had been assigned to placebos (unmedicated pills) while in the hospital and 45% to chlorpromzine (thorazine), a popular anti-psychotic medication. Personal interviews were conducted with 80 patients and information on 28 others was obtained either through the mail, telephone, or contact with relatives. The analyses reported here are based on the 80 patients on whom full information is available.

Patients accepted for the project met the following criteria: between 16 and 40 years of age; referred from the community mental health program with a diagnosis of schizophrenia; diagnosed as having an acute schizophrenic reaction at hospital admission on the basis of evaluation with a battery of psychiatric rating scales; having no gross adverse reaction to chlorpromazine; having had no electroshock therapy within six months preceding admission; having no gross organic impairment; no history of epilepsy; no history of drug "abuse" prior to admission; and no (or few) previous hospitalizations.

When a patient was admitted to the experimental ward he was assigned randomly to either of two treatment conditions—a chlorpromazine treatment group or a placebo treatment group. Ward personnel, psychiatric raters, and all but one of the research personnel were not told to which treatment condition patients were assigned. Periodically, staff were asked to judge which patients were on chlorpromazine. Consistently, 40 to 50 percent of the time wrong judgments were tallied, indicating that staff personnel were ignorant as to patients' actual drug status.

On the first or second day after admission to the project, two trained research personnel interviewed each patient and completed a battery of psychiatric ratings including the Brief Psychiatric Rating Scale and the Global Assessment Rating Scale. Ratings on these scales were repeated at the time of each patient's discharge. Two principal measures were used. A Severity of Illness score was derived which was a composite of the above mentioned ratings. A Clinical Change Index was derived; it represented the direction of change (improvement or worsening of symptoms) from hospitalization to discharge and from discharge to follow-up. A third measure, Overall Functional Disturbance, also was utilized.

All patients took nine tablets a day (three, three times a day). Those assigned to the chlorpromazine condition received a minimum of 300 milligrams a day. The physician could order up to 900 milligrams of chlorpromzine a day. However, he was never told by the research assistant in charge whether the patient actually received medication or placebos.

Follow-up ratings were obtained, wherever possible, at 1, 3, 6, 12, 18, 24, 30, and 36 months after discharge from the hospital project.

Nurses, attendants, and doctors on the experimental ward were specially selected. Of primary concern was their willingness to work closely and continually with even very dis-eased patients and to accept as much as possible (rather than avoid) their own fears and fantasies about madness. Ongoing intensive group-work sessions for staff focused on awareness of their own feelings and openness to the feelings of others.

Findings:

Clinical Change, Severity of Illness (SI), and Overall Functional Disturbance (OFD) scores were compared for the medicated and unmedicated groups; comparisons were made at admission, discharge, and at last follow-up.

On the Clinical Change Index, significant differences, admission to discharge, were found between placebo and chlorpromazine-drugged patients. Chlorpromazine-drugged patients tended to show greater clinical changes than placebo patients while in the hospital. Thus medicated patients showed a faster and greater symptom reduction than unmedicated patients. On the Severity of Illness and Functional Disturbance scales, no significant differences were found between the medicated and unmedicated groups, at admission or at discharge. However, at follow-up, Severity of Illness scores were significantly less for placebo patients who continued off medication than for other patients. In other words, patients given placebos who stayed off medication outside of the hospital were less dis-eased at follow-up than patients given chlorpromazine while in the hospital, regardless of whether or not the hospital medicated patients continued using medication outside of the hospital. Further, greater Functional Disturbance at follow-up tended to be found among chlorpromzine-drugged patients; Functional Disturbance was less in the placebo patients than in the medicated patients. Finally, it was found that overall, significantly fewer patients were rehospitalized who had been assigned to placebos (Table 1). This was clearly apparent among patients on placebo during the project who had not used medication in the follow-up period.

Table 1

Number of Patients Rehospitalized in Terms of Their Initial Hospital Medication Condition †

		Rehospi-talized	Not Rehospi-talized
Random Drug Assignment While Hospitalized	Placebo	12	30
	Clorpromazine	24	15

† Information for this analysis was available on 81 patients rather than 80.

Table 2

Rehospitalizations in Relation to Hospital and Follow-up Medication Conditions

Medication Grp.		Number of patients	Percent Rehosp.
In Hospital	At Follow-Up		
Placebo	Off Medication	24	8%
Chlorpromazine	On Medication	22	73%
Placebo	On Medication	17	53%
Chlorpromazine	Off Medication	17	47%

Conclusions:

In most research with acutely dis-eased patients, the foremost criterion for evaluating them favorably is still the reduction of overt and agitated psychotic behavior. The study reviewed here suggests that this criterion may, at least in certain instances, be an erroneous and unfortunate one. A significant lessening of psychotic symptoms during hospitalization, associated with phenothiazine treatment, is not related to long terms positive re-organization. Indeed it is suggested that certain acute patients, evidencing bizarre and regressive behaviors, will get better and stay better if their dis-ease is NOT interrupted with anti-psychotic chemotherapy.

Perhaps part of the reason why a significant number of placebo patients showed long-term improvements was the ward milieu that was established during the three-year period and the staff who worked on through the project. It was already known from earlier research that patients with a positive, "integrating" attitude to their dis-ease had higher levels of post-hospital adjustment several years later than those with an "isolating" (rejecting) attitude toward it. In the Agnews project, this knowledge was translated into a staff attitude and a way-of-being-in-relationship which was different from many conventional hospital settings. In effect, a "space" was evolved (in a hospital setting) in which patients were given room to express their energies in relative safety; this increased the probability for these dis-eased people to rebalance themselves.

This article was first published in January, 1987 in American Health Magazine. It indicates that either far more people are having spiritual experiences as time goes on, or, far more are willing to talk about these experiences.

Mysticism Goes Mainstream

Father Andrew Greeley

Nearly half of American adults (42%) now believe they have been in contact with someone who has died, usually a dead spouse or sibling. That's up from more than one-fourth (27%) in a previous national survey done 11 years earlier.

Still higher percentages of Americans report having had psychic experiences such as extra-sensory perception (ESP). In a new survey, two-thirds of all adults (67%) now report having experienced ESP. In 1973, it was 58% in a similar poll.

Both national surveys were done by my colleagues and me at the University of Chicago's National Opinion Research Council (NORC). I became interested in what psychologists call "paranormal" experiences back in the '70s, when I began to realize how many people have them (even if they don't tell anyone).

It may well be, as Shirley MacLaine argues in the next article ("Shirley MacLaine's Spiritual Dance"), that the incidence of such experiences is rising fast. But I favor a different explanation: Partly because of her and others, millions are less afraid to talk about the experiences. I've had no vested interest, religious or sociological, in the metaphysical reality of these experiences. I am a sociologist and novelist. I am also a parish priest, as suggested by my current book, *Confessions of a Parish Priest*. The Roman Catholic Church of this era is profoundly skeptical of paranormal phenomena. So am I. I doubt, for example, that the contact-with-the-dead experiences can ever be "scientifically" validated. But even though I've never had a psychic or mystical experience myself, most Americans have. We saw this in our first study in 1973 and in data from a repeat survey we have just analyzed.

Our new results, published here for the first time, show a clear trend: More people than ever say they've had such experiences. Other surveys confirm the trend (see "Mystical Americans," p. 49). And it's true whether you look at the most common forms of psychic and mystical experience, or the rarest.

Some experiences aren't too far from the ordinary, and may soon be explained by neurological or psychological processes—like *déja vu*, that eerie sense of going to a new place and feeling sure you've somehow been there before. 59% of Americans reported *déja vu* in 1973; today, the figure's 67%.

Other experiences, though, are profound. In 1973, a full 35% of Americans reported they had had a mystical experience; feeling "very close to a powerful, spiritual force that seemed to lift you out of yourself." And one-seventh of those who have had such experiences – 5% of

247

the whole population - have literally been "bathed in light" like the Apostle Paul. These experiences go way beyond intellect, and even beyond emotion. For a fifth of those who have them, they involve "a sense of tremendous personal expansion, either psychological or physical" - a form of body mysticism.

Such paranormal experiences—by definition, lying outside the normal—are generally viewed as hallucinations or symptoms of mental disorder. But if these experiences were signs of mental illness, our numbers would show the country is going nuts. What was paranormal is now normal. It's even happening to elite scientists and physicians who insist that such things cannot possibly happen.

Indeed, the nation is living with a split between scientific belief and personal reality. For example, 30% of the Americans who do *not* believe in life after death still say they've been in personal contact with the dead. My friend John Shea, a theologian, believes that these encounters could be real and the cause, not the result, of man's tenacious belief in life after death. But as a scientist all I can vouch for is the fact that millions of Americans have such experiences.

In any case, our studies show that people who've tasted the paranormal, whether they accept it intellectually or not, are anything but religious nuts or psychiatric cases. They are, for the most part, ordinary Americans, somewhat above the norm in education and intelligence and somewhat less than average in religious involvement.

248

We tested people who'd had some of the deeper mystical experiences—such as being bathed in light. We began with the Affect Balance Scale of Psychological Well-Being, a standard measure of the healthy personality. And the mystics scored at the top. Norman Bradburn, the University of Chicago psychologist who developed the scale, said no other factor has ever been found to correlate so highly.

When we reported our first NORC survey in 1973, a scientific sample of 1,467 adults, we soon discovered how nervous people can be about spirituality. Many, particularly in academia and the media, find it unthinkable that a sizable proportion of the people they see every day believe they have experiences outside the accepted limits of science. This discomfort has made it hard to carry on serious academic discussion about the mystical experiences of ordinary Americans.

I've been using my survey findings in a series of best-selling novels, beginning with *The Cardinal Sins* (Warner Books). While the incidents in my books are fictional, each is based on one or more personal interviews with people who tell their stories.

So, in *Lord of the Dance*, the heroine Noele Farrel is psychic. Annie Reilly in *Angels of September* sees her adolescent sweetheart—who'd been killed in the Hurtgen Forest battle 40 years earlier—walking along Chicago's Oak Street Beach. In this year's *Patience of a Saint*, Redmond Peter Kane is bowled over by an intense mystical experience on Wacker Drive as he walks by the ice-green

Wacker Drive Building. In the upcoming *Rite of Spring,* Brendan Ryan walks into his room in a Grand Beach summer home and finds his murdered wife, still lovely, calmly waiting for a chat with him. She has been guided to his room by Jackie Curran, a five-year-old who's psychic.

Some readers (and critics especially) raise a protest: Such events don't happen. They shouldn't be in fiction. Perhaps out of Celtic perversity, I disagree. To pretend that such perceptions do not occur to ordinary people in everyday life is like a Victorian novelist pretending that sexual intercourse does not occur. Either sham is, to say the least, nonscientific if not inhuman.

Despite years of attempts to study paranormal phenomena, there's been a scientific iron curtain raised against serious research on these experiences. But a crack in it opened a few years ago. Researchers in Japan and Wales, then in England, began to report on contact with the dead, especially among widowers in nursing homes. A University of North Carolina team led by associate professor of family medicine P. Richard Olson found that nearly two-thirds (64%) of widows at two Asheville nursing homes had at least "once or twice felt as though they were in touch with someone who had died."

That's not surprising by itself. What is surprising is the vividness of the experiences. Of those who reported such contact, 78% said they saw the dead one. 50% heard, 21% touched, 32% felt the presence, 18% talked with the departed and 46% had some combination of the above. Most found the encounter helpful, not scary, but none had ever mentioned the incident to their doctors. "It's not well known that such experiences are common, but they are," Olson says. In *Geriatrics Today,* he writes that even psychoactive drugs didn't end the "visits."

Our second NORC survey of paranormal experiences included a national sample of 1,473 adults in 1984. When I recently finished work with that data, it showed a marked increase in the number of men and women willing to report the encounters, at least in the anonymity of a polling interview. Among widows and widowers in the general population, our survey just about replicated Olson's findings in North Carolina.

We asked ourselves whether psychic and mystical beliefs cause the experience, or experience causes the belief. We turned to our national sample—this time to check for belief in life after death, intensity of religious commitment, and whether respondents envision a loving God or a judgmental one. We found, surprisingly, that many widows who experienced these visitations had not previously believed in life after death. So they were not hallucinating an image to match their beliefs (at least, not their conscious beliefs). This suggests, though it does not prove, that the experience is more likely to cause a belief in the hereafter than the other way around.

Pollster Andrew Greeley and colleagues at the University of Chicago have tracked our spiritual health since 1973. The data show that more Americans report paranormal experiences now than in the '70s ('73 results in Parentheses).

Americans Who:	1973	1987
Had contact with the dead (adult pop.)	(27%)	42%
Had contact with the dead (widows)	(51%)	67%
Had visions	(8%)	29%
Experienced ESP	(58%)	67%
Experienced déja vu	(59%)	67%
Experienced clairvoyance	(24%)	31%
Believe in life after death	(*)	73%
Believe the afterlife is Paradise	(*)	68%
Believe that after death they'll be reunited with dead loved ones	(*)	74%

no figures available

National surveys by The Gallup Organization bolster Greeley's polls showing paranormal experiences in the USA are on the rise:

Had an unusual spiritual experience	43%	('85)
Had a near-death experience	15%	('81)
Believe in life on other planets	46%	('81)
Believe in life after death	71%	('81)
Believe in reincarnation	23%	('81)
Believe in God or a Universal Spirit	95%	('81)
Believe Jesus is God	70%	('83)
Believe in angels	67% of teenagers	('86)
Believe in heaven**	71%	('80)
Believe in hell	53%	('80)
Expect the afterlife to be boring	5%	('81)

"Of those who believe, 20% ('81) think their chances of going to heaven are excellent.

We also asked whether people who'd lost a parent or child reported contact with the dead more than people whose siblings had died—on the theory that those who'd lost closer family members would have a greater "need" to hallucinate visitations. Again, we were surprised: People who'd lost a child or parent were less likely to report contact with the dead than those who'd lost siblings.

These findings make it difficult to explain such talks with the departed as simple psychological wish-fulfillment. But one finding does give a clue to the psychology of these experiences. For widows and for people who had lost siblings alike, the major factor associated with contacting the dead was a belief in a loving God, rather than a judgmental one. Though intriguing, however, this still doesn't prove whether belief or experience comes first. Feeling contact with a dead relative could certainly change one's mind about God, and make it easier to picture a warm, loving deity.

Whatever the cause of these "visitations," our work confirms the North Carolina suggestion that these experiences are common, benign and often helpful. What has been "paranormal" is not only becoming normal in our time—it may also be health-giving.

That has not made the news welcome to the routine scientist. There's an understandable resistance to studying phenomena, however benign, whose nature we really don't understand. It would be easier, certainly, to deny that these experiences exist.

But the data show clearly that they *do* exist, that people experience them in great numbers—and that they could even change the nature of our society. What may be most significant in our studies is not that the majority of adults now report experiencing ESP, or even that nearly half feel that they have talked with the dead. A small minority, maybe under 20 million, have undergone profoundly religious moments of ecstasy. They report out-of-body

trips, being bathed in light, or other encounters that transform their lives. They become profoundly trusting, convinced that something good rules in the world. Whether
their number is growing or they're just now ready to tell
about it, that many people capable of trust can have a lasting effect on the country.

The following article was published in the Journal of Nervous and Mental Disease, November, 1992, Vol. 180, No. 11. It addresses the need for a diagnostic code for spiritual problems, as well as clinical training regarding these problems.

Toward a More Culturally Sensitive DSM-IV:
Psychoreligious and Psychospiritual Problems

David Lukoff, Ph.D.[1], Francis Lu, M.D.[2] and Robert Turner, M.D.[3]

In theory, research, and practice, mental health professionals have tended to ignore or pathologize the religious and spiritual dimensions of life. This represents a type of cultural insensitivity towards individuals who have religious and spiritual experiences in both Western and non-Western cultures. After documenting the "religiosity gap" between clinicians and patients, the authors review the role of theory, inadequate training, and biological primacy in fostering psychiatry's insensitivity. In the next section, a new Z Code (formerly V Code) diagnostic category is proposed for DSM-IV: Psychoreligious or Psychospiritual Problem. Examples of psychoreligious problems include loss or questioning of a firmly held faith, and conversion to a new faith. Examples of psychospiritual problems include near-death experience and mystical experience. Both types of

[1]*Saybrook Institute, San Francisco/California. Send reprint requests to: Francis Lu, M.D., Department of Psychiatry, San Francisco General Hospital, 1001 Potrero Avenue, San Francisco, CA 94110*

[2] *Department of Psychiatry, University of California, San Francisco.*

The authors wish to thank Bruce Greyson, Stanley Krippner, Kenneth Ring, Richard Thurrell and Roger Walsh for their helpful comments on an earlier draft of this paper. We also wish to acknowledge the assistance of Bruce Flath, head librarian at the California Institute of Integral Studies, in conducting computer bibliographic searches.

problems are defined, and differential diagnostic issues are discussed. This new diagnostic category would: 1) improve diagnostic assessments when religious and spiritual issues are involved; 2) reduce iatrogenic harm from misdiagnosis of psychoreligious and psychospiritual problems; 3) improve treatment of such problems by stimulating clinical research; and 4) encourage clinical training centers to address the religious and spiritual dimensions of human existence.
- Journal of Mental Disorders 180:673-682, 1992

The need for a more culturally sensitive psychiatric classification system, one which acknowledges psychosocial and cultural factors, has been a topic of much debate (Fabrega 1987, 1992; Kleinman, 1988; Mezzich, Fabrega, and Kleinman, 1992). The religious and spiritual dimensions of culture are among the most important factors that structure human experience, beliefs, values, behavior as well as illness patterns (Browning, et al., 1990; James, 1961; Krippner and Welch, 1992). Yet psychiatry, in its diagnostic classification systems, as well as its theory, research and practice, has tended to either ignore or pathologize the religious and spiritual dimensions of life.

For instance, in the *Diagnostic and Statistical Manual of Mental Disorders (DSM-III-R),* religion is consistently negatively portrayed. All 12 references to religion in the Glossary of Technical Terms are used to illustrate psychopathology. These references are conspicuous because "with the exception of a single reference to politics, the glossary mentions no other particular area of human experience" (Post, 1990, p 813). Similarly, from Freud's writings through the 1976 report on mysticism by the Group for the Advancement of Psychiatry (GAP), there has been a tendency to associate spiritual experiences with psychopathology. Some clinical literature has described the mystical experience as symptomatic of ego regression (Freud, 1959; Leuba, 1929), borderline psychosis (GAP, 1976), a psychotic episode (Horton, 1974), or temporal lobe dysfunction (Mandel, 1980).

The first section of this article reviews the historical background, research, and theory highlighting psychiatry's insensitivity towards the religious and spiritual issues that patients bring into treatment. It documents the "religiosity gap" between clinicians and patients, the inadequate training in religious and spiritual issues, and the role that biological primacy has played in creating insensitivity towards these issues. Case examples are also provided in which sensitivity to the cultural dimensions of religious and spiritual experiences is essential for effective treatment. The second section presents a proposal for a new diagnostic category that would help remediate this long standing insensitivity. The authors introduce the category of "Psychoreligious or Psychospiritual Problem" to delineate those distressing experiences of a religious or spiritual nature that are the focus of psychiatric diagnosis or treatment, but are not attributable to a mental disorder.

While there is no consensus as to the boundaries between religiosity and spirituality, we adhere in this review to the distinction most frequently drawn between them. Religiosity refers to "adherence to the beliefs and practices of an organized church or religious institution" (Shafranske and Maloney, 1990, p 72). Spirituality describes the transcendental relationship between the person and a Higher Being, a quality that goes beyond a specific religious affiliation (Peterson and Nelson, 1987).

Background

The view that religion is associated with psychopathology has a long history in the theory, research, and practice of psychiatry. Early psychoanalytic theory drew parallels between religion and both neurosis and psychosis. Freud (1966) saw religion as a "universal obsessional neurosis" (although this position is being revised within some contemporary psychoanalytic circles [Laor, 1989]). While Skinnerian behaviorism ignored religious experience to focus exclusively on observable behavior, Albert Ellis, the originator of rational emotive (cognitive) therapy, promoted a highly critical view of religion, viewing it as equivalent to irrational thinking and emotional disturbance: "The elegant therapeutic solution to emotional problems is quite unreligious ...The less religious they [patients] are, the more emotionally healthy they will tend to be" (Ellis, 1980, p 637). Religion and psychiatry have also been viewed as competing belief systems for giving meaning to the world (Lovinger, 1985). In addition, the positivistic tendencies of psychiatry reject subjectivist and mentalistic ideas, resulting in a devaluation of religion.

The relationship between psychiatry and spirituality in many ways parallels the relationship between psychiatry and religion. Psychiatry has tended to ignore the spiritual dimension of life, and to view spiritual experiences as evidence of psychopathology. Freud (1959) promoted this view in *Civilization and Its Discontents,* where he reduced the "oceanic experience" of mystics to "infantile helplessness" and a "regression to primary narcissism." In the 1976 report by the Group for the Advancement of

Psychiatry (GAP) on "Mysticism: Spiritual Quest or Psychic Disturbance," "the authors follow Freud's lead in defining the mystic perception of unity as a regression, an escape, a projection upon the world of a primitive infantile state" (Deikman, 1977, p 214).

Research Literature

In research, psychiatry has largely ignored religion. A study of articles published in four psychiatric journals during a recent 5-year period showed that only 2.5% (59 of 2348) included religious variables, and these primarily involved the psychopathological uses of religion by patients (Larson, et al., 1986). In an invited address to the American Psychiatric Association in 1986, the renowned theologian Hans Kung spoke about the "repression of religion" in psychiatric practice (Kung, 1990). Similarly, much of the recent clinical literature has either understated the incidence and significance of spiritual experiences or ignored studies which indicate their positive impact on mental health.

These negative views of religion and spirituality are not warranted in light of recent studies showing no association between religiosity and psychopathology in the non-patient population. In fact, a meta-analysis of religiosity and mental health found them to be positively related. Church-affiliated individuals showed greater happiness and satisfaction with marriage, work and life in general (Bergin, 1983). Studies of the self-reported relationship between quality of relationships with divine others (e.g., Christ, God, Mary, etc.) and several measures of well-being also found a significant positive association

(Pollner, 1989). While there does seem to be a relationship between religiosity and psychopathology in the seriously mentally ill, (Feldman and Rust, 1989), for the vast majority of the population, religiosity is associated with positive characteristics of mental health.

In contrast to Freud and the authors of the GAP Report, other theorists have viewed mystical experiences as a sign of health and a powerful agent of transformation (Hood, 1974, 1976; James, 1961; Jung, 1973; Maslow, 1962, 1971; Stace, 1960; Underhill, 1955). Studies have found that people reporting mystical experiences scored lower on psychopathology scales and higher on measures of psychological well-being than controls (Caird, 1987; Hood, 1976, 1977; Spanos and Moretti, 1988). Allman, et al. (in press) found that most clinicians do not currently view mystical experiences as pathological.

Another widely-researched spiritual experience is the near-death experience (NDE). Numerous studies document its non-pathological nature (Flynn, 1982; Greyson, 1981, 1983a; Ring, 1984). People who have had a NDE consistently report: 1) an increased appreciation for life, self acceptance, concern for others, and sense of purpose; 2) a decreased concern for personal status and material possessions; and 3) an overall shift towards universalistic spiritual values regardless of previous religious affiliations or lack thereof (Ring, 1984).

Religiosity Gap

Surveys conducted in the United States consistently show a "religiosity gap." Both the general public and psychiatric patients report themselves to be more highly religious and to attend church more frequently than mental health professionals. In a 1975 survey conducted by the American Psychiatric Association (APA) Task Force on Religion and Psychiatry, about half of the psychiatrists surveyed described themselves as agnostics or atheists. A study of psychologists found that only 43% stated a belief in a transcendent deity (Ragan, et al., 1980). This contrasts with between 1-5% of the general population who consider themselves atheists or agnostics (Gallup, 1985). Studies have also found that both psychiatrists and psychologists are relatively uninvolved in organized religion. Over half of psychiatrists reported that they attended church "rarely" or "never" (APA Task Force on Religion and Psychiatry, 1975), while only 18% of psychologists agreed that organized religion was the primary source of their spirituality (Shafranske and Malony, 1990). In contrast, Gallup (1985) found that one third of the population consider religion to be the most important dimension of their life, and another third consider it very important. A study of psychiatrically hospitalized patients found that religious beliefs and practices also assumed an important and often central place in their lives (Kroll and Sheehan, 1989).

The spiritual beliefs and practices of mental health professionals have not been researched to the same extent. But the limited data available do not suggest the existence of a "spirituality gap." In one survey where only 18% of psychologists reported a high level of involvement with organized religion, 51% characterized their spiritual beliefs and practices as involving "alternative spiritual path which is not part of an organized religion" (Shafranske and Malony, 1990, p 74). Another survey (Bergin and

Jensen, 1990) of psychiatrists, psychologists, social workers and marriage and family counselors found that 68% endorsed the item indicating that they: "Seek a spiritual understanding of the universe and one's place in it." The authors concluded: "There may be a reservoir of spiritual interests among therapists that is often unexpressed due to the secular framework of professional education and practice" (p 3). They name this phenomenon "spiritual humanism" and indicate that it could provide the basis for bridging the cultural gap between clinicians and the more religious public.

Training

Despite the importance of religion and spirituality in most patients' lives, neither psychiatrists nor psychologists are given adequate training to prepare them to deal with issues that arise in these realms. In a survey of members of the American Association of Directors of Psychiatric Residency Training on the role of religion in psychiatric education, didactic instruction on all aspects of religion was infrequent. The study concluded that the significance of religion for psychiatry warrants greater consideration, including recognition of the full spectrum of religious experience from unhealthy to healthy (Sansone, et al., 1990). Anderson and Young (1988) observed that "All clinicians inevitably face the challenge of treating patients with religious troubles and preoccupations" (p 532). Barnhouse has pointed out that, "Sex and religion are, in some form, universal components of human experience...Psychiatrists who know very little about religion would do well to study it" (Barnhouse,

1986 p 103). Certain issues in differential diagnosis require knowledge of the patient's religious subgroup (Lovinger, 1984) and/or the nature of acceptable expressions of subculturally validated forms of religious expression (Spitzer, et al., 1980). Yet, Post (1990) noted that "Few psychiatrists are trained to understand religion, much less treat it sympathetically" (p 813).

Similarly, in a survey of members of the American Psychological Association, 83% reported that discussions of religion in training occurred rarely or never (Shafranske and Malony, 1990). A study of training directors of the Association of Psychology Internship Centers (APIC), found that 100% indicated they had received no education or training in religious or spiritual issues during their formal internship. Yet 72% reported that they had addressed those issues, at least occasionally, in clinical practice. This survey also revealed that most of the training directors did not read professional literature addressing religious and spiritual issues in treatment, and that little was being done at their internship sites to address these issues in clinical training (Lannert, 1991). Thus many psychologists and psychiatrists are operating outside the boundaries of their professional training, which raises clinical and ethical concerns.

Biological Primacy

The lack of sensitivity to the cultural forces of religion and spirituality reflects the ontological primacy that psychiatry assigns to biology over culture. Brody (1990) has pointed out that the term 'culture' is absent in the DSMIII and is mentioned only in passing in the DSM-III-R. For example, the DSM-III-R glossary definition of delusion notes that, "The belief is not one ordinarily accepted by other members of the person's culture or subculture (i.e., it is not an article of religious faith)" (p 395). Yet neither DSM-III-R nor the training of mental health professionals addresses the cultural dimensions of religious belief required to make such a discrimination. By emphasizing the biological system and overlooking the religious and spiritual factors in mental disorders and problems, psychiatry has ignored essential knowledge about the cultural basis of behavior and organism-environment interactions (Brody, 1990).

Cultural Sensitivity Issues in Clinical Practice

The narrow focus on biological factors, combined with the historical biases against religious and spiritual experiences, impede culturally sensitive understanding and treatment of psychoreligious and psychospiritual problems. This is particularly apparent when ethnic minorities and non-Western societies are considered. According to the United Nations World Health Organization, over 70% of the world's population relies on non-allopathic systems of medicine (Mahler, 1977), and the traditional healers who operate from these models often conceptualize and treat patients' complaints as having spiritual etiologies (Westermeyer and Wintrob, 1979). For a psychiatrist to effectively work with an indigenous healer or treat the patient directly, he or she must understand the patient's cultural construction of the illness. When the cultural context of the individual is considered, some problems which present with unusual religious or spiritual content are, in fact, found to be free of psychopathology.

For example, Eisenbruch (1992) has described the "cultural bereavement" syndrome which occurs among Cambodian refugees. They often show signs of distress which are not related to acculturation difficulties, such as being visited by supernatural forces and yearning to complete obligations to the dead, amidst difficulties with daily functioning. Given their experience of being uprooted under tremendously violent circumstances, these reactions "may be a normal, even constructive, existential response, rather than a psychiatric illness" (p. 9). Western medical intervention can compound the refugee's distress and inhibit healthy aspects of the cultural bereavement process. However, through the use of culturally validated ritual, a Buddhist monk or traditional healer may successfully restore the patient's link with the past and help reintegration into the community. Eisenbruch (1991) argues that adding cultural bereavement to the nosology would refine the diagnosis of post-traumatic stress disorder and would allow for greater recognition of the refugee's existential predicament. It is our view that cultural bereavement may exemplify a psychospiritual problem occurring within a non-Western ethnic group.

Non-Western traditional cultures distinguish between serious mental illness and the psychospiritual problems experienced by some shamans-to-be (Murphy, 1978; Noll, 1983). Anthropological accounts show that babbling confused words, displaying curious eating habits, singing continuously, dancing wildly, and being "tormented by spirits" are common elements in shamanic initiatory crises (Kalweit, 1990). For example, when one shamanto-be recuperated from an episode of such unusual behavior, the elder shamans declared, "You are the sort of man who may become a shaman; you should become a shaman. You must begin to shamanize'" (Halifax, 1979, p 50). In shamanic cultures, psychospiritual crises are interpreted as an indication of an individual's destiny to become a shaman, rather than a sign of mental illness (Walsh, 1990). Individuals in Western cultures occasionally experience similar shamanic psychospiritual problems (Achterberg, 1988; Lukoff, 1991; Lukoff and Everest, 1985).

In Asian cultures as well, psychospiritual problems are distinguished from psychopathology (Walsh, 1990). For example, a well-known pitfall of spiritual practice recognized in many Asian traditions is "false enlightenment," associated with delightful or terrifying visions, especially of light (Kornfield, 1989). When these spiritual traditions are transplanted into Western contexts, such problems still occur. Grof and Grof (1989) have collected case reports of persons experiencing difficulties when engaged in the intense practice of both Western and non-Western spiritual disciplines. They argue that such cases, whether they occur as part of a spiritual practice or spontaneously, should not be diagnosed or treated as mental disorders, but rather as "spiritual emergencies" that can result in long term improvements in overall psychological well-being and functioning.

Psychoreligious or Psychospiritual Problem

To redress the lack of sensitivity to the religious and spiritual dimensions of problems that become the focus of psychiatric treatment, the authors have proposed a new Z Code category[3] to the Task Force preparing the 4th edition of the DSM, due to be published in 1993. It is entitled Psychoreligious or Psychospiritual Problem, defined as follows:

Psychoreligious problems are experiences that a person finds troubling or distressing and that involve the beliefs and practices of an organized church or religious institution. Examples include loss or questioning of a firmly held faith, change in denominational membership, conversion to a new faith, and intensification of adherence to religious practices and orthodoxy. *Psychospiritual problems* are experiences that a person finds troubling or distressing and that involve that person's reported relationship with a transcendent being or force. These problems are not necessarily related to the beliefs and practices of an organized church or religious institution. Examples include near-death experience and mystical experience. This Z Code category can be used when the focus of treatment or diagnosis is a psychoreligious or psychospiritual problem that is not attributable to a mental disorder.

The incorporation of this nonpathological category in the diagnostic nomenclature would necessitate differentiating among three different types of problems: 1) purely religious or spiritual problems; 2) mental disorders with religious or spiritual content; and 3) psychoreligious or psychospiritual problems not attributable to a mental disorder.

---

[3] In order to be consistent with the ICD-10, the DSM-III-R category of V Codes will be relabelled Z Codes in DSM-IV, defined as "Other clinically significant problems that may be the focus of diagnosis and treatment" (Task Force on DSM-I V, 1991, p U:1).

Psychoreligious Problems Religious Problems

Religious problems involve conflicts over questions of faith and doctrine. These should be, and generally are, handled by clergy. For example, a religious woman may seek out a member of the clergy to discuss her religion's view on family planning alternatives. She may initially experience some distress over the correct way to handle this issue, but after consulting a trusted religious professional, the problem of what her religion allows adherents to do (therefore what she will do) is resolved. Religious problems are usually dealt with in a church setting by a religious counselor who typically does not have training in psychotherapy (Young and Griffith, 1989).

Mental Disorders with Religious Content

Some mental disorders present with religious content. For example, individuals with obsessive-compulsive disorder have reported scrupulous devoutness, but the religiosity is used as a metaphor for the expression of compulsive requirements (Salzman, 1986). Similarly, some individuals with psychotic disorders present with delusions of being Christ or receiving direct communication from God. Even in these cases, the treatment literature documents that there is often therapeutic value in addressing a person's religious ideation (Bradford, 1985; Hoffman, et al., 1990).

Psychoreligious Problems Not Attributable to
   Mental Disorder

Psychoreligious problems involve conflicts that concern a person's religious life and beliefs, and that are not attributable to a mental disorder. In *Psychiatry and Religion: Overlapping Concerns,* Robinson (1986) noted: "Some patients have troublesome conflicts about religion that could probably be resolved through the process of therapy" (p 22). Members of the American Psychological Association reported that at least 1 in 6 of their clients presented issues which involve religion or spirituality (Shafranske and Malony, 1990). In another study, 29% of psychologists agreed that religious issues are important in the treatment of all or many of their clients (Bergin and Jensen, 1990).

A frequently reported type of Psychoreligious Problem involves *loss of a firmly held faith.* Both religious and psychiatric issues are associated with such a loss. Shafranske (1991) described a man of professional accomplishment whose life was founded upon the conservative bedrock of Roman Catholic Christianity. He came to doubt the tenets of his religion and, in so doing, declared he had lost the vitality to live.

Another type of Psychoreligious Problem involves *patients who intensify their adherence to religious practices and orthodoxy.* If the patient is newly religious, the psychotherapist needs to help determine what potential conflicts exist between his former and current lifestyle, beliefs, and attitudes. Spero (1987) described the case of a 16-year-old adolescent from a reform Jewish family who underwent a sudden religious transformation to orthodoxy. The dramatic changes in her life, including long hours studying Jewish texts, avoidance of friends, and sullenness at meals, led to her referral to a psychoanalyst. A mental status examination determined that neither schizophrenia nor any other Axis I or II disorders were present. The analysis then dealt with the impact of religious transformation on her identity and object relations. The process of religious change challenges important areas of stability, and "to some degree the sense of historical dislocation represents a crisis for all nouveau-religionists" (Spero, 1987, p 69).

Psychospiritual Problems
Spiritual Problems

Spiritual problems, which are unrelated to the practice of institutionalized religion, involve conflicts about a person's relationship to the transcendent or arise from a spiritual practice. An example of the latter would be an individual who begins meditating as a spiritual practice and starts to experience perceptual changes. Walsh and Roche (1979) have suggested that: "Such changes are not necessarily pathologic and may reflect in part a heightened sensitivity to the (usually subliminal) perceptual distortions to which we are all subject (p 1086). Spiritual problems are usually handled by individuals proficient in the relevant spiritual teachings and practices.

Mental Disorder with Spiritual Content

Manic and psychotic episodes frequently present with spiritual content (Arieti, 1976; James, 1961; Lukoff, 1985;

Podvoll, 1987). However, in these cases, the spiritual conflicts are related to or possibly attributable to an Axis I disorder. Such cases can be diagnosed with the existing DSM-III-R diagnostic categories.

Psychospiritual Problems Not Attributable to a Mental Disorder

Psychospiritual problems are conflicts that arise from spiritual experiences, and that are not attributable to a mental disorder. Two types of spiritual experiences are prominent in the clinical and research literature: mystical experience and near-death experience (NDE).

Mystical experience. Definitions used by researchers and clinicians vary considerably (Lukoff and Lu, 1988), ranging from Neumann's (1964) "upheaval of the total personality" to Greeley's (1974) "spiritual force that seems to lift you out of yourself" to Scharfstein's (1973) "everyday mysticism." A definition of mystical experience both congruent with the major theoretical literature and clinically applicable is as follows: the mystical experience is a transient, extraordinary experience marked by feelings of unity, harmonious relationship to the divine and everything in existence, as well as euphoric feelings, noesis, loss of ego functioning, alterations in time and space perception, and the sense of lacking control over the event (Allman, 1989; Hood, 1974; Stace, 1960). Numerous studies assessing the incidence of mystical experience (Back and Bourque, 1970; Greeley, 1974, 1987; Hood, 1974, 1977; Thomas and Cooper, 1980) all support the conclusion reached by Spika, et al., (1985) that 30-40% of the population have had mystical experiences, suggesting that they are normal rather than pathological phenomena.

271

In addition, a recent survey (Allman, et al., in press) has demonstrated that the number of patients who bring mystical experiences into treatment is not insignificant. Psychologists in full-time practice estimated that 4.5% of their clients over the past 12 months brought a mystical experience into therapy. This clearly challenges the GAP report which claims that "mystical experiences are rarely observed in psychotherapeutic practice" (GAP, 1976, p 799).

Near-death experience (NDE). Considerable scientific research over the past decade has established that NDE is a clearly identifiable psychological phenomenon not attributable to a mental disorder (Basford, 1990). It is a profound subjective event experienced by persons who come close to death (or who are believed dead and unexpectedly recover) as a result of serious injury or illness, or who confront a potentially fatal situation and escape uninjured (Stevenson and Greyson, 1979). Phenomenologically, NDE includes: 1) a characteristic temporal sequence of stages (i.e., peace and contentment; detachment from physical body; entering a transitional region of darkness; seeing a brilliant light; and passing through the light into another realm of existence) (Ring, 1990); as well as 2) a cluster of subjective components (i.e., strong positive affect; dissociation from the physical body; and transcendental or mystical elements). A reliable, valid, and clinically useful NDE scale (Greyson, 1983b) has been developed, which measures the various subjective elements of an individual's experience.

Both medical research (Ring, 1990; Sabom, 1982) and a nationwide poll (Gallup, 1982) indicate that about one-third of all individuals who have had a close encounter with death have experienced NDE. In 1982, Gallup

272

estimated that approximately 8 million American adults have experienced NDE. Numerous studies of the aftereffects of NDE provide strong evidence of its nonpathological nature (Greyson, 1981, 1983a; Ring, 1984). The treatment literature has addressed the problems which can follow both mystical experiences and near-death experiences. For example, Nobel (1987) noted that although mystical experience may result in greater psychological health, the process is sometimes disruptive and may prompt individuals to seek treatment. Likewise, several clinicians have focused on the significant intrapsychic and interpersonal difficulties that frequently arise in the wake of a NDE. As summarized by Greyson and Harris (1987), specific *intrapsychic* problems include: 1) ongoing anger or depression related to losing the near-death state; 2) difficulty reconciling the NDE with previous religious beliefs, values or lifestyle; 3) the fear that the NDE might indicate mental instability. *Interpersonal* problems brought about by the NDE include: 1) difficulty reconciling attitudinal changes with the expectations of family and friends; 2) a sense of isolation; 3) a fear of ridicule or rejection from others; 4) difficulty communicating the meaning and impact of the NDE; and 5) difficulty maintaining previous life roles that no longer carry the same significance.

An example of a psychospiritual problem is the case study from the previously cited GAP report which illustrates how a mystical experience can become the focus of treatment. The patient was a woman in her early thirties who sought out therapy to deal with unresolved parental struggles and guilt over a younger brother's psychosis. Approximately two years into her therapy, she under-

273

went a typical mystical experience, including a state of ecstacy, a sense of union with the universe, a heightened awareness transcending space and time, and a greater sense of meaning and purpose to her life. This experience increasingly became the focus of her continued treatment, as she worked to integrate the insights and attitudinal changes that followed. As the study reported:

> Her mood was ecstatic (if you prefer a theological term) or euphoric (if you prefer psychiatric vocabulary); it persisted for about ten days. She felt that everything in her life had led up to this momentous experience and that all her knowledge had become reorganized during its course. For her, the most important gain from it was a conviction that she was a worthwhile person with worthwhile ideas, not the intrinsically evil person, 'rotten to the core', that her mother had convinced her she was.
>
> (GAP, 1976, p 804)

Due to the rapid alteration in her mood and her unusual ideation, the authors considered diagnoses of mania, schizophrenia, and hysteria. But they rejected these because many aspects of her functioning were either unchanged or improved, and overall her experience seemed to be "more integrating than disintegrating"(p 806). They concluded that "while a psychiatric diagnosis cannot be dismissed, her experience was certainly akin to those described by great religious mystics who have found a new life through them" (p 806). Her subsequent treatment focused on expanding the insights she had gained and on helping her to assimilate the mystical experience.

Although positive personality transformations frequently follow an NDE, significant intrapsychic and interpersonal difficulties may also arise. In their study, Greyson and Harris (1987) reported that many individuals doubted their mental stability, and therefore did not discuss the NDE with friends or professionals for fear of being rejected, ridiculed, or regarded as psychotic or hysterical. One person reported, "I've lived with this thing [NDE] for three years and I haven't told anyone because I don't want them to put the straight jacket on me" (Sabom and Kreutziger, 1978, p 2). Another found that, "After this happened to me [a NDE], and I tried to tell people, they just automatically labeled me as crazy" (Moody, 1975, p 86).

In addition, there are reports of individuals who have shared their experiences with professionals and received negative reactions. One woman stated, "I tried to tell my minister, but he told me I had been hallucinating, so I shut up" (Moody, 1975, p 86). A hospitalized patient recounted that, "I tried to tell my nurses what had happened when I woke up, but they told me not to talk about it, that I was just imagining things" (p 87).

Differential Diagnosis

At first glance, the diagnosis of Adjustment Disorder would seem to fit many of the cases presented as examples of Psychoreligious and Psychospiritual Problems. However, Adjustment Disorder is appropriate only when symptoms are in excess of what would be a normal and expectable reaction to a stressor. Mystical experiences as well as psychoreligious problems (e.g., change in denominational membership) often occur without an obvious stressor (GAP, 1976), and therefore do not meet the criteria for Adjustment Disorder. Conversely, when Psychoreligious and Psychospiritual Problems are triggered by an extremely stressful event (e.g., a near-death experience), they would be comparable to the DSM-III-R V Code category for Uncomplicated Bereavement. Even when the reaction to a death meets the diagnostic criteria for Major Depression, the diagnosis of a mental disorder is not given because the symptoms result from "a normal reaction to the death of a loved one" (DSM-III-R, p 361). Similarly, in the case of NDE, sequellae involving anger, depression and interpersonal difficulties occur so frequently that they should be considered normal and expectable reactions to the stressor (Greyson and Harris, 1987). Individuals in the midst of a tumultuous Psychoreligious or Psychospiritual Problem may appear to have an Adjustment Disorder when viewed out of context, but they are actually undergoing an entirely appropriate process. Sensitive to the multicultural context of contemporary Western psychiatry, Gabbard, et al. (1982) have stated:

> It is incumbent upon us as psychiatrists to be thoroughly familiar with the range and breadth of human experience, whether pathological or healthy. We must respect and differentiate unusual but integrating experiences from those which are distressing and disorganizing. (p 368)

Accordingly, it is important to have a Z Code available for disruptive religious and spiritual experiences, because inappropriately diagnosing them as mental disorders can negatively influence their outcome (Greyson and

Harris, 1987). The clinician's response can determine whether the experience is integrated and used as a stimulus for personal growth, or whether it is repressed as a bizarre event that may be a sign of mental instability: "Attempts to classify the experience as a pathological entity are neither accurate nor helpful" (pp 44-45).

Fortunately, there are assessment tools for making differential diagnoses among religious problems, mental disorders with religious content, and Psychoreligious. Problems. Spitzer, et. al, (1980), Pruyser (1984), and Lovinger (1984) have discussed methods for distinguishing pathological uses of religion from subculturally validated forms of religious expression. Barnhouse (1986) has pointed out that the pathological significance of religious language can seldom be determined by the immediate context alone. She suggests that a religious history be part of the standard evaluation.

Some groundwork has also been laid for differentiating problematic spiritual experiences from pathological disorders. Efforts to differentiate mystical experience from psychopathological phenomena have focused upon schizophrenia (Wapnick, 1969), psychosis (Buckley, 1981; Caird, 1987; Oxman, et al., 1988), psychoactive substance-induced organic mental disorders (Lukoff, 1985, 1991), and epilepsy (Sensky, 1983). NDE has also been differentiated from similarly appearing psychoactive substance-induced hallucinations (Bates and Stanley, 1985), meditative states (Bates and Stanley, 1985), and organic brain disorders (Greyson, 1983b).

Conclusion

Mental health professionals have not accorded religious and spiritual issues in clinical practice the attention warranted by their prominence in human experience. Surveys show that religion and spirituality play a central role in the lives of most of the population, including psychiatric patients. Religiosity and spirituality are linked to psychological well-being, involve issues of love and relatedness, and provide a source of meaning and purpose in life. Yet, theory and research in psychiatry and psychology have largely devalued or ignored the religious and spiritual dimensions of life. Furthermore, the clinical literature describing presentations, assessment, treatment, and differential diagnosis of problematic aspects of religious and spiritual life has been ignored in training.

Clinicians have begun to address gender, ethnic, and racial issues. It seems that psychiatry would also benefit from giving the same consideration and emphasis to religious and spiritual issues in treatment. Significantly, the nursing profession has already established a diagnostic category of Spiritual Distress to cover two treatment situations: 1) when religious or spiritual beliefs conflict with a prescribed health regimen; and 2) when there is distress associated with a patient's mental or physical inability to practice religious or spiritual rituals (Carpenito, 1983).

The DSM-IV Options Book (Task Force on DSM-IV, 1991) notes that the V Code section of DSM-III-R "excluded many important reasons for presentation to mental health practitioners" (p U:1). However, none of the proposed categories acknowledge psychoreligious or psychospiritual problems. Efforts to reconcile DSM-IV with the most recent revision of the World Health Organization's (1992) *International Classification of Diseases (ICD-10)*, include a number of new Z Code categories. Yet, none of the *ICD-10* categories acknowledge psychoreligious or psychospiritual problems either. The category for "life-cycle transitions" (e.g., retirement, empty nest syndrome) is not appropriate, because psychoreligious or psychospiritual problems can occur at virtually any point in the life-cycle from childhood to old age (Armstrong, 1984). Furthermore, assigning one of the Z Codes related to "social circumstances" or "social environment" would not alert clinicians to the available strategies for assessing and treating specific psychoreligious and psychospiritual problems.

We recognize that further research on psychoreligious and psychospiritual problems is needed, covering forms of presentation, prevalence, associated features, and differential diagnosis. However, the lack of definitive research at the present time should not preclude the recognition of such problems in the diagnostic classification system. As Wing (1977) points out, one of the key tests for the validity of a diagnosis is whether it results in improved treatment:

To put forward a diagnosis is, first of all, to recognize a condition, and then to put forward a theory about it. Theories are meant to be tested. The most obvious test is whether applying the theory is helpful to the patient. Does it accurately predict a form of treatment that reduces disability without leading to harmful side effects? (p 87)

The proposed new Z Code category for DSM-IV would redress the cultural insensitivity currently surrounding the treatment of religious and spiritual issues in the following ways: 1) increase the accuracy of diagnostic assessments when religious and spiritual issues are involved; 2) reduce the occurrence of iatrogenic harm from misdiagnosis of psychoreligious and psychospiritual problems; 3) result in improved treatment of such problems by stimulating clinical research; and 4) encourage clinical training centers to address the religious and spiritual dimensions of human experience.

References

Achterberg J (1988) The wounded healer: Transformational journeys in modern medicine. In G Doore (Ed), *Shaman's Path*. Boston: Shambala Publications.

Allman L (1989) *Mystical experience as a clinical issue in psychology*. Dissertation, Pepperdine University, Los Angeles.

Allman L, de la Rocha 0, Elkin D, Weathurs R (in press) Psychotherapists' attitude towards clients reporting mystical experiences. *Psychotherapy*

American Psychiatric Association (1987) *Diagnostic and statistical manual of mental disorders* (3rd ed, rev). Washington, DC: Author

Anderson RG, Young JL (1988) The religious component of acute hospital treatment. *Hospital and Community Psychiatry* 39:528-533.

APA Task Force on Religion and Psychiatry (1975) *Psychiatrists' viewpoint on religion and their services to religious institutions and the ministry*. Washington, DC: American Psychiatric Association. Arieti S (1976) Creativity: *The magic synthesis*. New York: Basic Books. Armstrong T (1984) Transpersonal experience in childhood. *Journal of Transpersonal Psychology* 16:207-230.

Back K, Bourque L (1970) Can feelings be enumerated? *Behav Science* 15:487-496.

Barnhouse RT (1986) How to evaluate patients' religious ideation, in *Psychiatry and religion: Overlapping concerns*, Washington, DC: American Psychiatric Press.

Basford T K (1990) *Near-death experience: An annotated bibliography.* New York: Garland.

Bates B, Stanley A (1985) The epidemiology and differential diagnosis of near-death experience. *American Journal of Orthopsychiatry* 55:542-549.

Bergin A (1983) Religiosity and mental health: A critical re-evaluation and meta-analysis. *Professional Psychology* 14:170-184.

Bergin A, Jensen J (1990) Religiosity of psychotherapists: A national survey. *Psychotherapy* 27: 3-7.

Bradford D (1985) A therapy of religious imagery for paranoid schizophrenic psychosis. In M Spero (Ed), *Psychotherapy of the religious patient.* Springfield, IL: Charles C Thomas.

Brody EB (1990) The new biological determinism in sociocultural context *Aust New Zealand Journal of Psychiat* 24:464-469.

Browning Browing D, Gobe T, Evison I (1990) Religious and ethical factors in psychiatric practice. Chicago: Nelson-Hall.

Buckley P (1981) Mystical experience and schizophrenia. *Schizophr Bull* 7:516-521.

Caird D (1987) Religion and personality: Are mystics introverted, neurotic, or psychotic? *Br Journal of Soc Psychology* 26:345-346.

Carpenito L (1983) *Nursing diagnosis: Application to clinical practice.* Philadelphia: J.B. Lippincott.

Deikman A (1977) Comments on the GAP Report on Mysticism. *Journal of Nervous and Mental Disorders* 165:213-217.

Eisenbruch M (1991) From post-traumatic stress disorder to cultural bereavement: Diagnosis of Southeast Asian refugees. *Soc Sci Med* 33:673-680.

Eisenbruch M (1992) Commentary: Toward a culturally sensitive DSM: Cultural bereavement in Cambodian refugees and the traditional healer as taxonomist. *Journal of Nervous and Mental Disorders* 180:8-10.

Ellis A (1980) Psychotherapy and atheistic values: A response to A. E. Bergin's "Psychotherapy and Religious Issues." *Journal of Consulting and Clinical Psychology* 48:635-639.

Fabrega H (1987) Psychiatric diagnosis: A cultural perspective. *Journal of Nervous and Mental Disorders* 175(7): 383-394.

Fabrega H (1992) Commentary. Diagnosis interminable: Toward a culturally sensitive DSM-IV *Journal of Nervous and Mental Disorders* 180:415-425.

Feldman J, Rust J (1989) Religiosity, schizotypal thinking, and schizophrenia. *Psychology Rep* 65:587-593.

Flynn C P (1982) Meanings and implications of NDEr transformations: Some preliminary findings and implications. *Anabiosis* 2:3-14.

Freud S (1959) Civilization and its discontents. In J Strachey (Ed, Trans) *The standard edition of the complete psychological works of Sigmund Freud* Vol. 20. London: Hogarth.

Freud S (1966) Obsessive actions and religious practices. In J Strachey (Ed, Trans) *The standard edition of the complete psychological works of Sigmund Freud* Vol.1, London: Hogarth.

Gabbard GO, Twemlow SW, Jones FC (1982) Differential diagnosis of altered mind/body perception. *Psychiatry* 45:361-369.

Gallup G (1985) 50 Years of Gallup Surveys on Religion. *The Gallup Report*. Report No. 236.

Gallup G Jr (1982) *Adventures in immortality: A look beyond the threshold of death.* New York, NY: McGraw-Hill.

Greeley A (1974) *Ecstacy: A way of knowing.* Englewood Cliffs, NJ: Prentice Hall.

Greeley A (1987) Mysticism goes mainstream. *Am Health* Jan/Feb 47-49.

Greyson B (1981) Near-death experiences and attempted suicide. *Suicide Life Threat Behav* 11:10-16.

Greyson B (1983a) Near-death experience and personal values. *American Journal of Psychiatry* 140:618-620.

Greyson B (1983b) The near-death experience scale: Construction, reliability, and validity. *Journal of Nervous and Mental Disorders* 171:369-375.

Greyson B, Harris B (1987) Clinical approaches to the near-death experience. *Journal of Near-Death Studies* 6:41-52.

Grof S and Grof C (Eds) (1989) *Spiritual emergency: When personal transformation becomes a crisis.* Los Angeles: Tarcher.

Group for Advancement of Psychiatry (1976) *Mysticism: Spiritual quest or mental disorder.* New York: Author.

Halifax J (1979) *Shamanic voices.* New York: Dutton.

Hoffman S, Laub B, Zim S (1990) Collaboration of clergy and psychotherapists in treating psychiatric patients. *Israeli J Relat Science* 27: 180-185.

Hood RW (1974) Psychological strength and the report of intense religious experience. *J Sci Study Religion,* 13:65-71.

Hood RW (1976) Conceptual criticisms of regressive explanations of mysticism. *Rev Relig Research* 17:179-188.

Hood RW (1977) Differential triggering of mystical experience as a function of self-actualization. *Rev Relig Res* 18: 264-270.

Horton PC (1974) The mystical experience: Substance of an illusion. *American Psychoanalytic Assoc Journal* 22(1-2):364-380.

James W (1961) *The varieties of religious experience.* New York: MacMillan.

Jung CG (1973) *Psychology and religion.* Princeton, NJ: Princeton University Press.

Kalweit H (1989) When insanity is a blessing: The message of shamanism. In S Grof and C Grof (Eds), *Spiritual emergency: When personal transformation becomes a crisis.* Los Angeles: Tarcher.

Kleinman A (1988) *Rethinking psychiatry.* New York: Free Press.

Kornfield J (1989) Obstacles and vicissitudes in spiritual practice. In S Grof, C Grof (Eds), *Spiritual emergency: When personal transformation becomes a crisis.* Los Angeles: Tarcher.

Krippner, S, Welch, P (1992) *Spiritual dimensions of healing.* New York: Irvington Publishers.

Kroll J, Sheehan W (1989) Religious beliefs and practices among 52 psychiatric inpatients in Minnesota. *American Journal of Psychiatry* 146: 67-72.

Kung H (1990) *Freud and the problem of God.* New Haven, CT: Yale University Press.

Lannert J (1991) Countertransference and spirituality. *J Humanistic Psychology* 31:68-76.

Laor N (1989) Psychoanalytic neutrality toward religious experience. *Psychoanal Study Child* 44:211-230.

Larson DB, Pattison M, Blazer DG, Omran A, Berton K (1986) Systematic analysis of research on religious variables in four major psychiatric journals, 1978-1982. *American Journal of Psychiatry* 143:329-334.

Leuba JH (1929) *Psychology of religious mysticism.* New York: Harcourt Brace.

Lovinger R (1985) Religious imagery in the psychotherapy of a borderline patient. In MH Spero (Ed), *Psychotherapy of the religious patient.* Springfield, IL: Charles C Thomas.

Lovinger R (1984) *Working with religious issues in therapy.* New York: Aronson.

Lukoff D (1985) Diagnosis of mystical experiences with psychotic features. *Journal of Transpersonal Psychology* 17: 155-181.

Lukoff D, Everest H (1985) The myths in mental illness. *J Transpersonal Psychology* 17:123-153.

Lukoff D (1991) Divine madness: Shamanistic initiatory crisis and psychosis. *Shaman's Drum* 22:24-29.

Lukoff D, Lu F (1988) Transpersonal psychology research review topic: Mystical experience. *Journal of Transpersonal Psychology* 20: 161-184.

Mahler H (Nov 1977) The staff of Aesculapius. *World Health* Nov: 3.

Mandel A J (1980) Toward a psychobiology of transcendence: God in the brain. In RJ Davidson and JM Davidson (Eds), *The psychobiology of consciousness*. New York: Plenum.

Maslow A (1971) *The farther reaches of human nature*. New York: Viking.

Maslow A (1962) *Toward a psychology of being*. Princeton, NJ: D. Van Nostrand.

Mezzich J, Fabrega H, Kleinman A (1992) Editorial: Cultural validity and DSM-IV. *Journal of Nervous and Mental Disorders* 180: 4

Moody RA (1975) *Life after life*. New York: Bantam Books.

Murphy J (1978) The recognition of psychosis in non-Western societies. In RL Spitzer, DF Klein (Eds), *Critical issues in psychiatric diagnosis*. New York: Raven.

Neumann E (1964) Mystical man. In J Campbell (Ed), *The mystic vision*. Princeton, NJ: Princeton University Press.

Nobel KD (1987) Psychological health and the experience of transcendence. *The Counseling Psychologist* 15: 601-614.

Noll R (1983) Shamanism and schizophrenia: A state specific approach to the "schizophrenia metaphor" of shamanic states. *American Ethnologist* 10: 443-459.

Oxman T, Rosenberg S, Schnurr P, Tucker G, Gala G (1988) The language of altered states. *Journal of NervMental Dis* 176: 401-408.

Peterson EA, Nelson K (1987) How to meet your clients' spiritual needs. *Journal of Psychosoc Nursing* 25:34-39.

Podvoll E (1987) Mania and the risk of power. *Journal of Contemplative Psychotherapy* 4:95-122.

Pollner M (1989) Divine relations, social relations, and well-being. *Journal of Health and Social Behavior* 30:92-104.

Post SG (1990) DSM-III-R and religion (ltr). *American Journal of Psychiatry* 147:813.

Pruyser PW (1984) Religion in the psychiatric hospital: A reassessment. *Journal of Pastoral Care* 38:5-17.

Ragan C, Maloney HN, Beit-Hallahmi B (1980) Psychologists and religion: Professional factors and personal belief. *Rev Religious Res* 21:208-217.

Ring K (1984) *Heading toward omega: In search of the meaning of the near-death experience*. New York: William Morrow.

Ring K (1990) *Life at death: A scientific investigation of the near-death experience*. New York: Coward, McGann & Geoghegan.

Robinson L (1986) Psychoanalysis and religion: A comparison. In L Robinson (Ed), *Psychiatry and religion: Overlapping concerns* Washington, DC: American Psychiatric Press.

Sabom MB, Kreutiziger S (1978) Physicians evaluate the near-death experience: *Theta* 6:1-6.

Sabom MB (1982) *Recollections of death: A medical investigation*. New York: Harper & Row.

Salzman L (1986) Religion as metaphor in mental illness. In L Robinson (Ed), *Psychiatry and religion: Overlapping concerns*, Washington, DC: American Psychiatric Press.

Sansone RA, Khatain K, Rodenhauser P (1990) The role of religion in psychiatric education: A national survey. *Acad Psychiatry* 14:34-38.

Scharfstein B (1973) *Mystical experience*. New York: Bobbs-Merrill.

Sensky T (1983) Religiosity, mystical experience and epilepsy. In FC Rose (Ed), *Research Progress in Epilepsy*. New York: Pitman.

Shafranske E (1991) Beyond countertransference: On being struck by faith, doubt and emptiness. Paper presented at the annual conference of the American Psychological Association, New Orleans, LA.

Shafranske E, Malony HN (1990) Clinical psychologists' religious and spiritual orientations and their practice of psychotherapy. *Psychotherapy* 27:72-78.

Spanos N P, Moretti P (1988) Correlates of mystical and diabolical experiences in a sample of female university students. *Journal for the Scien Study of Religion*, 27:105-116.

Spero MH (1987) Identity and individuality in the nouveau-religious patient: Theoretical and clinical aspects. *Psychiatry* 50:55-71.

Spika B, Hood R, Gorsuch R (1985) *The psychology of religion: An empirical approach*. Englewood, NJ: Prentice-Hall.

Spitzer RL, Gibbon M, Skodol A, Williams JBW, Hyler S (1980) The heavenly vision of a poor woman: A down to earth discussion of DSM-III differential diagnosis. *Journal of Oper Psychiatry* 11(2):169-172.

285

Stace WT (1960) *Mysticism and philosophy.* Philadelphia: Lippincott.
Stevenson I, Greyson B (1979) Near-death experiences. JAMA 242:265-267.
Task Force on DSM-IV (7/1/91) DSM-IV *options book.* Washington, DC: American Psychiatric Association
Thomas L, Cooper P (1980) Incidence and psychological correlates of intense spiritual experiences. *Journal of Transpersonal Psychology* 12(1): 75-85.
Underhill E (1955) *Mysticism: A study in the nature and development of man's spiritual consciousness.* New York: Meridian Books.
Walsh R (1990) *The spirit of shamanism.* Los Angeles: Jeremy Tarcher.
Walsh R, Roche L (1979) Precipitation of acute psychotic episodes by intensive meditation in individuals with a history of schizophrenia. *American Journal of Psychiatry,* 136: 1085-1086.
Wapnick K (1969) Mysticism and schizophrenia. *J Transpersonal Psychol* 1:49-67.
Westermeyer J, Wintrob R (1979) "Folk" explanations of mental illness in rural Laos. *American Journal of Psychiatry,* 136:901-905.
Wing J (1977) The limits of standardization . In V Rakoff, H Stancer, H Kedward (Eds), *Psychiatric Diagnosis* New York: Bruner/ Mazel.
World Health Organization (1992) *The International Classification of Mental and Behavioural Disorders.* Geneva: WHO
Young JL, Griffith EE (1989) The development and practice of pastoral counseling. *Hospital and Community Psychiatry* 40:271-276.

Appendix D

Referrals

This section is divided into four headings. "SEN and the Conferences of 1985" gives a brief introduction to SEN and the people who contributed to this book. "References to Referral Networks" gives the names, addresses and phone numbers of networks that refer people to Helpers. "24 Hour Care Centers" gives the names and addresses of sanctuaries for people in crisis. "Literature on the Phenomenology of Spiritual Emergence and Emergency" is a list of books that would be helpful for anyone wanting to know more about the topic. "Movies and Audio Tapes" is an annotated list of resources for audio and audio-visual presentations that illustrate themes pertaining to spiritual emergence.

SEN and the Conferences of 1985

The Spiritual Emergence Network conferences of 1985 were held for the following purposes:

1. To enhance communication between clinicians working with people in spiritual emergency.
2. To increase our understanding of diagnosis where phenomena of spiritual emergence are present.
3. To understand the role of residential treatment centers for people in spiritual emergency.
4. To understand the role of Helpers who support people in spiritual emergence and emergency.
5. To consider the elements that catalyze spiritual emergence within individuals and within collective groups.
6. To support the development of the Spiritual Emergence Network.

The conferences each focused on producing particular products. The October, 1985, conference participants collected ideas towards creating a "Training Manual" for teaching professionals and paraprofessionals how to work with people undergoing crises of spiritual emergence. The May, 1985, conference dedicated some intensive work toward questions of enhancing communication and networking SEN on a worldwide basis.

Note: To preserve the privacy and exploratory nature of the work at the SEN conferences, 1985, we decided not to make the tapes of the conferences available to the general public. Our agreement with the participants is that none of the discussions or presentations would be quoted in publications without their prior consent.

The participants who attended the conferences were psychologists, psychiatrists, administrators, social workers, spiritual teachers, monastics, and students of transpersonal psychology. Following is a list of these people, a short description of their work, and the topic of their talk, if they gave one.

The May, 1985, Conference Participants:

Anne and Jim Armstrong: Anne is a psychic counselor who, together with her husband, Jim, teach people how to use their intuition. They spoke on "Psychic Opening and Spiritual Emergence."

Angeles Arrien, M.A.: symbol consultant, anthropologist and teacher of universal symbols and Shamanism. Arrien spoke about "Universal Symbols in Spiritual Emergence."

Dominie Cappadonna, Ph.D.: teacher of transpersonal psychology, healer, and tour guide. Cappadonna spoke about "Global Spiritual Emergence."

Susanna Davila, Ph.D.: administrator of the Transpersonal Counseling Center at the Institute of Transpersonal Psychology, supervisor for the Spiritual Emergence Network.

Christina Grof and Stanislav Grof, M.D.: authors and founders of SEN; S. Grof has done over 20 years of research in the area of consciousness studies. Dr. Grof dialogued with Lama Sogyal Rinpoche on the subject of "Diagnosing Spiritual Emergency." He and Christina also dialogued with the Hendricks on the similarities and differences in their respective work with the body using the breath.

Gay Hendricks, Ph.D. and Kathlyn Hendricks, Ph.D., A.D.T.R.: therapists and teachers of transpersonal breathwork, the Hendricks spoke on "Spiritual Emergence/ Emergency as a Somatic Experience."

Voyce Hendrix and Betty Dahlquist: administrators of California Association of the Social Rehabilitation Agencies. They participated in the discussion led by Telles on "Organizing Residential Treatment Centers and Educational Models for Training Counselors."

Charles Lonsdale, M.A.: (then) administrator of SEN.

Francis Lu, M.D.: psychiatrist and assistant clinical professor at the University of California. Dr. Lu spoke about his work and dialogued with Ralph Metzner on "The Use of Pharmaceuticals for People in Spiritual Emergency."

Ralph Metzner, Ph.D.: psychologist, author, administrator at California Institute of Integral Studies. Metzner spoke on "Diagnosing Spiritual Emergence" and dialogued with Dr. Lu on "The Use of Pharmaceuticals for People in Spiritual Emergency."

Lama Sogyal Rinpoche: an honored spiritual teacher from Tibet, spoke on "Diagnosing Spiritual Emergency."

Sharon Solfvin, M.A.: administrator at J.F.K. University and counselor.

Lawrence Telles, Ph.D.: academic philosopher, coordinator of invited conferences on "Psychosocial Alternatives to Traditional Psychiatric Care." Telles spoke about his work "Organizing Residential Treatment Centers and Educational Models for Training Counselors."

Bryan Wittine, Ph.D.: transpersonal therapist and (then) administrator at J.F.K. University's School of Consciousness Studies. Wittine spoke about "Transpersonal Therapy and the Dark Night of the Soul."

Frances Vaughan, Ph.D.: professor of transpersonal psychology, author, and psychologist. Vaughan spoke about "Transpersonal Psychotherapy and Ego Development."

Karen Paine-Gernee: educator and counselor, spoke about "Spiritual Emergence and Adult Children of Alcoholics."

Mitchell May, M.A.: healer and educator. May spoke about "Physical Emergencies which Precipitate Spiritual Emergence."

Dick Price: (then) president of Esalen Institute.

Father Thomas: Benedictine monk, dialogued with Brother David and Dick Price on "Communities which Foster Spiritual Emergence."

Brother David Steindl-Rast: Benedictine monk, author and lecturer on Eastern and Western Spirituality. Brother David dialogued on "Communities which Foster Spiritual Emergence."

Peggy Taylor and Paul Taylor, Ph.D.: (then) coordinators for SEN at Esalen, and transpersonal counselors.

Emma Bragdon, William Brater, Eric Lehrman, Megan Nolan, Ph.D., David Rasch. SEN Volunteers.

290

The October, 1985 SEN Conference Participants:

Jamie Baraz: spiritual teacher within the Vipassana community. Baraz spoke on "Managing Spiritual Crises in Spiritual Communities."

Mara Suzana Behlau and Roberto Zeimer: SEN Regional Coordinators from Brazil. They spoke about "Supporting Spiritual Emergence in South America."

Roger Bunting: administrator of Metasystems Design Group, Inc. Bunting discussed "Networking" and, more specifically, "Metasystem Computer Technology."

Elizabeth Campbell, Ph.D.: moderator of the conference, (then) administrator of the External Degree program at the Institute of Transpersonal Psychology, teacher. Campbell spoke on "Networking."

Cecil Chamberlin, M.D.: psychiatrist at the Menninger Foundation, and SEN Regional Coordinator in Kansas. Dr. Chamberlin spoke about his work and "Supporting Spiritual Emergence in North America."

Susanna Davila,Ph.D.: Administrator of the Transpersonal Center and supervisor for SEN at the Institute of Transpersonal Psychology.

Christina Grof and Stanislav G rof, M.D.: founders of SEN. They spoke about "Supporting Spiritual Emergence Internationally."

Willis Harman, Ph.D.: President of the Institute of Noetic Sciences, professor at Stanford, Senior Social Scientist at Stanford Research Institute, and author. Harman spoke on "The Emerging Global Consciousness."

Michel Henry: administrator of a philanthropic organization and teacher. Henry spoke about "Global Networking."

Frank Kretschmer, M.A.: Regional Coordinator for SEN in Germany, transpersonal therapist. Kretschmer spoke with Pennington on "Supporting Spiritual Emergence in Europe."

Alicia Mayo: SEN Regional Coordinator in Mexico, counselor and educator. Mayo spoke on "Curanderismo: A Healing System of Mexico" and her work supporting spiritual emergence in Mexico.

Megan Nolan, Ph.D.: (then) Administrator of SEN. Nolan gave current information about SEN.

Judith Orloff, M.D.: psychiatrist and regional coordinator for SEN in southern California.

George Pennington: SEN regional coordinator in Germany, transpersonal counselor, administrator of a residential treatment facility in Germany, "Esse." Pennington spoke on "Supporting Spiritual Emergence in Europe."

John Perry, M.D.: psychiatrist, author, past coordinator of Diabasis- a residential treatment center in San Francisco. Dr. Perry spoke about "Residential Treatment Centers: A Model for World-Wide Use."

Dick Price: (then) president of Esalen Institute. Price dialogued with Perry on "Residential Treatment Centers."

Swami Radha: spiritual teacher from Canada. Swami Radha spoke about "Managing Spiritual Crisis in Spiritual Communities."

Aminah Raheem, Ph.D.: teacher of Jin Shin Do at Institute of Transpersonal Psychology, Transpersonal Integration Practitioner. Raheem spoke on "Identifying Crises of Spiritual Emergence and Facilitating Transformation."

Lee Sannella, M.D.: psychiatrist, opthalmologist, author. Sannella discussed "What Makes a Good Helper?"

Jacquelyn Small, MSSW: author, teacher, and counselor. Small talked about "Identifying Crises of Spiritual Emergence and Facilitating Transformation." She also led an experiential session in Holotropic Breathwork.

Brother David Steindl-Rast: Benedictine monk, lecturer, and author. Brother David spoke about his experiences "Supporting Spiritual Emergence Internationally."

Peggy Taylor and Paul Taylor, Ph.D.: (then) SEN coordinators at Esalen, transpersonal counselors. Paul Taylor spoke on "The New Physics and Spiritual Emergence."

Larry Telles, Ph.D.: academic philosopher and administrator in the field of psycho-social rehabilitation. Telles dialogued with Perry on "Residential Treatment Centers."

Emma Bragdon, David Warren, Ph.D., Edris Head, Eric Lehrman, Ruth Norman. SEN Volunteers.

References to Referral Networks

The Spiritual Emergence Network began in 1980 to educate people about spiritual emergence phenomena and refer individuals to qualified Helpers for support and/or therapy.

The Spiritual Emergence Network has been renamed the "Center for Psychological and Spiritual Health" and is located at the California Institute for Integral Studies, in San Francisco, CA. They offer information, referrals, and support for individuals experiencing difficulty with psycho-spiritual growth. As of November, 2005, their website reports " It may take up to one week for emails and calls to be returned". They offer phone consultations and referrals, PST, only at: (415) 575-6299. Email: mailto:cpsh@ciis.edu Their website http://www.cpsh.org/ is an excellent resource. If you search "spiritual emergence network" on the WWW, you will find other resources in other countries.

The Spiritual Competency Resource Center, http://www.virtualcs.com/ offers a roster of information and general referrals on its website.

24-Hour Care Centers:

Pocket Sanctuary is a retreat center close to Tucson, Arizona committed to honoring the transformational potential in all psychological crises, including spiritual emergencies. A dedicated, licensed staff are trained in a variety of modalities. Programs incorporate expressive therapies such as art and sand-tray, guided imagery, emotional release work, integrative bodywork, meditation, sweat lodge, and transpersonal approaches such as breathwork. This center is not set up to work with people who require assistance with medications.

293

Barbara Findeisen, MA, MFC, the originator of the Star Program, is available for outpatient psychotherapy tailored to the needs of individuals who come to Pocket Sanctuary for retreat. She can be reached at (520) 398-8073.

The Star Program is a 10-day process that addresses childhood issues, adult dysfunctional behaviors, and/or a desire for personal growth. Star Programs are held in Arizona at 'Pocket Sanctuary'. **The Star Foundation, (888) 857-STAR * (707) 857-3359. mailto:starfoundation@pobox.com**

Soteria Associates in San Diego, CA. is dedicated to referring people to healthcare professionals and care centers who use a miniumum of psychiatric drugs. Contact: Judy Schreiber. Email: **Mosher_Schreiber@yahoo.com. Website: http://www.moshersoteria.com/**

Literature on the Phenomenology of Spiritual Problems

The following books are appropriate to educate yourself further on the experiences people have had as they reach transpersonal states of consciousness. These books are also educational for clients looking for more information about transpersonal states of consciousness.

Beggin, P. *Toxic Psychiatry: Why Therapy, Empathy and Love Must Replace the Drugs, Electroshock and Biochemical Theories of the 'New Psychiatry'*. New York: St. Martin's Press, 1991.

Capra, F., *The Tao of Physics*, Boulder, Co.: Shambhala, 1975.

Capra, F., *The Turning Point*, N.Y.: Simon and Schuster, 1982.

Da Free John, *The Dawn Horse Testaments* San Rafael, CA: Dawn Horse Press, 1985.

Dass, Ram, *The Only Dance There Is*, New York: Doubleday and Co., 1974.

Golas, T., *The Lazy Man's Guide To Enlightenment*, New York: Bantam, 1972.

Gopi Krishna, Kundalini, *The Evolutionary Energy in Man*, Berkeley, CA: Shambhala, 1971.

Greenwell, B., *Energies of Transformation: A Guide to the Kundalini Process*, CA: Shakti River Press, 1990.

Grof, S., *Beyond the Brain*, Albany, NY: State University of New York Press, 1985.

Grof, S.,(Ed.) "Revision", *Journal of Consciousness and Change*, Vol.8,#1,1985.

Grof, S. and C. Grof, (Ed), *Spiritual Emergency When Personal Transformation Becomes a Crisis*, Los Angeles: Tarcher, 1989.

Grof, S. and C. Grof, *The Stormy Search for the Self*, Los Angeles: Tarcher, 1990.

Haich, E., *Initiation*, Palo Alto, CA: The Seed Center, 1974.

James, W., *Varieties of Religious Experience*, NY: Collier Books, 1961. Hastings, A. *With the Tongues of Men and Angels; A Study of Channeling*, Orlando, FL: Holt, Rinehard and Winston, 1991.

Hixon, L., *Coming Home: The Experience of Enlightenment in Sacred Traditions,* Los Angeles, CA: J. P. Tarcher, 1989.

Keyes, K., *Handbook to Higher Consciousness,.* Coos Bay, Oregon: Living Love Publications, 1972

Lucas, W.B., *Regression Therapy: A Handbook for Professionals, Vol. I &II.,* Creset Park, Ca.: Deep Forest Press, 1993.

Maslow, A.H., *Religions, Values, and Peak Experiences,* NY: Viking Press, 1970.

Monroe, R., *Journeys Out of the Body,* Garden City, NJ: Doubleday, 1971.

Podvoll, E., *The Seduction of Madness.* New York: HarperCollins, 1990.

Nelson, J., *Healing the Split, Madness or Transcendence?* Los Angeles: J. Tarcher, 1990.

Rama, Swami, Ajaya, Swami, and Ballentine,R., *Yoga and Psychotherapy: The Evolution of Consciousness,* Honesdale, PA: Himalayan International Institute, 1976.

Ring, K., Heading Toward Omega, NY: William Morrow and Co., 1984.

Ring, K., *The Omega Project: Near-Death Experiences, UFO Encounters, and Mind at Large.* NY: William Morrow and Co., 1992.

Sannella, L., *Kundalini: Psychosis or Transcendence,* San Francisco: H.S. Dakin, 1976.

Schaef, A.W., *Beyond Therapy, Beyond Science,* San Francisco, CA: Harper San Francisco, 1992.

Shepard, L., *Living with Kundalini: The Autobiography of Gopi Krishna.* Boston: Shambhala, 1993.

Small, J., *Transformers: The Therapists of the Future,* Marina Del Rey, CA: DeVorss and Co., 1982.

Sogyal Rinpoche, *Tibetan Book of Living and Dying,* San Francisco, CA: Harper, 1992.

Trungpa, C., and Freemantle, F., *Tibetan Book of the Dead,* Berkeley, CA: Shambhala, 1975.

Walsh, R., and Vaughan, F., *Beyond Ego,* LA: Tarcher, 1980.

Weil, A., *The Natural Mind, a New Way of Looking at Drugs and Higher Consciousness,* NY: Houghton Mifflin, 1972.

Weiss, B., *Many Lives, Many Masters.* New York: Simon & Schuster, 1988.

White, J., *What is Enlightenment?* L.A.: Tarcher, 1984.

Wilber, K., *Atman Project: A Transpersonal View of Human Development,* Wheaton, Ill.: Theosophical Publishing House, 1980.

Yogananda, P., *Autobiography of a Yogi,* LA: Self-Realization Fellowship, 1946.

Movies, CDs, and Audiotapes

A broad selection of audiotaped interviews on spiritual emergence phenomena with authors, teachers and health professionals are avalilable through:

New Dimensions Radio
1-800-935-TAPE
http://www.newdimensions.org/

Audiotaped and videotaped presentations from conferences in various parts of the world on topics related to spiritual emergence are available through:

Conference Recording Service/New Medicine Tape
1308 Gilman Street
Berkeley, CA 94706
510-527-3600

Conference recordings from the International Transpersonal Association and the Association of Transpersonal Psychology are highly recommended.

Videos on topics related to transformative visions, alternative realities and creativity are available through:

Mystic Fire Video
Website: http://www.mysticfire.com/
800-292-9001

A series of thought-provoking interviews between Jeffrey Mishlove, Ph.D., and pioneering health professionals representing transpersonal psychology is available through:

Thinking Allowed Productions
http://www.thinking-allowed.com/
800-999-4415

Especially recommended is the video titled "Spiritual Psychology" with Frances Vaughan, Ph.D. (Spirituality and Psychology), Seymoor Boomstein, M.D. (Psychology and Spiritual Paths), Edith Fiore, Ph.D. (Past-Life Regression and Depossession), and John Weir Perry, M.D. (Visionary Experience or Psychosis?).

Duvall Media
PO Box 15892
Newport Beach, CA 92659

Especially recommended are "Journey to the Edge and Milestones to Recovery" as well as an interview by Naomi Steinfeld.

The following major motion pictures highlight reflections on spiritual emergence phenomena. They are readily available through major video stores.

Emergence of a Karmic Pattern

Groundhog Day	Dead Again
Defending Your Life	Truly, Madly, Deeply
Flat Liners	Grand Canyon

Mystical Experience
including Near Death Experience

Resurrection   Fearless
Brainstorm   Always

Shamanic Journey

Emerald Forest   The Wave
Birdie   A Man Called Horse
Dances With Wolves   Altered States
The Dark Crystal   Never Cry Wolf

Activation of the Central Archetype

The Fisher King   Legend
Star Trek Series   Excalibur
Star Wars Trilogy   Zardoz
The Never Ending Story   Jason and the Argonauts
The Magic Flute (Bergman)
The Adventures of Baron VonMunchausen

Psychic Opening

Resurrection   Regarding Henry
The Abyss   Carrie
Bliss   Dead Zone

Possession

Big   All of Me
Switch   King Lear

Extraterrestrials

E. T.
Cocoon
Enemy Mine
Brother from Another Planet
Close Encounters of the Third Kind

Starman
Communion
Fire in the Sky

Spectrum of Spiritual Experiences

Baraka
Dreams

The Seventh Seal

Confusion: Psychosis, Religious and/or Spiritual Problem

The Rapture
Jesus of Montreal
Gospel According to Matthew
The Last Temptation of Christ

Thornbirds
Man Facing Southeast

Psychotic Experience/Creative Individuals

Frances
An Angel at my Table

Crazypeople

Trancending Physical Disability Through Spiritual Strength

My Left Foot
The Miracle Worker

Gaby

Appendix E _____

Glossary

Atman: A level or state of consciousness described as the radically perfect integration of all prior levels of consciousness.

Bio-energy: The fundamental source that pulsates and charges the body; the root of all subjective experience, body expression (including emotion) and movement (Lowen,1958; Kelley, 1970).

Breathwork: A therapeutic modality using amplification of breathing to energize and support the psychic/somatic homeostatic process.

COEX system: System of condensed experience; intense experiences from previous personal history including birth and past-lives, which have not yet been metabolized and exist in one's psychic structure inhibiting further development to some extent (Grof, 1985).

Ego: The organizing principle of the lower self.

Helper: A professional or paraprofessional who acts as a companion and guide to a person in spiritual emergence/emergency.

Kundalini: The creative energy of the universe which lies dormant at the base of the human spine until activated; when activated it rises up the spine as active energy—opening, clearing, and lighting the energetic centers of the body (Mookerjee, 1982).

Psychosis: An episode of impairment of higher mental faculties, with abnormalities in reality testing, memory, language, rational thinking, and speech.

Self-structure: The level or structure of consciousness attained in an individual's development. It is assumed that once a level of consciousness emerges in human development, it tends to remain in existence in the life of the individual during subsequent development (Wilber, 1985 a & b).

Spiritual emergence: The process of personal awakening into a level of perceiving and functioning that is beyond normal ego functioning. It involves having spiritual experiences and integrating these experiences into a positive framework for increased well being.

Spiritual emergency: Profound disorientation and instability that sometimes accompany intense spiritual experiences. Spiritual emergency appears as an acute psychotic episode lasting between minutes and weeks. It has a positive, transformative outcome.

Spiritual experience: Any experience of the transpersonal level of consciousness.

Subtle: A level or state of consciousness where there may be manifestations of psi phenomena, out-of-body experience, expanded sensory perceptions, and deep inspiration. At this level of consciousness one may have direct experience of archetypes and perceptions of God.

Transpersonal: Having to do with experiences that are beyond normal ego states, i.e., extraordinary well-being, optimal psychological health.

Permissions

The author is deeply appreciative for permissions granted to reprint articles.

The article entitled "Mysticism Goes Mainstream" was originally published by American Health Partners in 1987. It is reprinted by permission of the author, Andrew Greeley.

Jossey-Bass, Inc., Grune and Stratton, and the authors, L. Mosher and A. Menn gave permission to reprint the article "Soteria: An Alternative for Schizophrenics." It first appeared in 1979 in *New Directions for Mental Health Services*. A version of this article edited by Masserman in 1982 was published in *Current Psychiatric Therapies, Vol. 21*.

The Spiritual Emergence Network gave permission to reprint the article "Forms of Spiritual Emergency."

Permission to reprint the article, "Toward a More Culturally Sensitive DSM-IV," was given by Williams and Wilkins for the Journal of Nervous and Mental Disease. *Vol. 180*, #11, pp 673-682, Nov. 1992.

Permission to reprint the review article "Schizophrenics for whom Phenothiazines are Contraindicated or Unnecessary" (1971) was given by Dr. Julian Silverman.

304

Bibliography

(Note: References to the articles "Soteria: An Alternative to Hospitalization for Schizophrenics," and "Toward a More Culturally Sensitive DSM-1V" are included with those articles in Appendix C.)

Allison, F. (1967). Adaptive Regression and Intense Religious Experience. *Journal of Nervous Mental Disorders, 145, 452-463.*

Allman, L.S., de la Roche, 0., Elkins, D.N. & Weathers, R. S. (1992). Psychotherapists' attitudes towards clients reporting mystical experiences. *Psychotherapy, 29 (4), 564-569.*

American Psychiatric Association (1980). *Diagnostic and Statistical Manual of Mental Disorders (3rd ed.)* . Washington, D. C.: Author.

American Psychiatric Association (1987). *Diagnostic and Statistical Manual of Mental Disorders (4th ed.).* Washington, D. C.: Author.

American Psychiatric Association (1993). DSM-IV *Draft Criteria.* Washington, D.C.: Author.

Armstrong, A. (1985, May). SEN conference.

Armstrong, A. (1986). The Challenges of Psychic Opening: A Personal Story. *ReVision. 8 (2).*

Armstrong, T. (1985). *The Radiant Child.* Wheaton, Ill. : Quest Books.

Arroyo, S. (1992). *Astrology, Karma and Transformation.* Sebastopol, Ca.: CRCS Publications.

Assagioli, R. (August, 1981). Self-realization and psychological disturbances. *Mandalama*, 4-11.

Baraz, J. (1985, Oct.). SEN conference.

Bly, R. (1971). *The Kabir Book.* Boston: Beacon Press.

Boisen, A. T. (1962). *The Exploration of the Inner World.* NY: Harper and Brothers.

Bolen, J. (1984). Seminar on "The Heroine's Journey." San Francisco: Jung Institute.

Bragdon, E. (1990). *The Call of Spiritual Emergency: From Personal Crisis to Personal Transformation.* San Francisco, Ca: HarperSanFrancisco.

Breggin, P., (1991) *Toxic Psychiatry.* New York: St. Martin's.

Cappadonna, D. (1985, May). SEN conference.

Chamberlin, C. (1986). Supporting Spiritual Emergence. *SEN Newsletter.*

Crabtree, A. (1985). *Multiple Man: Explorations in Possession and Multiple Personality.* New York: Prater Publishers.

Cusack, C. (1974). Transcendental Runner. Runner's World (eds.) *The Complete Runner* . New York: Harper and Row, pp. 18-25.

Cucuruto, P. (1977). training seminar. San Francisco.

Dabrowski, K. (1964). *Positive Disintegration.* Boston: Little Brown.

Da Free John (1985). *The Dawn Horse Testament.* San Rafael: Dawn Horse Press.

Eliade, M. (1964). *Shamanism: Archaic Techniques of Ecstasy.* Bollingen Series, vol. 76. New York: Pantheon Books.

Esalen Institute (1971). Schizophrenics for whom Phenothiazines are Contraindicated or Unnecessary. Big Sur: Author.

Ferguson, M. (Ed.) (1985). Psychotherapists Report on Drugs' Clinical Outcome. *Brain-Mind Bulletin* 10 (8), 1&3.

Gallup , G. Jr. (1982). *Adventures in Immortality: A Look Beyond the Threshold of Death.* New York: McGraw-Hill.

Gallup, G. (1985). *Fifty Years of Gallup Surveys on Religion.* The Gallup Report, No. 236.

Goldstein, J. (1976). *The Experience of Insight.* Boston: Shambhala.

Goldwer, M. (1992). *The wounded healers: Creative illness in the pioneers of depth psychology.* Lanham, D.: University Press of America.

Greeley, A. M. (1975). *The Sociology of the Paranormal.* Beverly Hills, CA: Sage.

Greeley, A. M. (1987, January-February). Mysticism goes Mainstream. *American Health.*

Greer, G. (1983). MDMA: *A New Psychotropic Compound and its Effects in Humans.* Santa Fe, NM: Author.

Grof, C. (1993) *Thirst for Wholeness.* San Francisco: HarperSanFrancsico.

Grof, S. (1980). *LSD Psychotherapy.* Pomona, CA: Hunter House.

Grof, S. (1985, May). SEN conference.

Grof, S. (1985). *Beyond the Brain.* Albany, NY: State University of New York Press.

Grof, S. & Grof, C. (1985). Forms of Spiritual Emergency. SEN Newsletter, 1 (3). Menlo Park, CA: ITP.

Grof, S. & Grof, C. (1986). Spiritual Emergency: The Understanding and Treatment of Transpersonal Crises. *ReVision.* 8 (2), 7-20.

Grof, S. & Grof, C. (Ed.) (1989). *Spiritual Emergency: When Personal Transformation Becomes a Crisis.* Los Angeles: J. Tarcher.

Grof, S. & Grof, C. (1990) *The Stormy Search for the Self* Los Angeles: Tarcher.

Harman, W. (1985, Oct.). SEN conference.

Hendricks, G. (1985, May). SEN conference.

Hendricks, K. (1985, May). SEN conference.

Hood, R. (1974). Psychological Strength and the Report of Intense Religious Experience. *Journal of the Scientific Study of Religion.*13, 65-71.

Huxley, A. (1931). In Horowitz & Palmer, (eds.) (1977) *Moksha.* Los Angeles: Tarcher.

Jackson, E. (1984). training seminar. Berkeley.

James, W. (1961). *The Varieties of Religious Experience.* New York: Collier-Macmillan Ltd.

Johnstone, R. (1973). A Ketamine trip. *Anaesthesiology.* 39, 460-461.

Jung, C. G. (1961). *Memories, Dreams and Reflections.* New York: Random House.

Jung, C. G. (1968). *Analytic Psychology: Its Theory and Practice.* New York: Random House.

Kabir in Bly, R. (1971) *The Kabir Book.* Boston: Beacon Press.

Kelly, C. (1971). *Education in Feeling and Purpose.* Ojai, CA: Radix Institute.

Kennett, J. (1982). Teaching seminar. Institute of Transpersonal Psychology.

Krippner, S. & Welch, P. (1992). *Spiritual dimensions of healing.* New York: Irvington Press.

Krishna, Gopi (1971). *Kundalini: The Evolutionary Energy in Man.* Boston: Shambhala.

Krishna, Gopi (1975). Science and Kundalini. A paper presented at the seminar on Yoga, Science and Man. New Delhi.

Laing, R. D. (1972). Metanoia: Some experiences at Kingsley Hall, in Ruitenbeek (Ed.), *Going Crazy* (pp.11-21) New York: Bantam.

Lievegoed, B. (1979). *Phases: Crisis and Development in the Individual.* London: Rudolf Steiner Press.

Lindberg, A. M. (1955). *Gift from the Sea.* New York: Pantheon.

Lowen, A. (1958). *The Language of the Body.* New York: MacMillan.

Lowen, A. & Lowen, L. (1977). *The Way to Vibrant Health.* New York: Harper and Row.

Lucas, W. (1993). *Regression Therapy: A Handbook for Professionals, Vol. I & II,* Crest Park, Ca. : Deep Forest Press.

Lukoff, D. (1985). Diagnosis of Mystical Experiences with Psychotic Features. *Journal of Transpersonal Psychology.* 17 (2), 155-181.

Lukoff, D. (1991). Divine Madness: Shamanistic initiatory crisis and psychosis. *Shaman's Drum,* 22, 24-29.

Lukoff, D. & Everest, H. (1985). The Myths of Mental Illness. *The Journal of Transpersonal Psychology.* 17 (2), 123-153.

Lukoff, D., Lu, F. and Turner, R. (1992). Transpersonal psychology research review: Psychoreligious dimensions of healing. *Journal of Transpersonal Psychology,* 24 (1), 41-60.

Lukoff, D., Lu, F. and Turner, R. (1992). Toward a More Culturally Sensitive DSM-IV, *Journal of Nervous and Mental Disease* , 8 (11).

Lukoff, D., Lu, F. and Turner, R. (1992). Transpersonal psychology research review: Psychoreligious dimensions of healing. *Journal of Transpersonal Psychology,* 25 (1), 11-28.

Mack, J. (April/1992). An Authentic Mystery, *Harvard Magazine.* Cambridge, Mass.

MacLaine, S. (1983). *Out on a Limb.* New York: Bantam.

MacLaine, S. (1984). *Dancing in the Light.* New York: Bantam.

Maslow, A. (1971). *The Farther Reaches of Human Nature.* New York: Viking Press.

McGlashan, A. (1970). *The Savage and Beautiful Country.* London: Chatto and Windus.

McKenna, T. (1992). *Food of the Gods.* NY: Bantam.

Metzner, R. (May, 1985). SEN Conference.

Mindell, A. (1988). *City Shadows: Psychological Interventions in Psychiatry.* London: Routledge.

Mosher, L. and Menn, A. (1979). Soteria: An Alternative to Hospitalization for Schizophrenics. *New Direction for Mental Health Services, 1,* San Francisco: Jossey-Bass, pp. 73-84.

Moyers, B. (1993). *Healing and the Mind.* Public Affairs Television and D. Grubin Productions.

Ossof, J. (1993). Reflections of shaktipat: psychosis or the rise of kundalini? A case study. *Journal of Transpersonal Psychology,* 25, (1), 29-42.

Parush, D. (Oct.,1993). "Finding God in the Three Pound Universe: The Neuroscience of Transcendence in *Omni Magazine.*

Peck, S. (1993). Psychiatry's Predicament in *Further Along the Road Less Traveled.* New York: Simon & Schuster.

Perry, J. (1974). *The Far Side of Madness.* N. J. : Prentice-Hall.

Perry, J. (1986). Spiritual emergence and renewal. *ReVision.* 8 (2), 33-38.

Pirsig, R. (1974). *Zen and the Art of Motorcycle Maintenance.* New York: William Morrow and Co.

Platt, J. (1983). in Russell, P., The Global Brain. Los Angeles: Tarcher, p. 74.

Raheem, A. (1985, October). SEN conference.

Rama, Swami, & Ballentine, R. & Ajaya, Swami (1976). *Yoga and Psychotherapy,* Honesdale, PA: Himalayan Institute.

Ring, K. (1980). *Life at Death.* New York: Quill.

Ring, K. (1984). *Heading Towards Omega.* New York: William Morrow. Roberts, H. K. (1973) personal communication.

Rogo, D. (1984), Ketamine and the Near-Death Experience. *Anabiosis – The Journal of Near Death Studies* 4 (1), 87-96.

Russell, P. (1983). *The Global Brain.* Los Angeles: Tarcher.

Sannella, L. (1976). *Kundalini: Psychosis or Transcendence?.* San Francisco: H.S. Dakin, Co.

Shafranske, E., & Malony, H., (1990). Clinical psychologists' religious and spiritual orientations and their practice of psychotherapy. *Psychotherapy,* 27, 72-78.

Siegel, R. (1992) *Fire in the Brain.* NY: New American Library.

Silverman, J. (1971). A Paradigm for the Study of Altered States of Consciousness. *Journal of Psychedelic Drugs.* 3 (2), 89-103. Small, J. W. (1985). Floodtide. San Francisco: J. W. Small.

Sogya Rinpoche (May, 1985). SEN Conference.

Speeth, K. (1982). On Psychotherapeutic Attention. *Journal of Transpersonal Psychology,* 14 (2), 141-160.

Stein, M. (Ed.) (1984). *Jungian Analysis.* Boulder: Shambhala.
Steindl-Rast, D. (1985, May). SEN conference.
Strassman, R. (1984). Adverse Reactions to Psychedelic Drugs: A Review of the Literature. *Journal of Nervous and Mental Disease,* 172 (10), 577-595.
Suzuki, S. (1970). *Zen Mind, Beginner's Mind.* New York: Weatherhill.
Szasz, T. (1961). *The Myth of Mental Illness* NY: Hoebes-Harper.
Tarnas, R. (1993). *The Passion of the Western Mind.* NY: Ballantine.
Telles, L. (October, 1985). SEN Conference.
Thomas, L. & Cooper, P. (1977). Incidence and Psychological Correlates of Intense Spiritual Experiences. Paper presented at East Psychological Meeting, Boston.
Toufexis, A. (1985, June 10). A Crackdown on Ecstasy. *Time Magazine,* p. 64.
Vaughan, F. (1985, May). SEN conference.
Vaughan, F. (1986). *The Inward Arc.* Boston: Shambhala.
Vaughan, F. (1991). Spiritual Issues in Psychotherapy, *Journal of Transpersonal Psychology,* 23 (2),105-120.
Waldman, M. (1992). The Therapeutic alliance, kundalini, and spiritual /religious issues in counseling: The case of Julia. *Journal of Transpersonal Psychology,* 24 (2), 115-151.
Walsh, R. & Vaughan, F. (1980). *Beyond Ego.* Los Angeles: Tarcher Press.
Weil, A. (1972). *The Natural Mind.* New York: Houghton Mifflin. Weiss, B. (1988). *Many Lives, Many Masters.* NY: Simon & Schuster.
Weiss, B. (1992). *Through Time into Healing.* NY: Simon& Schuster.
White, J. (Ed.) (1984). *What is Enlightenment?* Los Angeles: J. Tarcher.
Wicks, R., Parsons, R., & Capps (eds.). (1985). *Clinical handbook of pastoral counseling.* Mahwah, NJ: Paulist Press.
Wilber, K. (1980). *The Atman Project.* Wheaton, Ill.: Theosophical Publishing House.
Wilber, K. (1984). The Developmental Spectrum and Psychopathology. Part I , *Journal of Transpersonal Psychology.* 16 (1), 75-118.
Wilber, K. (1984). The Developmental Spectrum and Psychopathology. Part II, *Journal of Transpersonal Psychology.* 16 (2), 137-166. Wittine, B. (1985, May). SEN conference.
Yogananda, P. (1946). *Autobiography of a Yogi.* Los Angeles: Self-Realization Press.
Young, V. (1983). *Working with Death: A Trainer's Manual.* (doctoral dissertation, ITP).

Index

mind technologies *187*
Mindell, A. *26, 83*
miscarriage *63*
monastic community *55, 56*
moral crisis *63*
morphine *72*
Mosher, L. *217*
Mother Theresa *24*
Motion Quest *144*
Moyers, B. *188*
mudras *209*
multi-dimensional awareness *20*
multiaxial evaluation *92*
multiple personality disorder *36*
muscular spasm *34*
mystic *151*
mystical *224*
mystical experience *8, 10, 47, 255, 260, 271, 274*
mysticism *246*

N

Native American Medicine Wheel *153*
natural disasters *64*
near-death experience *8, 38, 40, 41, 44, 59, 255, 260, 272, 273*
Network Chiropractic *144*
Nolan, M. *292*
NORC *249, 251*

0

object relations *270*
obsessive-compulsive disorder *268*

OOBE *36*
opiates *72*
opium *72*
organic imbalance *98*
Orloff, M. *292*

P

Paine-Gernee, K. *290*
paranoia *107*
paranoid *87, 107*
paranoid ideation *10*
paranormal *248*
paranormal abilities *213*
past-life *136*
Pennington, G. *292*
perceptions of light *34*
Perry, J.W. *26, 83, 210, 292*
persecutory voices *209*
Persinger, M. *188*
personality disorders *100*
personality shifts *59*
phenothiazine *126, 220, 226*
physical diseases *98*
plant spirits *34*
Pocket Sanctuary *294*
Polarity *144*
possession *36, 86, 215*
Prana *189*
prayer *50, 128*
precognition *11*
pregnancy *62, 65*
Price, R. *290, 292*
priests *54*
Process Acupressure *144*
Psychedelics *73, 74, 230*
psychiatric drugs *99, 106, 126*
psychic opening *36, 86*

A Sourcebook for Helping People
with Spiritual Problems
by Emma Bragdon, PhD

The E-Book can be purchased at
http://www.emmabragdon.com/products.html

Softcover perfectbound copies can be purchased at
http://www.emmabragdon.com/products.html

For Bulk Orders of perfectbound copies contact:

Lightening Up Press • P.O. Box 325
Woodstock, VT 05091
Phone: 802-674-2919
Email: pr@emmabragdon.com

Also available:
*Spiritual Alliances: Discovering the Roots of Health
at the Casa de Dom Inácio*
*Kardec's Spiritism: A Home for Healing and Spiritual
Evolution*
*The Call of Spiritual Emergency: From Personal
Crisis to Personal Transformation* – revised in
2006

If you would like to be on our mailing list for future
publications, and receive our quarterly newsletter,
please **mailto:pr@emmabragdon.com** with the
following info:

Name: _____

Email: _____

Privacy: We will not sell or give our mailing list to anyone else, and are committed to maintain the privacy of
those on our list.

CPSIA information can be obtained at www.ICGtesting.com
Printed in the USA
BVOW050502041011

272641BV00001B/5/A